PASSIONATE PILGRIM

PASSIONATE PILGRIM

THE EXTRAORDINARY LIFE OF ALMA REED

ANTOINETTE MAY

Marlowe & Company

NEW YORK

First paperback edition, 1994

Published in the United States by
Marlowe & Company
632 Broadway, Seventh Floor
New York, New York 10012

Distributed to the trade by Publishers Group West.

Manufactured in the United States of America

ISBN 1-56924-887-7

To another passionate romantic,
Clara Trusel.

CONTENTS

ACKNOWLEDGMENTS

This book owes its existence most directly to a very special friend and mentor, John Wilson, whose editorial skill, creative instincts, and strong personal involvement once again proved invaluable.

Passionate Pilgrim is the story of a reporter and her times. Its telling owes much to the friends and colleagues of Alma Sullivan Reed: Pablo Bush Romero, Jim Budd, Bill Shanahan, Pearl Gonzalez, and Joe Nash; and to the Sullivan family, most particularly Jane Wallach and Kevin Forsberg, as well as Patsy Berman and Kim Haney.

Alma Reed's writings—her books, articles and letters—comprise another primary source. The story could not have been told without the assistance of Maria Teresa Gullotti and the Departmento de Desarrollo Tourism in Mérida, Mexico, as well as the *Mexico City News*, and the Fremont Older Collection of Mort and Elaine Levine.

The author is further indebted to Vern Appleby, C. J. Marrow, Ruth Shari, and Vickie Von Arx, who provided the very best kind of aid—moral, technical, and practical.

Support for *Passionate Pilgrim* was provided by the Peninsula Community Foundation in San Mateo, California.

PROLOGUE

"You simply can not bury her next to him—not with his wife and family still alive!"

"But, Your Excellency"—Pablo Bush Romero forced himself to speak the words slowly, with quiet emphasis—"she was his fiancée. They were to be married. Within a month they would have been man and wife."

Luis Torres Mesias, the present governor of Yucatán, shook his head. "She was his mistress. It is a question of honor, the honor of the family."

"The fact remains that Felipe Carrillo Puerto was divorced. His life was his to do with as he chose."

"That, too, Don Pablo, was a scandal—a very old scandal that continues to divide the state."

"The martyred governor, great leader that he was, was nonetheless a man."

"Yes, a man who, some might say, made some great mistakes. I'm certain his widow would say that Alma Reed was the greatest of them.

The divorce—the law that he himself created, the law to make it possible . . ."

Bush sighed wearily. It was an old story still hotly debated after more than forty years. "The burial, your excellency—it was the life long wish of a great lady, a very great lady. Remember, sir, Alma Reed was the beloved not only of the governor, but of the city of Mérida, of Mexico itself. This extraordinary woman's efforts on behalf of archeology, of art, of Mexico are known throughout the world—but most particularly in her native United States. How would it look if this, her last request, was denied?"

It was Torres's turn to sigh. He tried to look away, but the other man's eyes held him. They were the eyes that had sought sunken treasure ships in the Caribbean, that had stalked man-eating tigers in India. Almost of their own accord, his hands sought paper, pen.

There was no sound but that of a pen scratching. Torres signed his name with a flourish. "You have my permission to inter Mrs. Reed's ashes in the General Cemetery. But *not,* you understand, not with Felipe Carrillo." His voice softened. "I'm certain that you can find some appropriate spot for the lady."

Bush could scarcely contain his relief. He'd been custodian of his friend's ashes for nearly a year, waiting patiently for this concession. He was not a patient man, but in this case—what other choice? "You are most kind, Your Excellency." Bush took the proffered paper and quickly bade his benefactor good day. As Bush passed out of the Governor's Palace, Alma Reed and the many facets of her life continued to fill his mind. It was here, more than forty years before, that she had met Felipe Carillo Puerto for the first time. Finally their story would be complete.

Maneuvering skillfully through the teeming streets of Mérida, narrow lanes laid out some four hundred years before in a time of conquistadores and carriages, he reached the General Cemetery. As he approached the grave sites, Bush passed an old stone wall. It was here, he knew, that Carrillo had been shot. Bougainvillea cascaded downward, flaming fingers delineating a plaque that commemorated the spot.

On this brilliant October day it was difficult to conjure up the grim specter of the firing squad that must have stood just behind him, or of Felipe and his three brothers standing with their backs against the wall, their arms bound behind them. How many times had Alma come here, how many times had her fingers caressed these old stones?

Not far beyond was the magnificent tomb that enshrined the murdered man. As Bush approached it, his eyes fell almost immediately upon a small plot directly opposite the massive monument and only a few feet from it. He couldn't believe his luck! The site was perfect, and it was unoccupied. There was, of course, the question of proximity. The two graves would be very close, only a few feet apart, the effect almost like that of two lovers gazing into each other's eyes. The family would not like that, nor would Torres. Yet, Bush reasoned, once the interment had taken place, who would dare dig up the remains of a national heroine?

With no hesitation, he strode to the cemetery office and presented the governor's signed document. The arrangements were quickly concluded. Returning to his hotel, Bush placed a call to Torres's office. "I've found a suitable place for Mrs. Reed."

"I'm delighted to hear it," Torres replied.

"The interment will be in two days."

"Oh! What a pity, my duties will take me out of town."

"Yes, indeed, a pity."

With a sigh of relief, Bush replaced the receiver. Torres had not asked the location of the site. Very possibly, he did not want to know.

Alma Reed's funeral cortege began at 9:30 on the morning of October 22, 1967, eleven months after her death. The ashes were transported by limousine from the United States consulate on fashionable Montejo Boulevard to the cemetery, where a simple ceremony was held. The participants ranged from schoolchildren to prestigious dignitaries. All the towns and villages of Yucatán were represented. A Boy Scout troop did the honors. Taps was sounded. The United States consul, William Harbin, officiated. He spoke with a diplomat's eloquence of Alma Reed's contribution to a more harmonious relationship between the United States and Mexico, a contribution that had begun more than forty years before, when she, a pioneer reporter on a San Francisco newspaper, had changed the course of history by saving the life of an unknown Mexican national, a teenage boy sentenced to be hanged.

Bush's mind wandered as he scanned the crowd around him. The speech droned on. There was mention of Alma's concern for the masses, her efforts to make known to the world the work of Mexican artists. Her pivotal influence on the career of José Clemente Orozco was lauded. Did many of the mourners gathered there speculate, as he did, that the great muralist was Alma's lover as well as her friend? Most probably.

Certainly all of them knew of her notorious connection with Felipe Carrillo Puerto, known today as the Abraham Lincoln of Mexico. Looking about at some of the older faces, Bush was certain that many of them recalled that liaison. One of them, Dr. Prospero Martinez Carrillo, Bush recalled, had been reminiscing about it quite recently. *"Amor calido,"* "a romance of the steam," he'd called the affair.

Bush started at the sudden recognition of a face in the crowd. It was the dead governor's only son. The "young" Felipe must now be nearly the age his father had been when he fell suddenly, devastatingly in love with the beautiful North American journalist. Surely the son's presence must mean that he understood and had forgiven the passions that once ruled his father.

U.S. consul Harbin scrupulously avoided mention of one of Alma's greatest triumphs. It hardly seemed politic to mention the recovery of Mayan treasures valued at more than two million dollars that had been smuggled out of the country by his predecessor some years before. The pioneer archeologist-consul, Edward Thompson, possibly befuddled by Alma's youthful charm, had made her his confidant. How he must have regretted that decision later, but the damage was done. Alma's "scoop" had made headlines that would eventually change the rules of the game for archeologists in all parts of the world.

Then the poets had their say. Mérida had always been a city of poets, Alma Reed a prime subject. One of the greatest, Luis Rosada de la Vega, had been her dear friend as was his composer-collaborator, Ricardo Palmerín. Now both men were buried nearby. It was inevitable that one of their most beloved compositions would be played, the ballad that the governor, Felipe Carrillo Puerto, had commissioned in honor of his American sweetheart.

As two young guitarists began to strum the strains of "La Peregrina"— "The Pilgrim"—tears came to the eyes of nearly everyone.

> *Wanderer of the clear and divine eyes*
> *And cheeks aflame with the redness of the sky,*
> *Little woman of the red lips,*
> *And hair radiant as the sun,*
> *Traveler who left your own scenes—*
> *The fir trees and the snow, the virginal snow—*
> *And came to find refuge in the palm groves,*

Under the sky of my land,
My tropical land,
The little singing birds of my fields,
Offer their voices in singing to you—
And they look at you
And the flowers of the perfumed nectars
Caress you and kiss you on the lips and temples,
When you leave my palm groves and my land,
Traveler of the enchanting face,
Don't forget—don't forget—my land,
Don't forget—don't forget—my love.

And so it had finally come to pass that Felipe's *peregrina,* his lovely pilgrim, had at last joined him forever.

Alma Reed had been a hummingbird, always in flight, always busy, stirring things up and writing them down. Bright, beautiful, forever darting here and there, it was difficult for Bush to realize that she was silent at last. Memories of the complex woman he'd met late in her life were vivid: an impassioned writer, a diver whose fascination for the sea and its hidden treasures never waned, a woman who loved parties, midnight drinks, and lively arguments. This was an individual who lived life as high adventure, a life beyond the wildest dreams of most.

Many of Alma's exploits had been eulogized, others pointedly ignored. And, perhaps, that was as it should be. His friend had been a reporter to the end, determined to ferret out and interpret the facts; but the facts about herself—well, that was quite another matter. Alma's whole life was about myth—not only myth in a universal sense, but in a uniquely personal one. This was a woman who'd artfully succeeded in creating her own. Alma Reed's world was itself a myth, myth lived as life and life as myth. The story had begun long ago in a distant land. Would anyone ever know it all?

PART I

CHAPTER · 1

The Making of a Great "Sob Sister"

B ehind Fremont Older's head the wall was battered. The "greatest editor of the West" did that when he was angry, tossing his massive head back like a charging bull.

"What," he demanded, "makes you think you can write?"

Alma looked around the small, spare room flooded with proofread copy, marked newspapers, unfiled letters and noted the battle-scarred desk rimmed with the butts of some twenty cigars—Havana, she supposed. She'd heard that the man sitting opposite her read every line of every edition of the *San Francisco Call.* Surveying the discarded sheets littering the floor, she believed it.

Enclosed in the shabby room to which she'd fought hard to gain access, Alma felt the magnetism of the man and his power. She was certain that people rarely talked back to Fremont Older. Alma steeled herself to meet his challenge.

She knew her man and was ready. "I don't *think.* I know."

Politicians, financiers, people in trouble—they all flowed through Older's office. He was well acquainted with most of the powerful men in the city and state government; "riffraff" he called them, and he battled their chicanery with headlines of a violence never seen before. They fought back—sometimes with dynamite. For years, the editor had walked a dangerous path. Alma loved the stories of his legendary escapes. Once a gunman hired by political bosses came up one elevator as Older slipped down the other. When another would-be assassin trapped him in his office, Older suggested that they sit down and talk it over. An hour later, so the story went, the two were smoking cigars and exchanging life philosophies. And, when kidnapped on the street, Older simply talked the gangsters hired to kill him out of their mission. Alma liked to believe all of it.

Studying the warrior-editor, well into his sixties but still a handsome giant with a conqueror's bearing, Alma was more determined than ever to work for him. There was another side to Older, and she played to it: "San Francisco's poor need a champion. So do the homeless, the unlucky." Alma almost shouted the words in her effort to gain his attention. "Their tragedies could happen to anyone, and, on some level, we all know it. I can sell papers for you with their stories."

Quickly, she outlined a prospective column, its uniqueness and scope, the limitless possibilities from which to draw, the mass appeal to readers. Feeling like Scheherazade, Alma rushed on, her voice soft now, controlled and beguiling, her words fresh, colorful, full of enthusiasm, compassion, and sometimes humor. She was desperately hoping to divert Older's attention from two appalling facts. She had neither experience nor formal education. Nothing objectively qualified her for the position she so eagerly sought. Perhaps she would have to, well, lie a little. It would certainly not be the first time, nor the last.

One fiction related to her very birth itself. Alma Marie Sullivan was born in San Francisco on June 17, 1889—not 1894, as she would later claim.

A scant forty years had elapsed since the Gold Rush transformed a sleepy village into a boom town. Despite the impracticality of its location—a cold, foggy windswept peninsula where water and trees were in short supply—the city had grown from a population of three hundred to nearly three hundred thousand. To its inhabitants, San Francisco was *the* City, City with a capital *C,* and so it remains.

Prefabricated buildings had been brought from nearly every East Coast port city as well as from England, France, Germany, Belgium, China, Australia, even Tasmania, and set down at such incredible angles on hills that rose so steeply that it wouldn't have surprised anyone to see the city slide into the sea, whole streets at a time.

Perhaps the secret of the city—and its inhabitants—was to be found in its bay, which curved and lapped and arched and stretched as if at some time the very sands had been instilled with joy and invitation and passion and rest. Surely the difference between stern, inaccessible cliffs, against which waters dash but cannot prevail, and soft, wooing beaches, up which waves sweep as far as they like, is telling. Does anybody imagine that if the pilgrims had landed in California, witches would have been hanged there? Or that if gold had been found in New England, a Massachusetts man would spend it like a Californian?

The survivor instinct was inherent in Alma. Her grandparents on both sides were among the thousands who but for the discovery of gold might never have thought of migrating to remote Pacific shores.

The parents of Eugene J. Sullivan left their home in County Cork, sailed to New York, and then boarded another ship that would take them around the Horn. It was one of the most hazardous sea journeys known, a voyage of seven months with the ever-present danger of shipwreck. The vessel, past its prime and hastily refitted, was a floating tenement. Squeezed into dark and fetid cabins, some argonauts fell to deadly fevers; others died from tainted food. Off the coast of Central America, ships were often becalmed. The waveless sea, the unbearable heat, the vacant horizon, drove men to violence and madness. For many, the California adventure ended before it ever began.

Adelaide Frances Murphy's parents, descendants of revolutionary patriots, left their native Kentucky and traveled westward by covered wagon. Measured painfully by plodding hooves and creaking wheels, the continental crossing was a weary succession of prairies, mountains, deserts, and more mountains. Animal bones marked the way, along with broken wagons, abandoned furniture, shattered china, trunks of clothes, cases of books, graves, and crosses.

Tattered, weather-beaten, the survivors of both land and sea journeys found further perils awaiting them in the mining camps: cholera, malaria, dysentery, typhoid, landslides, cave-ins. Even worse was the violence that erupted among themselves. Life was shockingly cheap; murder commonplace. Thousands died; thousands more returned to their homes.

Neither of Alma's grandparents were among them. Neither family struck it rich, but both survived, and both began new lives for themselves in California. Adelaide Murphy grew up in the rough-and-tumble Gold Country, while the Sullivans settled in Petaluma, a village situated in an area of lush, green farmland, solace for the soul to many Irish expatriates.

Eugene Sullivan had different tastes. He was drawn to San Francisco, a city of adventuring strangers obsessed with the idea of the quick buck. There was a harshness to life, an underlying instability, an ethos of survival of the fittest. San Francisco was a city of hope in defiance of fact; it suited him well. Sullivan was excited by the combined elegance and frontier ramshackle. Wet fogs and capricious chilliness did nothing to dampen his enthusiasm. Eugene determined to make it big in real estate. He would grasp the city by its ears, and climb on top.

The beautiful Adelaide Murphy, in town for a visit and introduced to him by friends, listened to Eugene's plans. In the Mother Lode Country of the Sierra Nevada, the sixteen-year-old, wise beyond her years, had seen firsthand what could happen to men who lived by their wits alone and yet let the years go by without achieving lasting recognition and prominence; but the pursuit of a dream was compelling, and Eugene a handsome man. His optimism proved infectious.

In 1888, the couple was married; Alma Marie was the first of their ten children, two of whom died in infancy.

One of the first things that Alma learned was never to count on anything or anyone. Eugene made fortunes with astounding speed, then lost them even faster. A true visionary, his timing rarely kept pace with his vision.

Adelaide was strong, but there was a touch of the fey about her. Reading tarot cards for family and friends was a pleasant diversion, and it kept everyone hopeful. Somehow, despite all the triumphs and failures, she held the family together. After seven children, she preferred to stop, but Eugene—a devout Catholic backed by a zealot priest—was adamant and persistent. Three more sons, Prescott, Stanley, and Desmond, would follow, but only after a ten-year interval.

Active, spirited, often defiant, Alma questioned everything. She soon rejected traditional religion in the light of Darwin and Spencer, looking to her own intelligence and instincts for guidance. There was so much to explore, to investigate. She would make up her own mind and only when it suited her. Of one thing Alma was certain, a decision that helped to determine the course of her life. She did *not* want a life like her mother's. She would not tie her fortunes to the whims of a man; she would not fill her life with babies. As the oldest child, Alma had more than enough of babies; much of her own childhood had been lost to changing diapers, quieting teething infants, amusing obstreperous toddlers. By 1906, when Prescott—named for the Arizona town, the site of Eugene's last speculation—came along, Alma was seventeen and ready to give notice.

An honor student at Polytechnic High School, she'd hoped to attend the University of California. Another financial reversal curtailed that plan. Alma was kept busy helping her mother in lieu of the dismissed maid, dreaming all the while of independence from her family, of a writing career, of an apartment of her own.

Eugene and Adelaide were horrified. They looked at their oldest child and saw in wonderment a tall, willowy beauty with golden brown hair and a smile that was almost heartbreaking in its appeal. This was a young woman who might capture a millionaire, Eugene speculated. Alma, even then scornful of the posturings of San Francisco's Nob Hill society, showed little enthusiasm. It was hell to be poor, but wealth in itself held little appeal. She admired creativity and accomplishment. Alma's idols were innovators and achievers, originals in every sense; she was determined to be one of them.

The dreams of privilege and position that kept the elder Sullivans going had scant appeal to her. *Heart Line,* Frank Gellet Burgess's novel of San Francisco's bohemia, was Alma's bible. She imagined herself another Fancy Gray, described as having "that free, fearless gaiety, the almost abandoned good nature of San Francisco girls."

More than a little disturbed, Adelaide pointed out that the same character had ended up throwing herself off a ferry boat in despair and that Fancy Gray's real-life counterpart, journalist Nora Mae French, had recently taken cyanide at a Carmel writer's retreat. Some of the nervous mother's suspicions were valid. French's tragedy proved prophetic. Many of Alma's girlhood idols, literary luminaries of the day, would take their own lives.

Jack London; then Carrie Sterling—beautifully gowned, Chopin's "Funeral March" on the gramophone; and finally George Sterling, the self-styled emperor of San Francisco's bohemia, dead of cyanide in his room at the Bohemian Club. The list went on.

Alma wasn't listening. The possibility that failed expectations could backfire into bitterness or result in fatal indulgence was as foreign to her as suicide itself. Alma wanted to *live*. Unfortunately, this was the last gasp of the age before Freud. *September Morn,* a sentimental painting of a chaste maid hiding her nudity with her hands, was considered lascivious. Pregnant women modestly remained at home after the fourth month. The Gibson Girl, crisply covered from neck to ankles in shirtwaist and skirt, was an icon. In the eyes of Eugene and Adelaide, bohemia was inextricably linked with irresponsibility and sin. Women left home to be wives or prostitutes. With no desire to be either, Alma wracked her brains for another means of support and ran into the ideal of duty. It was insidious. What kind of daughter would even think of leaving home? With a new baby, Adelaide needed all the help she could get.

For a time Alma was forced to content herself with a vicarious existence.

Much of Eugene's money—when he had it—was spent on books. The succession of homes, each reflecting the family's mercurial fortunes, invariably contained a library. Whether it was a spacious room with ample shelves and comfortable chairs, or merely a small corner with homeless books stored in and on packing boxes, "the library" was an integral part of life for both father and daughter.

A complex man with an Irishman's love of poetry, Eugene collected the very best of writing. "You think you know it all, then be your own teacher," he challenged Alma, handing her his latest acquisition, *Vanity Fair.* She quickly identified with Becky Sharpe and renewed her resolve to extricate herself somehow from middle-class life and values. If self-education was the only path open to her, it was time she began. Longing for the romance and adventure of the Great World, Alma read the *Aeneid* and dreamed of Carthage, puzzled over the dialogues of Socrates and Plato; she loved the ancient civilization from which they'd sprung.

From the age of eight on, Eugene had taken Alma with the younger siblings in tow on regular Sunday pilgrimages to the M. H. de Young Museum in Golden Gate Park. The Egyptian Hall, with its mummies shrouded in fragments of age-yellowed linen, frightened the other children but fascinated Alma, evoking in her eager imagination strange patterns of life and death forces long since forgotten.

Their second stop was invariably the art gallery, where huge academic canvases in broad, gilt frames were on display together with striking engravings from the days of the forty-niners, reconstructions of authentic interiors and costumes of the Gold Rush period. For the most part, the enormous paintings were portraits of the makers of California's history and scenes depicting the major events in the story of the Bear Flag State. The painting that impressed her most and would remain forever in Alma's memory—largely because of Eugene's civic enthusiasm and forensic powers—was a huge canvas that commemorated the ceremony of the driving of the last spike, a gold one, by the Union Pacific Transcontinental Railroad. Central to the theme were the men still idealized by Eugene as "empire builders." In later years, when Alma occasionally returned to the museum on her own, she was more apt to think of them as robber barons.

The demographic mix of San Francisco and its evolution was another element in her education. Suddenly, Alma was liberated from her domestic service. This time it was her father who needed her. Eugene's speculative interests took him and, consequently, Alma to many areas of the city. Cosmetically, San Francisco had changed and was continuing to change before her eyes. On April 18, 1906, the Sullivans were jolted from their beds by an earthquake of such magnitude that it would achieve a permanent place in American history. Hundreds of buildings collapsed. Scarcely had the tremors stilled before fires began, ultimately destroying 490 blocks and 28,000 buildings. The Sullivans were among the lucky ones, their small flat on Jones Street one of the few that remained standing.

On April 12, while the fire continued to rage, *Chronicle* headlines promised: "SAN FRANCISCO WILL RISE FROM THE ASHES A GREATER AND MORE BEAUTIFUL CITY THAN EVER."

Some believed the earthquake and fire had been a form of divine retribution for San Francisco's pervading sinfulness. Notorious for vice and corruption, the city, many thought, had passed through an ordeal by fire. Now it was purified, the slate wiped clean.

When Mayor Gene Schmitz announced, "Our fair city lies in ruins, but these are the damnedest, finest ruins ever seen on the face the earth," most cheered, choosing to forget that Schmitz was the puppet of a brutally crooked machine headed by Abraham "Boss" Reuf.

Almost as quickly as San Francisco had been destroyed, a second instant city arose, reminding old-timers of the early days. The Gold Rush dynamic had returned full force. That sense of purpose and regeneration appealed to Eugene, who saw a fortune to be made and borrowed heavily. He was a true San Franciscan.

Alma's days were spent running errands, pushing her way through streets crowded with horse-drawn buggies, bicycles, and even a few motor cars. Immediately after the quake, many had predicted that the new San Francisco would be built on a different model. No longer would it be a city of privilege, a closed corporation, run at the whim of the old families who shared a credo: "I've made mine, you stay out—so I'll have more for myself." Instead, everyone would have a share of its glories and its riches. The City with its capital *C* would be a City of the People.

Eugene, who'd just opened a new office at 145 Montgomery Street, was, as could be expected, one of the optimists. He insisted that anyone willing to work, anyone willing to take a few chances, could make it big. But Alma, watchful, curious, learned quickly. Her cable car jaunts to city hall and to Chinatown, the sorties down the slot south of Market and out to the Barbary Coast, were eye-openers. The odds, she realized, were still stacked against anyone outside the inner circle. Some would make it, of course, the lucky ones—she prayed her father would be among them; some never would.

As time passed, she became convinced that there were many who *had* to be helped, if only so they might help themselves. Eugene disapproved of his daughter's newfound radicalism; it was almost as threatening as her romance with bohemia. Moving up in the world, the last thing he needed was a revolutionary daughter! Conversations were lively around the Sullivan dinner table.

In 1909, the family moved into a large, pretty house at 458 Divisadero. At last Alma had a room of her own, a place where she could retreat from the newest baby's anguished wails. Stanley was teething. She knew that sound too well.

Alma made a decision. If she must sacrifice the academic education she longed for to assist her father with his real estate ventures, then she might just as well take full advantage of the opportunity. At twenty-one, Alma became a licensed broker. Eugene proudly insisted that she was a born saleswoman. Alma hoarded her commissions, hoping to eventually accumulate enough to pay tuition and living expenses. Mostly she dreamed of a place of her own. One day on an impulse Alma bought a small lot west of Twin Peaks in an area of dunes and ice plant. Someday, she felt certain, the city would overtake these dunes, but now the land was going for a song. There was simply too much of Eugene in her to resist the gamble.

Eugene smiled benignly. He now owned the Chutes, a square-block amusement park on Fillmore Street. The young Sophie Tucker and Al Jolson were among those who performed there. Some of Alma's craving for excitement and variety was stimulated by this contact with the raffish entertainment world.

The Chutes brought a new element into her life. The majority of the laborers were Mexican, most of them native Californians. She found the earnestness and industry of many to be at striking variance with the lazy mañana stereotype. A sense of camaraderie developed as Alma, who had almost a genius for language, quickly picked up Spanish phrases. Aware that California had once belonged to the forebearers of these very men, she began to study state history from a new perspective. Of all the minorities, the Mexicans had been treated the most unfairly, Alma felt.

"Actually, it's a lot like what the British did in Ireland," she attempted to explain to Eugene; but, he, having bought into the imperialist world of California's elite, was unsympathetic to the comparison. Now founding president of the Sierra Blue Lakes Water and Power Company, he was riding high. However, the year 1913 began on a euphoric note but ended with abrupt and total disaster. With devastating swiftness, the tide turned against him. Overextended, unable to meet his creditors, Eugene had lost it all. On December 25, the *San Francisco Examiner* carried a notice that Eugene J. Sullivan had filed a petition for bankruptcy. It would have been small consolation then to know that his scheme was a sound one that would one day bring millions into the coffers of the Pacific Gas and Electric Company. Within a year, the Sullivans had moved from the big house on Divisadero to a tiny cottage at 753 Clayton.

Eugene was depressed, crushingly so; but not for long. A new career soon beckoned. He would engage in the insurance brokerage business. Its potential, in his renewed optimistic perspective, was limitless.

Alma, despondent that her lot was worthless at the time when they most needed it, was weary of real estate, weary too of the close confinement of the cramped house, the noise of the younger children. She was twenty-four years old and determined at last to do what *she* wanted to do.

Dark, airless, noisy, crowded beyond belief, Alma had never encountered anything like a newspaper office. The city room was a dust bowl, a firetrap, a wall-to-wall wastebasket. No factory owner would have dared ask his laborers to work under such conditions, nor would the state—even then— have allowed it if he had.

Alma adored it.

Emerging from the cubicle that was Fremont Older's office with the grudging promise of a trial position as a cub reporter, she thought herself the luckiest woman alive. Naturally, Eugene and Adelaide were aghast. No nice woman worked for a newspaper. Bad as things were for the Sullivans, they hadn't, surely, come to *that!*

Alma thought of the grime, the cigar fumes, the men shouting expletives as casually as her mother said good day, and smiled inwardly. "Lots of great writers began on newspapers," she reminded her parents, playing on Eugene's love of literature. "Just think of Thackeray, Dickens, Kipling— I'm sure there must be many, many more." Eugene and Adelaide were unconvinced; it made no difference.

Savings that Alma had attempted to stash away over the years had vanished long ago to help defray family expenses, but now, with her younger brother, Walter, working, Alma's time had come. With her first paycheck, she rented a small room—hardly more than a closet—in a woman's residence club at 635 Sutter. Clean, shabbily respectable with the mismatched furniture peculiar to transient places, Alma thought it heaven to return to the privacy of the tiny space—a space that was all her own, to the sanctity of possessions that remained just where she placed them.

Actually, she spent little of her time there. Alma all but lived at the *Call.* She was learning the newspaper business and took to it from the very beginning. Soon there was no question of a "trial position"; she was part of the team, the city room her true home.

Its hub was the city desk. A newspaper story—"copy," Alma was soon calling it—went as the last of many steps from the copy desk, built blackjack table–style with the city editor in the slot and his copy editors around the rim, to the composing room where overalled linotype operators set the copy for the big presses.

On the wall of the city room hung the credo of both Fremont Older and the *Call*'s publisher, William Randolph Hearst: "SPEED AND ACCURACY." Alma learned very quickly that if she couldn't manage the first, adherence to the second wouldn't save her.

Naïvely, she'd imagined herself writing in some quiet corner. Her immediate introduction to the large, boxlike Underwood with its stiff, sticking keys quickly shattered that illusion. She learned with the speed born of necessity to type with two fingers, deaf to the turbulence going on around her. Each sheet of her story was a "take"—perhaps because it was frequently taken away piecemeal to be set in type. The flow grew more frenzied as the deadline of each edition approached.

On a few never-to-be-forgotten occasions, Older towered over her as she hammered away, snatching the take from the machine when she completed it, scanning the page gimlet-eyed. "Boy!" he bellowed and a copyboy appeared to race the page to the next room, where the hungry presses waited. Once those presses began to roll and roar, there was a brief respite, and then in an hour or so another edition to prepare. The big clock on the wall above Alma was her constant enemy, racing her relentlessly toward deadline.

Alma had made a good case for charity as a circulation builder. Older was intrigued by her plan to write human interest stories about the needy. She would be known as "Mrs. Goodfellow," he decided, and, in addition to writing a column, would act as a kind of clearinghouse for charitable gift giving. One day Mrs. Goodfellow was delighted to write:

> *Here is proof of the false prophesies voiced by the alarmists who predicted that if women ever went into a voting booth or a jury box, they would lose the essentially feminine qualities of mercy, tenderness and forbearance; that crops would fail, all children would sass their parents, and the race would generally peter out. For the failure of crops and the biological destiny of the race, consult other authorities, but for the effect of jury service on the essentially feminine qualities of mercy, tenderness and forebearance, note this letter from a lady. . . .*

The letter was from a woman who'd received two dollars for jury duty and wanted to contribute it to the subject of a recent Mrs. Goodfellow column, a destitute mother of two, who'd been burned badly by an exploding gas stove.

Another time, Mrs. Goodfellow challenged her audience:

> *Have you ever had men, sick and weak and hungry, come and ask for your help? Not the gentlemen of the road to whom this is no new experience, but real men who have been accustomed to hold down men's jobs and positions. Do you know what it means to one of these clean, whole-souled citizens to have to appeal to some agency, or someone more fortunate than they for assistance; to ask for groceries to keep their families from starvation?*
>
> *Today a man seventy years of age, frail and speaking almost in a whisper, called on Mrs. Goodfellow and asked for a shirt so that he might be presentable while applying for a job. He had left the hospital a few days ago. He apologized for asking for aid. His manner was gentle and refined. He had lost a son in France; his wife was dead. He was alone in the world.*
>
> *"And perhaps you'd like some food supplies also?" Mrs. Goodfellow inquired.*
>
> *"Oh, no. I could not ask for that. That would be begging. But," he added hesitatingly, "I have not eaten, well, since yesterday." He was so weak, he could hardly stand.*

The column went on to thank recent contributors for donations that included two union suits and other new underwear from "an employee of the Emporium" and two hundred tickets to a display of California wildflowers to be held at the St. Francis Hotel. The latter had been supplied by a society woman who went so far as to offer transportation for the infirm. Alma speculated as to how many takers there'd be for the latter offer. She was tempted to add a wry comment of her own or at least an exclamation mark or two, but restrained herself.

Alma's efforts were definitely catching on. Older rewarded her with a "due bill," an age-old newspaper practice in which free advertising was exchanged for the product of the advertiser. Alma, at no out-of-pocket expense to herself, moved into a room in the elegant Fairmont Hotel atop Nob Hill—small, but the Fairmont. She was pleased to learn that her new quarters meant an additional assignment. Besides being Mrs. Goodfellow, Alma was now a reporter with a beat of her own; her job was to cover the hotels.

Starting each morning at the Fairmont, Alma picked up a list of the conventions, club meetings, and banquets. She'd repeat the process across the street at the Mark Hopkins, then hop a cable car at the corner of California and Powell down to Union Square and the St. Francis. From there she'd scurry across Market Street, the main thoroughfare with its four streetcar lines, to the Palace, and finally, as time permitted, to the lesser hostelries.

Hotel life was racy, exciting. Soon Alma knew all about what actors or actresses were staying where, with whom, and under what names. She was fascinated too by the bright, breezy, show girls with their stylish hobble skirts, which virtually shackled them at the knees. Some colored their hair, she was certain. Occasionally Alma saw a politician, a famous lawyer, or a judge slip a five-dollar bill to a bell captain, utter a few discreet words, and presumably get whatever it was he wanted: liquor, gambling, or possibly one of the show girls. Nothing really surprised her, San Francisco had never been accused of being innocent.

Predictably, Alma soon tired of her beat. The stories she uncovered were either dull—the winner of the annual Native Daughters of the Golden West award—or unprintable. She was bored. Not so her parents. Eugene and Adelaide, admiring the modish new Mission-style furniture and commanding bay view, were flabbergasted by their daughter's Fairmont digs. Perhaps reporting wasn't *quite* as bad as they'd imagined. Besides, they allowed, what Alma was doing as Mrs. Goodfellow was really quite refined, a little like the charity work the society women did. When Prescott announced that he wanted to sell newspapers on the street, they agreed. The money he brought in helped; by now a new baby, Desmond, had shouldered Stanley out of the playpen.

The Sullivans might have been pleased with Alma's career, but she'd become restless. Satisfying as it was to make a success out of doing good, she still craved excitement. Alma wanted to be Mrs. Goodfellow all right, but she also wanted to write real news stories.

Older, recognizing the instinct of a true "sob sister," suggested, "What about San Quentin? Go out to the Big House and see what you can come up with."

In less than an hour, Alma was on the ferry headed across the bay to the state penitentiary in Marin County.

Warden James Johnston was anything but pleased to see her. "We don't want women reporters here," he bluntly announced. Alma, fresh and brisk in her shirtwaist and tie, tawny hair pulled loosely back into a twist, refused to be dismayed. "Warden, women have the vote now," she reminded him. "They're very interested in your prisoners. If you don't let me see and talk with them, somehow my women readers might just get the idea that you're working those men over with a hose or something. I might even get to thinking something like that myself. I can't go back without *some* kind of story. . . ."

What was a warden to do? Alma got her story and many more. After a time, Johnston even began to look forward to her visits. She might be a pushy girl, but she was so pretty, and you knew her heart was in the right place from the things she wrote. The guards loved her; the prisoners loved her. Soon they were calling her "The Rose of Condemned Row."

But Alma was about to acquire another name as well; it was Reed, Alma Reed. The woman who said she'd never marry was in love. Alma had always had admirers, many of them, yet for some reason the spark she sought had never appeared. So many of the men she met seemed banal or shallow, and, occasionally, when someone just a bit different did appear on the scene, his inevitable talk of marriage and children frightened her. In an age when young women married without the slightest idea of what the future involved—the consensus being that anything was better than spinsterhood—nine siblings had given Alma Sullivan a very clear view of what marriage was all about. From girlhood, she had been almost obsessed with the determination to break out of the traditional feminine ideal, the conventional mold that she believed served only to narrow a woman's interests, limit her aspirations, and hamper her development as an individual. From the very beginning, she had confounded her parents by refusing to see her place as in the home, taking no interest whatsoever in domestic affairs. She had been, in fact, almost militantly negative.

Now at last a man had appeared who'd caused her to rethink her views. Perhaps marriage *could* be different. Samuel Payne Reed was different. Like herself, he was a thoughtful idealist. Like herself, he was struggling to make a difference. Alma met Reed at San Quentin, where he was teaching volunteer classes in simple math, electricity, mechanics, and automobile maintenance. He'd paid his way through college working for Royal Daggett, a pioneer car dealer, and now had a job at Heald's Business College teaching English and electrical engineering. It was just a stopgap, he assured her. Sam Payne Reed wanted to write, to lecture on social reform. His destiny, he was certain, was to make a difference in the world.

Alma applauded her new friend's efforts at the prison. Having observed the inner workings of San Francisco's city government while helping out her father, she agreed with Reed that some of the worst miscreants were outside prison. She admired his practical attempts to assist inmates at a time when many believed they should be educated with crowbars.

Alma's colleagues at the *Call* thought Reed ideally suited to her. So did Eugene and Adelaide, until they discovered that he was not only a Protestant but a divorced one. Perhaps her parents' outspoken disapproval added piquancy to the match. Perhaps Alma, at twenty-six, was eager for a greater degree of intimacy than she'd yet experienced. Certainly she was very weary of her parents' constant refrain that no woman could really be a woman without marriage. Sam Reed was handsome and charismatic, and he possessed a keen intellect. The two had much in common; perhaps they really were "made" for each other. Why wait longer?

Alma and Sam were married at a simple ceremony on August 8, 1915. Reed moved in with her at the Fairmont, where his salary added to Older's due bill enabled them to move to slightly larger quarters—a tiny suite. Nob Hill living, even on the modest scale achieved by the Reeds, was heady. There were happy, tender times, and wild, exciting times. For a while, Alma thought she'd somehow managed to break the dreaded middle-class mold. But a union that others thought "perfect" ended abruptly when Alma discovered that her husband of scarcely a year was having an affair with her closest friend.

Divorce may have been anathema to Eugene and Adelaide, but it was the only solution that Alma would consider. The relationship was severed as quickly as possible, but Alma decided to keep the name. She liked "Reed."

Brisk, breezy, it suited the image she was cultivating—wavy, bobbed hair, bee-stung lips, a "new woman"; she would keep it.

Once again, the *Call* was Alma's full-time love. She found solace in the ringing telephones, the clatter of typewriters, the sight of copyboys racing up and down the aisles snatching takes from reporters at their desks. Mrs. Goodfellow was as busy as ever. ("Four little children—ranging in age from five months to six years—are hungry today, and have been hungry for weeks. They are suffering this terrible need because their father has been out of employment for months. . . .")

She covered everything now: murders, riots, deathwatches, but her main beat remained San Quentin, and Alma had a flare for the bizarre. On February 4, 1920, she wrote:

A convicted bigamist! YET, he doesn't know either of his two wives.

Twice wedded, YET he has never consciously been a party to a marriage contract!

Tried and found guilty under the law which guaranteess him the right to plead his case, YET he had never had the chance to make the most feeble defense!

These are the startling inconsistencies surrounding the imprisonment of twenty-three-year-old Fred M. Hope, according to the strange story he tells at San Quentin Penitentiary.

If that story be false, it is among the most skillfully contrived tales ever hatched in the imagination of a criminal to thwart the ends of justice.

If it be true, an innocent boy is being deprived of his liberty.

If his statement be founded in fact, then he is the victim of as baffling a trick of memory as science has ever recorded or fiction has conceived.

Fred M. Hope insists that he went to sleep in a tent at Camp Fremont as a soldier in Uncle Sam's army on the night of March 25, 1918 and that he awakened to find himself a convict in a prison cell on December 30, 1919.

All the events, including his two marriages, and every incident of his daily life during that interim of twenty-one months have left not the slightest trace on his memory. The whole period is a total blank. He does not recall a moment of the trial.

He would not, he declares, recognize either of his two
wives—Rosie Lair Hope and Theresa Raballo—if he were to meet
them face to face. . . .

Alma's words were not without irony. There was something to be said for memory loss. She would have preferred it. But if her own loss and humiliation, her crushing sense of disillusionment, could not be forgotten, then perhaps the circumstances might be altered somewhat to suit herself. She and Sam were divorced now, though in later years there would be a different story. "My husband was a wealthy industrialist—a fine and generous man," she would invariably explain when asked about her past. "Shortly after our marriage, he became mortally ill. I was very young, scarcely more than a girl; he insisted that we part so that I might be free. The marriage was annulled."

Once again she was bending the facts to suit herself, to enhance the legend of Alma Reed that had already begun to evolve.

CHAPTER 2

The Power of Alma

Alma never got used to San Quentin. Every time its heavy iron doors clanged shut behind her, a feeling of panic swept over her. It was useless to argue that she was free, that she could leave at any time; the sense of confinement, desolation, and abandonment defied rationalization. "I won't come back, I won't go through this again," she promised herself; yet each week she did go back.

And then one day, seemingly by chance, she realized why.

"What's all this?" Alma asked Warden James Johnston, nodding at a stack of white envelopes on a table beside his desk.

"Invitations. We're having a hanging Friday morning. Want to come?"

"Who is it this time?"

"Mexican kid. Doesn't understand English—didn't even know he was going to die until last week. One of the other prisoners had to tell him."

Alma inwardly braced herself. "I don't understand."

"Apparently the lawyer appointed by the state down in Ludlow told him that no one under twenty-one was executed for murder if they pleaded guilty."

"He didn't even have an interpreter?"

"Yeah, he did, but no one bothered to tell him that the lawyer had lied—probably trying to get the whole thing over with in a hurry. No one bothered to mention the sentence either. The kid found out he was going to hang accidentally. During a prison vaudeville show, he asked another Spanish-speaking con why they were sitting in the balcony rather than down with the others on the ground floor. When Ruiz—the kid—was told that the condemned men always sat in the balcony, he argued that he shouldn't be there, that his sentence was life imprisonment. Everyone just laughed."

Alma looked at him in shocked disbelief. "I can't believe this."

"Yeah, it's pretty bad—and gets worse. When the kid finally realized that what they were telling him was true, he began to scream—got so bad it broke up the show."

"The *kid?* It's another boy hanging, isn't it? How old this time?"

"Seventeen."

"This boy—I'd like to see him."

"A waste of time, Mrs. Reed; he's as good as gone. Nobody cares about a Mexican national."

Alma shrugged. At least Johnston hadn't said "greaser." "I care. It might cheer him to have a visitor. I speak a little Spanish."

Reluctantly, Johnston agreed. Alma was shown into the small room, where the condemned men met their visitors. While waiting, she looked out at the prison garden. The previous summer Alma had thought it surprisingly pretty, but now the winter wind wailed forlornly through bare rosebushes. It had been raining all day. The view from the window was as bleak and desolate as the high gray wall just beyond.

Simon Ruiz was small, slight, with large luminous dark eyes. His shy friendliness shone through despair as Alma began to question him, struggling with her halting Spanish. Gratitude showed in his eyes as he recognized her effort. Simon, too, spoke slowly and precisely, for he was anxious that she understand his words. As they talked, Alma was aware of the clock striking ominously a half hour, then an hour—one less of the precious few that remained to him. Eventually, with much effort and patience on her part, Alma understood the essentials of the story.

Five months earlier Simon had left his sixteen-year-old bride with his parents and set off for the United States, hoping to make enough money to return to Mexico and buy a farm. He found a job the first day. Then a Mexican friend told him that better pay was to be made from railroad work. The two traveled together to Ludlow, California—"Lulu," as Simon called it—where they obtained work as section hands.

Almost immediately the boys were befriended by Eduardo Mirando, an older man who'd ridden with Pancho Villa six years before coming to California. Mirando had recently been fired by John Miller, the foreman of the section gang, and was bitter about it. Miller was an evil man, he told the boys. They could be certain that he would treat them as badly as he himself had been treated. Mirando urged Simon and his friend to join him in robbing Miller's house, but they refused.

All the following day, he continued to work on them, sometimes bullying, other times cajoling, until finally, late in the evening, the boys reluctantly accompanied him to Miller's house. It was empty. Mirando stood watch while the youngsters entered and took the foreman's gun, knife, and some World War I Liberty bonds. Hearing Miller's approaching footsteps, Mirando told Simon to shoot the foreman with the gun he'd just stolen, but the boy refused. When Miller spotted Simon and angrily berated him, Mirando again urged Simon to kill the foreman, calling him a coward for standing such abuse.

"I did not want to kill him—he'd done me no harm," Simon told Alma, "but Mirando—he kept urging me, taunting me. Finally he pointed a gun at me and threatened to shoot if I did not shoot Señor Miller. At last I turned my head away and fired. I hoped that I had missed, but the bullet killed him."

Alma listened to the story carefully, studying the young man opposite her. She could feel Simon's anguish and believed him when he said, "I am very sorry, oh so sorry for what I have done. I was wrong to listen to Mirando. I know now I should have thought before it was too late, but now it is done and I deserve punishment. I should be in prison all my life or for a very long time, because I killed a man who did me no wrong. But I have never wronged anyone else, and I have always believed in peaceful living and hard work. I have been working hard since I left school—when I was fourteen. My great misfortune was that I met Mirando.''

Hours later, Alma emerged from the interview, exhausted and badly shaken. "What happened to the older man, Mirando?" she asked Warden Johnston.

"He turned state's evidence, testified against Ruiz. He's out now, free as a breeze.''

"That's so unfair.''

"Yes, I suppose it is, but it's perfectly legal. Kind of a shame, Ruiz really isn't such a bad kid. Once he finally got it into his head that he was scheduled to be hung, he settled down. He's religious; guess he thinks his saints'll save him.''

"*Somebody* had better, but I don't suppose anyone cares one way or the other.''

"Well, actually he does have one friend—the consul general of Mexico heard about him somehow. Circulated a petition among Mexicans living around here which he gave to the governor. Didn't get very far with it.''

Alma brightened. "The consul general! I'd like to talk to him. Could I use your phone?''

"Sure, sure, help yourself," he said, and he led her back to his own office.

She found the number quickly in the thin phone book and was soon talking to Alberto Mascarenas, who was delighted by her interest. "There is one factor that is difficult for your countrymen to understand," he told her. "Simon was born and raised in an environment of revolution and bloodshed. Some kind of warfare has been going on almost continuously in Mexico for nearly twenty years. Human life may mean less to a boy who has seen friends and relatives slaughtered before his eyes. I tried to explain to your governor that Simon had been in your country less than a month when he obeyed the order of an older man, a man who'd befriended him in a strange land. To kill is wrong, we know; but in the context of revolution—all he has ever known . . .''

"Yes, but he *is* in this country," Alma reminded him.

"That is his misfortune. In Mexico there is a law which holds the 'actor intellectual' or the person who plans the crime, as the responsible party. If this law were in operation here, I am convinced that it would reach, and reach rightfully, the man who urged and coaxed and bullied Simon into shooting John Miller. Instead, that man, by turning state's evidence, is free, while a seventeen-year-old boy is faced with the gallows."

Alma thanked him for the telephone interview, replacing the receiver on the cradle of the large black phone. "He makes a good case," she said, turning to face the warden.

"Not good enough to sway the governor. Mascarenas's already tried— four hundred names on that petition. The kid's going to hang. Nothing'll stop that."

Alma gathered her purse and notebook as the warden watched her despondently. Like the trusties in his office, Johnston looked forward to Alma's visits and was always sorry to see her leave. "I don't suppose you'd like to see how it works?"

Alma looked at him uncomprehendingly. "The hanging," he explained. "Maybe you'd like to see how we do it—no, I don't suppose you'd care for that."

"Oh, yes, I would. Just show me; I want to see it all."

On the ferry headed back to San Francisco, Alma found a seat by the window. No one seeing the prison from the outside could ever imagine the interior. It was like a medieval fortress. And somewhere inside a boy waited to die. Alma felt his sense of isolation almost as if it were her own. Warden Johnston had said it was hopeless, but Alma didn't accept that. Who was it who'd said the pen was mightier than the sword? Resolutely, she took out her notebook. Perhaps if she could convey some of the horror of what she'd seen. Slowly Alma began to write:

All the "props" are in readiness. The rope, the scales, the trap door, the three iron balls suspended from taut cords and concealed beneath the gallows floor—each has been carefully examined and passed upon as efficient.

And the Mexican boy who is to be the principal actor in tomorrow's tragedy of hideous realism? He, too, is ready—and awaits his fate with a stoicism, a calmness that surpass anything in the traditions of San Francisco's death row. . . .

Alma's story ran the following morning on the front page of the *San Francisco Morning Call* under the banner headlines: "BOY HANGS TO-MORROW UNLESS STEPHENS INTERVENES."

All the next day the switchboards were jammed with calls to Alma. Her story had struck a responsive cord. "What will stop it? What can I do?" callers asked. "Call the governor's office," she urged. "Send telegrams. Governor Stephens is the only one who can save Simon's life."

For Simon, lying on a cot in the corner of his cage, the day passed quietly. Under the flickering light of the gas jet, he read books loaned him by a padre in nearby Benicia, *The Glory of Mary* and *The Crown of Precious Pearls*.

In the afternoon a guard informed him that because this was his last night on earth, he might have anything that he wished to eat for dinner. Simon chose fried chicken, fried potatoes, bread, butter, coffee, blackberries with cream, and a little cake.

The final day passed with no action by the governor. Simon was taken to the death cell where he would spend his last night. The clanging door echoed eerily as the boy collapsed on the narrow cot. He lay quietly in his cell, the minutes ticking away.

Finally, in the distance, he heard the sound of approaching footsteps. Were they coming for him? Simon prayed for forgiveness and for courage. He rose slowly.

The door swung open. It was Warden Johnston, his ruddy face wearing an expression of a man immensely relieved of some great burden as his hand went instinctively to Simon's shoulder. The boy turned to the interpreter with desperate, but cautious, optimism.

"Governor Stephens has granted you a reprieve until January twenty-eighth—two weeks. The warden says to tell you a lot can happen in two weeks."

Hardly had the door closed behind Johnston when another sound was heard. Soft, gentle, yet exultant knuckles tapping on steely partitions.

Tap, tap, tap. Cell to cell: tap, tap, tap. "Reprieve!" it said. "Reprieve!" By the mysterious underground system of a giant prison, word was conveyed—Ruiz will not swing tomorrow. And then once again silence brooded over the great, grim penitentiary. In their dark guardhouses armed men peered down into the brilliantly lighted compounds. From the stations went up the cry: "Eleven o'clock, and all is well!"

That was the only sound heard. But throughout the prison there was quiet jubilation. In every blockhouse, in every corridor, in every cell were silent cheers, for the condemned boy had been granted a reprieve.

In Palo Alto, some fifty miles south of San Quentin, Ethel Scott settled down with a cup of cocoa. It was nearly 11:00 P.M., and upstairs her husband was sleeping. Soon she would join him, but for the moment she needed some quiet time to think. The day had been such a busy one. So many calls, so many pep talks. Club women, school and college friends, women she had known as far back as grammar school, anyone she'd ever met at a wedding or baby shower, wives of her husband's business associates. Ethel Scott had called them all, pleaded with them all: *"Send a wire. Call all your friends; get them to send wires. The governor must be persuaded to stop the murder."*

She should have been exhausted, but thoughts of the condemned boy kept her wide awake. The idea that her native state of California would have the name and infamy of executing the youngest prisoner ever put to death in any penitentiary in the United States quite appalled her. Only that morning she had read Alma Reed's story in the *Morning Call.* She was galvanized by its cry for help.

When she'd at last been granted the right to vote, when she and her friends had driven off together in her new blue Oldsmobile to cast their first ballots, they'd shared a grand sense of purpose and adventure. They reminded one another more than once that they were making history! Now, ten years later, she wondered if things had really changed. What good did it do to vote, what good did it do to be president of the California Club, if life was just as grim, just as cynical, and just as inhuman as before?

Ethel Scott had been on the phone immediately after reading the article, calling Alma Reed at the San Francisco newspaper. The line had been busy, and she'd had to wait a long time to get through. She could imagine her husband's raised eyebrows at the toll charges; Ethel winced at the time, not realizing that this call was only the beginning. Then at last the reporter was on the line, with a soft, gentle, but slightly throaty voice.

"I—I want to help," Ethel said. She was a bit unnerved to be talking to a newspaper woman. Many thought them a bit mannish, coarse even. Ethel didn't even want to contemplate the things they saw and wrote about. She inwardly chided herself; surely all women were sisters in this common cause.

"Thank you so much for calling," Alma greeted her warmly. "We need all the help we can get. Where do you live?"

"In Palo Alto."

"Do you know many people there? Perhaps if you could call your women friends and ask them to send telegrams to the governor. Even ten—five—any—would help."

"I can do a little better than that. I'm president of the California Club. We've got many chapters and a membership of some twenty thousand women."

That had been the beginning. Ethel had been at her phone all day, pleading and cajoling friends, acquaintances, acquaintances of acquaintances, club after club, contact after contact. Had it all been useless? she wondered now. Would the governor really care what a bunch of women thought?

She rose wearily and was carrying the cup into the kitchen when the sound of the phone pierced the nighttime stillness. Ethel very nearly dropped the cup. No one ever called at this hour. Something terrible must have happened to one of the children. Rushing to the table in the hallway, she grasped the telephone with trembling fingers.

"It's Alma Reed. I'm sorry to call so late, but I just had a feeling that you'd be up. You'll read about it in tomorrow's paper, but I thought you'd like to know the good news tonight. Governor Stephens granted a stay of execution."

"Thank God! We've won. We did it! We really did it!"

But on the other end of the wire, Alma sighed. She knew the fight had only begun.

"Governor William D. Stephens is convinced that the women of California are opposed to the hanging of Simon Ruiz," Alma announced in a page one article in the *Call,* dated March 5, 1921.

The story didn't mention that it was she who had activated the twelve club leaders representing some sixty thousand women to converge on the executive office in Sacramento, nor was there any suggestion that her own plea was by far the most eloquent.

It was good, but not good enough. The issue, now known as "boy hanging," had divided the state. Richard Bright, deputy sheriff of San Bernardino County, where Miller had been shot, countered Alma's efforts by urging the governor to carry out the sentence. Hundreds, professing to fear a resulting massive crime wave, agreed with him. Their letters and wires also poured in.

In her efforts to dispel the impression left by Bright, Alma traveled to Ludlow herself and interviewed the attorney who had represented both Simon and his friend as well as Eduardo Mirando. The man reluctantly admitted to her that he'd advised the boys to plead guilty, believing that their youth would influence the court in their favor. When this strategy failed and Simon was given the death penalty and his young friend life imprisonment, the attorney turned his attention to the remaining client, Mirando. Discharging what he blandly called his ethical obligations to Mirando, he'd deliberately withheld information regarding Mirando's part in the crime.

Stephens considered this testimony; he listened to Alma's arguments and to the pleas of the club women, many of them mothers, who grieved at the prospect of a boy losing his life in a strange land.

The best they were able to wrest from him was one more reprieve. The original hanging had been postponed to January 28, then February 11, then March 11. Now it would take place April 11. At last Alma realized that words alone were not going to save Simon.

Assemblywoman Anna Saylor looked as if she might just run into the kitchen and bring out a pan of hot biscuits and some good old-fashioned marmalade. It wasn't the persona Alma had expected.

For the first time the reporter had serious doubts about her course of action. Alma had herself written a bill that would—if passed—raise the minimum hanging age from fourteen to twenty-one. Now she needed a legislative sponsor. None of the men she'd approached would touch it; each had rejected the concept as fit only for "bleeding hearts." Finally, Alma realized that only a woman would rise to this kind of challenge.

Unfortunately, there were no choices. There was only one woman in the state legislature, Anna Saylor. Setting the cup and saucer down on the polished mahogany tea table, Alma glanced around at the comfortably furnished Berkeley home. Anna was watching her expectantly. It was now or never, Alma realized. Proceeding with what she hoped was engaging confidence, the reporter launched into the speech she'd prepared and memorized on the Oakland ferry coming over.

"I was one of many women—many people—who voted for you. Naturally I wanted to see a woman in government, but also I liked what you said. I've never forgotten the story in the *Call.* 'I don't want special consideration,' you said. 'My platform is on the equality, not the sex, basis. What is good for men is good for women. Copartnership and good fellowship must supplant rivalry.' "

"Yes, I did say that"—Anna paused, thinking back over her campaign days—"but I have to admit that I had, and still have, a lot to learn. I need all the help I can get. I assume you're here to write an article for your paper. Oh, there are so many issues that must be addressed. Do you have children? Well, you will have one day; believe me, the elementary schools desperately need more money."

"I'm certain that's true and it's because of your interest in young people that I'm here—"

"Elementary schools are just one thing," Anna cut in. "I'm vitally concerned about equal property rights for both husband and wife. You can surely see the need for that."

"Absolutely! I'd like to do a special feature on that one, but you can see right now I—"

"Oh"—Anna brightened. "You're here to do a story on my proposed industrial home for women. That's wonderful! Yes, I can see that you're just the sort of modern young person who can see beyond the hypocrisy clouding that issue. I said there would be no fight on a sex basis, but there *are* some questions that concern women vitally. This is one of them. It's up to us women to see that new pursuits are opened up to these tragic victims. They can't be treated as outcasts. We have no right to talk of 'fallen women.' There are no absolute standards. Don't you agree?"

"Oh, yes, certainly!" Alma was torn, it was another good story. Later, she promised herself, when the bill had passed, but now all her attention must go to Simon and the hanging age. "Actually," she began again, "I have here—"

Anna ignored her, rushing on, "Because they have a past we should not deprive them of a future. Under proper guidance, the best of them can be reclaimed—if we make the road back to righteousness a bit easier."

It was the perfect opening. Alma took advantage of a pause for breath and plunged in once more. *"No,"* she emphasized. "I'm here about something else entirely—an issue of even greater immediacy. This one involves young people really being deprived of their futures, *permanently* deprived. I looked you up in the library at the *Call,"* she admitted. "When you were elected two years ago you said, 'As the pioneer woman in the California Legislature, I expect to be riddled with criticism. If I vote for a measure, I will be questioned. If I vote against it, I will be questioned. So there's only one thing to do—the thing that seems right at the time.' "

Anna pushed back her fluffy, slightly out-of-control gray hair. "Yes, I did say that. Now I suppose you're here to discuss the Ruiz case. I feared as much when I got your call. I've followed your stories; everybody has. The Simon Ruiz matter is what they call a hot potato. Many of the legislators really want to put an end to boy hanging, but are afraid their constituents will think them soft."

Alma sighed heavily. "It *is* indeed a controversial issue. Perhaps too controversial for a woman to handle effectively. Some will undoubtedly say that a woman legislator should stick with domestic issues. Well, of course, you and I both know what they'll really say: 'A woman's only true job is taking care of her home and family.' " Alma sighed even louder. "It's a tough challenge, really too tough for a woman."

"Fiddlesticks! I have never seen the time when a woman couldn't run a home and take an interest in government as well"—Anna's ample bosom heaved expansively. "It's the poorest housekeeper who is always at it." The words had a familiar ring to Alma; she was certain she'd read them verbatim in the same news story. She braced herself for the bottom line. Anna obviously had a politician's love of her own voice, but the reporter's earlier estimate was changing. Anna *could* be a powerful ally—if she chose to be. "The woman who fritters her time making fancy salads and doing elaborate hand embroidery takes the husk of life and leaves the kernel. My motto is plain living and high thinking with a lemon pie and a few doughnuts thrown in once in a while."

"Very well said," Alma broke in, hoping to forestall more rhetoric. She removed the carefully drafted bill from her purse.

"Why shouldn't a woman take her place in the legislature?" Anna continued determinedly. "It takes both men and women to offer tolerance. They kept us out of the schools for ages. They allowed us entrance grudgingly in the churches. But there never was a time when we were not allowed to get up a benefit to buy a library for the college or a new carpet for the sanctuary. We'll 'buy in' with our work in the legislature too."

Alma was ready, the bill in her hand. "Does that mean a measure to save boys?"

Anna squared her shoulders, reached forward and took the paper. "Let's see what you've got."

"BILL IN MOTION TO STOP HANGING BOYS—ASSEMBLYWOMAN WILL PRESENT BILL: STATE-WIDE CAMPAIGN IS MAPPED." Fremont Older had handed Alma a copy of the first edition himself. The whole newsroom crowded around, excited and admiring. Alma wasn't just writing headlines; she was making them. They were all proud of her; even the toughest of the old hands were forced to admit that it wasn't bad at all for "a skirt."

Beneath the eight-column banner headline, Alma's story began:

> *Aroused to action by the proposal to hang a 17-year-old boy in California for murder, club women of the state today started a movement for the abolition of capital punishment for all persons under 21.*
>
> *The bill which would make this a law will be introduced at the present session of the Legislature by Mrs. F. L. Saylor, assemblywoman of Berkeley. With the introduction of the bill, a statewide fight will be made to force its passage.*
>
> *The first gun will be fired Friday when a delegation of prominent club women will wait upon Governor Stephens with a plea for the life of Simon Ruiz, a 17-year-old Mexican boy, who will be hanged April 11. The bill will be placed in the hands of Assemblywoman Saylor for presentation, and the various members of both houses will be asked to support it.*
>
> *Action which resulted in the framing of the bill was taken by Mrs. Alma Reed—Mrs. Goodfellow of the Call—who received the support and endorsement of the executive board of San Francisco Center at a special meeting at the St. Francis Hotel. The endorsement was unanimous and the clubwomen promised to give their active support for the measure.*

Hanging of persons under the age of 21 years must be stopped, the club women declare, and they have united to present their bill. Among the women who are active in the fight are . . .

"I've got the best boss in the world," Alma acknowledged. Fremont Older was not only backing her cause with a series of stirring editorials, but he'd agreed to send her to Sacramento to lobby for the bill.

"Actually, I think you'd go anyway," he admitted. "I might as well have you there as our correspondent covering the story."

Alma made a quick call to Anna. "Hurry!" the assemblywoman urged. "Wait till you see the Sacramento papers. They're dead set against the bill. We need all the help we can get. Can you bring Ethel Scott and some of the others?"

Soon the telephone chain was in motion. Overriding the objections of her husband, Ethel Scott led a small but vocal band of club women to Sacramento. Others would soon follow. Before long, they'd set up a command office at the Senator Hotel. Ethel admitted, "It's the most exciting thing that's ever happened to me."

But the enemy was formidable. Angry headlines deplored the bill, demanding instead that the present law be strengthened. Headlines in the *Sacramento Union* warned: "MEASURE PRESUMED TO PROTECT MISGUIDED YOUTHS, BUT WOULD ACTUALLY PERMIT SHREWD CRIMINALS TO 'USE' THEM."

That night, the proponents held an emergency strategy meeting. "This bill will never make it as it is now," Anna told them. "There's just too much pressure against it. We've got to bring the hanging age down from twenty-one to eighteen. There's a chance for eighteen; twenty-one's impossible."

Alma sadly agreed; she'd reached the same conclusion. "Maybe later—next year."

"Yes, perhaps next year or the year after—give them a little time; but for now . . ."

The following day in a special dispatch to the *Call,* Alma wrote: "At a conference here today it was decided to amend the bill before the Legislature forbidding capital punishment in the case of minors. The amendment will lower the age limit from 21 to 18 years, making it impossible to execute boys who are under 18 years of age at the time of their offenses."

It had been a wise decision—the only decision possible—Alma realized when the bill was presented. In an article for the *Call,* she announced:

The way has been cleared for California's forward step.

The bill aimed to prevent the hanging of minors survived its initial hearing last night before the committee on revision of criminal procedure. Although the measure did not receive the recommendation of the committee, it will be given a chance on the floor of the Legislature, where Mrs. Anna Saylor, its proponent, and her most ardent supporters believe that it will triumph.

Attended by a score of the state's leading clubwomen, social and prison workers, and humanitarians in many lines of service, the hearing was the occasion for the display of forensic ability by speakers who favored and opposed the bill.

The rhetoric of the proponents notwithstanding, across the board voters still opposed the bill. The *Sacramento Union* continued its attack in bold headlines: "SAYLOR BILL WOULD EITHER BRING ABOUT INJUSTICE IN LAW ENFORCEMENT OR WOULD SERVE TO LET ALL GUILTY ESCAPE."

Within the assembly the fight was a bitter one, but Alma and her team of lobbyists were gathering strength. The bill was returned to committee. This time, after a minimum of "further study," it came back with the recommendation that it be passed. On March 24, 1921, the Saylor bill was approved. It would now move to the Senate.

Appalled by this victory, the *Sacramento Union* warned of the appeals being made to the sympathy of senators. "Stripped of sentimentality, the Sayler bill is an anti-capital punishment measure. If the age limit were set at any figure the danger to the capital punishment law still would be present. Women lobbyists are exacting promises from senators to vote for the bill. . . ."

But not enough of them. Alma was growing desperate. The senators' resistance was steely, seemingly ingrained. Simon's precarious existence, the passage of the amendment that might save him, had taken over her life. Every waking moment was centered on this cause. Sometimes during one of the rare occasions when she had time for introspection, it seemed to Alma that her meeting with the boy was somehow predestined, that it was her purpose in life to save not only Simon but hundreds, perhaps thousands, of boys who had no one to speak for them. Now, for the first time confronted with the seemingly impregnable resistence of the Senate, Alma began to have serious doubts. All her pleas, her strategy, her desperately hard work—was it all for nothing?

Then a surprise telephone call reached her from San Bernardino County. It seemed heaven-sent. As senators squared off to debate the measure, Alma brought in her big gun, T. W. Duckworth, the deputy district attorney who had prosecuted Simon. "If I were clothed with the direct responsibility of deciding whether Simon Ruiz should be hanged or imprisoned for life, I would spare his life," he told legislators.

The senators were courteously silent, but debate resumed with no apparent acknowledgment of Duckworth's testimony. Alma and Anna looked at each other in consternation. What more could they do?

Among the fiercest opponents of the bill were two clergymen who cited Mosaic Law. "An eye for an eye," they sternly reminded their peers.

As the days passed, feelings heightened. An article in the *Sacrameto Bee* described the situation:

> *With the files of both houses crowded with bills, the Legislature today began the final week of the forty-fourth session. Adjournment is scheduled to take place at noon Friday, but in all likelihood the clock will have to be stopped for at least a day to permit the houses to complete their work.*
>
> *There are on the Assembly files approximately 500 measures that must be disposed of while the Senate is faced with more than 400 bills. The big fights of the closing week are expected to take place in the Senate. Under consideration is a strong bill raised by Assemblywoman Anna Saylor of Berkeley to prevent the hanging of boys under eighteen years of age. Mrs. Saylor and women lobbyists have been working hard in the interests of the measure, the outcome of which is doubtful. Many of the members are determined to oppose the passage. . . .*

These hard-liners, Alma quickly learned, were primarily prohibitionists and ministers, who spoke with righteous eloquence of families pulled asunder by the evils of alcohol, but found no inconsistency in extracting the last bit of vengeance from "wrongdoers." No one, no matter how young, how innocent, how uninformed, should be allowed to escape their righteous wrath.

It seemed that nothing could penetrate their hard-line stance. "Do you hold yourself to be higher, wiser than God?" they thundered at Alma, Bibles in hand. At times she expected to be struck by the holy book, so frequently was it waved in her face. These men, she reluctantly realized, were hopeless, beyond her reach. Stern, unyielding Calvinists, they would never allow themselves the luxury of pity. State-sanctioned murder was God's work. They weren't about to interfere with it.

But there were others in the Senate whose negativity was more pragmatic. Many were concerned that a yes vote might cause them to appear soft in the eyes of constituents. One of the most powerful men in the Senate, John Inman of Sacramento, disavowed these reservations, yet his rebuttal to the Saylor Bill was the most vocal.

From the beginning, he'd listened to Alma's arguments and those of the other lobbyists, smiled politely, and then shook his head. Alma, noting his easy geniality, had thought him an easy target. "Couldn't we have a bite to eat?" she suggested, smiling up into his florid face.

"Why, I'd be honored to have lunch with such a pretty lady," he agreed. Alma left the Senate floor feeling confident. She returned defeated. Inman had merely been amusing himself at her expense. Wondering at her own naïveté, she recognized his political savvy. There were a number of bills of much greater personal concern that Inman was anxious to see pass. In exchange for other senators' vote on these matters, he was more than willing not only to cast his vote against her bill but to curry favor with its hard-line opponents by speaking out against it. His speeches were strong, well-worded, and convincing. Senator John Inman was a formidable opponent.

It had been a hard fight. Now at last the voting had begun. Alma's heart pounded as she searched the faces of the Senate members. Each pause was an agony, each "nay" a wound that seemed to penetrate her very heart.

The final roll was tallied. It was nineteen for the measure, twenty against it. As she desperately surveyed the room, Alma realized that Senator Herbert Jones of San Jose was absent. "Oh, my God, where can he be?" she gasped. "He was for the bill; I know he was for it. Where could he have gone?"

"Perhaps the men's room," Ethel timidly suggested.

Alma was ready to follow him there if need be, but Senator Jones soon reappeared and insisted on another vote.

This time the tally was twenty to twenty.

"I'm sorry, dear. We really tried," Anna said, pressing Alma's hand.

"The lieutenant governor—he can break the tie," Alma ventured.

"Of course. He *will* break the tie, but you know how he'll break it."

Alma nodded wordlessly. They were both too well acquainted with the conservative sentiments of Lieutenant Governor C. C. Young. The president of the Senate had made his views very clear. His vote would defeat the amendment.

"I—I just have to go out," Alma said, rising. "I'll be right back, but I need some water." Quickly, she fled the gallery, unwilling that anyone see her tears. It was just too much. After all those long weeks of hard work, soon the vote would be over and for nothing. The vision of Simon as she had last seen him in San Quentin haunted her, his dark eyes watching her so trustingly as he talked earnestly about learning carpentry in prison. The thought of having to tell him was unbearable. Heedlessly, Alma ran the length of the corridor, then slumped down on the building's marble steps. The tension of the past months overwhelmed her as she began to sob quietly.

Senator Inman had hoped to have a quick cup of coffee prior to the business of the afternoon. He was relieved to have this boy-hanging matter out of the way. Other issues were far more important to him, and he was impatient to confront them. Then, fatefully, as Alma would always believe, his eyes happened to fall upon her as she sat slumped, face buried in her hands. Inman paused in his stride, shrugged slightly, and turned to face her.

Anna Saylor was gathering her papers, wearily stuffing them into a briefcase. Ethel Scott and the other lobbyists were milling about, trying to comfort one another. Each moved leadenly, unable to believe that it was really over. Someone said something about an early-afternoon train. Should they try to catch it? Perhaps it was best to have lunch first, but who wanted to eat?

"Quiet!" the assemblywoman silenced their babble. The women looked up surprised. Alma had reentered the room and was walking toward them. Senator Inman was back, too, talking now with Lieutenant Governor Young.

Anna studied the two men intently. They appeared to be arguing.

Young's face was literally turning purple. The assemblywoman edged closer. What was that they were saying, a *reconsideration?* But that was impossible. It was all over—Young's nay vote merely a formality. But, yes—Anna could scarcely believe it—they were talking about a reconsideration. John Inman wanted to change his vote and was insisting that the amendment be formally reconsidered. Now the Senator motioned her toward them.

"Assemblywoman Saylor"—Inman took her arm, drawing her closer—"surely you must agree that your bill as it now stands is unfair to law enforcement."

"Unfair?" Anna looked at him puzzled.

"This is absurd, every aspect of this damn fool bleeding-heart bill has been discussed"—Young's voice rose angrily. "The session ends today and we've got all the other bills—all of them have to go back to the assembly for their concurrence. We'll never adjourn, we'll never be out of here."

"I'm afraid I really don't understand"—Anna ignored Young, studying Inman's face for some clue.

"Dear lady, surely you must agree with me that as your bill now stands, the burden of proof lies unfairly upon the shoulders of the prosecution."

"Well, doesn't it always?"

"But surely not in the matter of age. Don't you feel that it is the boys—the defendants—who should be responsible for proving that they're under eighteen?"

Anna's sigh of relief was almost audible. Her worst adversary had for some unknown reason changed his mind. He was clearly seeking some face-saving solution to allow passage of the amendment.

"Why, of course, Senator, you're absolutely right. It hadn't crossed my mind, but the defendants should most certainly be required to establish their ages."

"I'm glad you see it that way. We will then open the bill up for reconsideration and vote once again."

"That's preposterous!" Young stormed. "People have left—"

"The sergeant at arms will just have to round up the absentees."

Quickly Anna turned to Alma and the others, who were watching anxiously. "Go to it, ladies. We've been given a second chance, but we can't afford any backsliding now. Talk to *everyone.*"

A call of the Senate was dutifully ordered. While the sergeant at arms rushed about searching for absent senators, Alma and the others swarmed over the Senate floor. Each argued desperately with every man who would listen, realizing that it was her last chance.

Young was furious. "There's been more pressure brought to bear on this measure than all the other bills put together," he argued. But at last everyone was back in place, and the voting began again. As before the senators were solidly divided; the vote was tied until the twenty-first ballot was cast by Senator John Inman.

The boy-hanging bill had passed. Many rushed forward to shake hands with Anna Saylor. She smiled proudly, but when the furor began to subside, the assemblywoman pushed her way through the exuberant lobbyists who were hugging one another. In the thick of it was Alma, her slim young body almost obscured by the matrons who were thumping her affectionately on the back.

Anna pulled the young reporter free from her admirers. "My dear, what happened? Senator Inman followed you back in; I saw him. He'd changed his mind—I knew almost immediately from the expression on his face. What in the world could you possibly have said that you hadn't already said many times before?"

"Nothing really"—Alma shook her head dazedly. "I didn't say anything. He saw me outside. I'm afraid I was sobbing. He took me by the shoulders, lifted me up, and said, 'Okay, honey, if it means all that much to you, I'll change my vote.' Maybe he just can't stand to see a woman cry."

CHAPTER · 3

Hail the
Conquering Gringa

"Mexico! You'll be murdered in your bed!" Adelaide shrieked. Eugene was only slightly more restrained. "What was it that newspaperman, that hero of yours, Ambrose Bierce—"Bitter" Bierce, wasn't it?—what was it that he wrote? 'To be a gringo in Mexico is euthanasia.'—and that was the last that anyone ever heard of him."

Alma shrugged. "It's so typical; 'Bitter' *is* bitter. That's just the sort of man he is."

"Was," her father corrected her. "Bitter" *was* bitter. The man is dead—murdered in Mexico."

"Nobody knows that. I'm sure he'll turn up one day with some wild, wonderful story."

"Alma! Be sensible; he went off to report on Mexico for Hearst. He's been missing for nine years. Nine years!"

"Well, all right—nine years. He dropped out nine years ago. Things were a little unsettled in Mexico then, but now—"

"Now they're just as unsettled. No one knows where that crazy Pancho Villa will turn up next or what he'll do."

"But Papa"—Alma was growing indignant—"don't you realize that this is an honor? I've been invited to Mexico by President Obregon himself. It's his way of saying thank you for my helping Simon. Do you imagine that he'd allow anything to happen to me?"

Eugene snorted.

"I suppose the man means well," Adelaide interjected, "but Mexico's a big place. A week never passes without a story telling of the murder or disappearance of an American traveler. Why, only last week I read in the *Bulletin*—your very own paper—that a train was derailed by bandits. Hundreds were slaughtered, some of them innocent Americans."

"I don't think Americans are very innocent," Alma contradicted. "Our country has huge oil interests in Mexico; we own half the oil fields. Mr. Hearst has an immense ranch in Chihuahua. There's been much too much interference in Mexican affairs."

"Now, Alma, we're not going to get into that," her father admonished.

"No, we're not. I've learned there's no point in it. The important thing is that I'm going to Mexico. This is the greatest opportunity of my life. Perhaps the story that Ambrose Bierce was unable to tell—perhaps that story will actually be *my* story. Wouldn't that just serve the great man right after all the awful things he's said about women writers? 'Gray batter of their brainettes!' "—Alma sniffed. "Can you imagine it, me scooping Bitter Bierce!"

Adelaide was horrified; Eugene, secretly proud and a bit envious.

Life had taken an exciting turn for Alma. The boy-hanging bill had scarcely passed when R. A. Crothers, editor of the *Bulletin,* had made her an offer too good to refuse. Competition between the two papers was fierce. Fremont Older himself had left the *Bulletin* for the *Call.* The loss had affected circulation drastically. Now the *Bulletin* was fighting desperately to regain its former position. What better way than to lure away the *Call*'s star reporter?

And Alma was a star. Her amazing success with Simon and her popularity as Mrs. Goodfellow had made her a household name in San Francisco. Crothers was anxious to capitalize on that. Not only would she receive more money, but he promised Alma a column with her picture. She would be the only staff reporter to receive that kind of recognition.

Delightedly, she had posed for a photograph that would be inset into her column; her profile, a winsome silhouette in a stylish broad-brimmed hat. As an additional inducement, the *Bulletin* would sponsor a charity and place her in charge. Alma decided on a summer camp for underprivileged children. "Happyland" was exactly the sort of place that she had longed to attend as a child. Her columns frequently extolled the contributions Happyland was making to San Francisco's youth and implored readers to donate funds.

Occasionally, there was a more lively assignment, such as Mrs. Nettie Farewell, a singularly unattractive woman, who complained: "A man wants what he can't get. I don't want to marry any man or to have any man in love with me. That's why my life is burdened with men." (The headline read: "WOOER BRAVES CROWBAR, BULLETS, ALL FOR LOVE.") But for the most part, Alma's stories focused on Happyland and the not-so-happy residents of a city facing a postwar depression. "FAMILY OF 6 IN DIRE NEED, FAMILY OF 9 HAS ONLY $3 TO LIVE ON" was a typical headline. Though aware of the value of what she was doing, there were times when Alma feared that sugar dripping from her typewriter might induce diabetes.

And then it had come: an invitation to Mexico as the personal guest of President Alvaro Obregon. Undaunted by the very real dangers involved, Alma never considered refusing. Crothers, delighted by her daring, looked forward to a series detailing her adventures.

Alma was busy making plans for her departure when another letter came—a plea from the suspect in a notorious murder case. The Reverend John Spencer had been accused of drowning his wife in Clear Lake, the center of a northern California resort area. He wanted her money, the neighbors said, and there were rumors of another woman. Spencer stoutly maintained both his virtue and his innocence but would discuss the case with no one. Now he was literally begging to see Alma, "the girl who'd saved Simon Ruiz." He would tell his story to her and her alone.

"You've got to go!" Crothers was adamant. "This is the story of a lifetime. Mexico can wait." Intrigued and flattered, Alma agreed.

It was settled. She would represent the *Bulletin* at what promised to be a most sensational trial. Of course, Eugene and Adelaide were delighted—anything to keep their daughter out of Mexico. Besides, as time passed, many of their earlier prejudices passed with it. Prescott, now a teenager with a thriving paper route, was cutting classes to hang around the *Bulletin*. Adelaide didn't need her tarot cards to tell what his career would be.

Alma interviewed the clergyman in his cell; he related a touching tale of conjugal bliss. Married fourteen years, he and his wife had been "chums and comrades, one rarely without the other." The only event that ever marred their happiness had resulted from stories told by a "designing woman to further her own ends." The gossip had upset his wife greatly, and to calm her nerves Spencer had taken her out rowing one summer evening.

According to the story, Mrs. Spencer had fallen while climbing from the boat to a wharf. His attempts to save her proved fruitless. Spencer's case wasn't enhanced by the fact that he'd shared a love nest in San Jose with another woman, a woman he had referred to in letters as "my only sweetheart," or that the clergyman had—only days before the drowning—obtained his wife's signature on a deed naming him the owner of her property.

"You preach the ten commandments and then break every one," the district attorney sonorously intoned early in the state's case. "Thou shalt not commit adultery, thou shalt not kill—each one of these you have broken."

Spencer's attorney opened his argument for the defense by remarking that if every man were hanged for going out with another woman, the hangman would be busy and the women lonesome.

After listening to a week of testimony, Alma was glad that her job was merely to report the facts, not to determine—much less act upon—them. As the jury filed out, she left the court and drove her borrowed Model T out to Clear Lake. Spencer was obviously guilty, but guilty of murder? How frightening that a man's fate could rest on circumstantial evidence alone.

Her thoughts strayed as they had more than once in the past few days to her marriage. Sam Reed had married Theoline Pohlson, who'd temporarily forsaken her career as a concert violinist to devote herself to him. They were expecting a baby. Would that be enough for him—for either of them? Now leavened by experience, Alma's earlier cynicism regarding the endurance of love and marriage had returned.

Returning to the courtroom, she settled down to wait. The jury deliberated seven hours. There were four ballots before a verdict was reached. At last it came: the Reverend John Spencer, found guilty of murder in the first degree, was sentenced to life imprisonment.

Alma raced to the phone. Within minutes, Crothers was on the line. "Glad you called," he said before she could say anything. "I've been trying all day to get you, but the circuits have been busy."

"You've got me now. They've found Spencer guilty; it's life. I'll see if he'll talk to me."

"No, no—the hell with that. I'll get someone on the line to take the story, then I want you out of there and back here on the double."

"Why, what's up? What's happened?"

"A big bash in Fatty Arbuckle's suite at the St. Francis. Some girl's dead. The D.A.'s out for blood. He's promised to clean up Hollywood. This will be a big one. I want you here."

"But Mexico—you promised. I was leaving as soon as Spencer's trial was over."

"Mexico will have to wait."

And it did.

Roscoe "Fatty" Arbuckle's income, people said, made the president's look like a sick nickel. In six years he'd risen from a five-dollar-a-day extra to receiving three hundred dollars for a single day—the highest paid film star in the world. Born in a sod hut in Kansas, America's favorite funny man paid the then–unheard-of sum of two hundred fifty thousand dollars for a house owned by Hollywood's first vamp, Theda Bara.

Touted as the "greatest pie slinger of all times, the grand lama of the meringue," the ambidextrous comedian threw with such deadly accuracy that he could hit any target up to ten feet away with ease. Sometimes he hurled two pies at once—in opposite directions. Within a year, Roscoe Arbuckle had risen to stardom and was writing and directing his own films, an instant success as a movie comedian, while a contemporary, Charlie Chaplin, still struggled for recognition. Known as "Fatty" to millions around the world, off screen, the comedian gently reminded friends, "I've got a name, you know." On camera, he played to his fatness. He was outrageous, some thought vulgar; children adored him.

As Arbuckle's career soared, his private life took a different direction. His wife of nine years, the elegant and lovely Minta Durfee, left him and moved to New York. The comedian was popular with women and had many friendships, most of them platonic. Perhaps his weight made him shy. It was conjectured by those who knew him well that Arbuckle was the most chaste man in Hollywood.

His passion was reserved for motor cars. The comedian's collection included a Pierce Arrow worth twenty-five thousand dollars, an astounding sum for those times. Extras included a cocktail bar and toilet. There was a chauffeur as well, but he usually rode in the back while Arbuckle drove. On a fateful Friday afternoon in September 1921, Arbuckle headed north for San Francisco sans chauffeur, telling his friends: "I'm going to the City to celebrate."

San Francisco enjoyed a reputation for lively élan. With New York a four-day train ride away, Hollywood celebrities fled north to play. When Arbuckle was invited to San Francisco to promote the World's Fair, Mayor Rolf had been only too proud to be photographed with him. Now the comedian was eager to return. A man known for giving parties on the slightest provocation, he had good cause for celebration. He'd signed a contract with Adolph Zukor of Paramount ensuring himself an income of one million a year. Having just completed three feature films simultaneously—one of them *The Life of the Party*—Arbuckle was ready for a party of his own.

Fifteen years earlier, John Barrymore, famous actor and alcoholic, was sleeping it off at the St. Francis Hotel when the great earthquake of 1906 tumbled him unceremoniously from his bed. The hotel had survived that cataclysm only to be shaken once again to its very foundation.

Prohibition, enacted in 1920, had never stopped anyone from getting a drink when he or she wanted it, and San Francisco, with more speakeasies per capita than any other U.S. city, would boast that many of its bars never closed a single day during the entire Prohibition era. Naturally, a man as wealthy and admired as the world's most popular comedian had no need to go out looking for a drink. For this occasion, the supply—several cases of whiskey and gin—came to him right through the front doors of the St. Francis Hotel.

From then on, Alma quickly discovered, no one knew what had happened. Only a few details could be agreed upon. The party began September 5, 1921—Labor Day Monday—in Arbuckle's three-room suite. One of the guests, Virginia Rapp, a failed starlet who'd recently insisted upon a new spelling and pronunciation of her name—Rappe (Ra-Pay)—was dead, and Roscoe "Fatty" Arbuckle was implicated. Some hinted that he'd raped her, crushing her to death with his own weight.

Alma, interviewing District Attorney Matthew Brady, recognized almost immediately that he was doing much more than his job. By prosecuting a star, the district attorney sought stardom for himself. "The charge?" he repeated. "Don't you read your own paper? Well, I'll tell you right now that no man—not even Arbuckle—can pull a thing like that in San Francisco and get away with it!"

Brady's star witness was one Maude Delmont, who claimed to have been the dead Virginia's dearest friend and who had accompanied her to the party. Alma found Maude sequestered in another suite at the St. Francis. Attired in an oriental dressing gown of brilliant orange and peacock blue, the woman sobbed hysterically.

"In her wild, incoherent ravings," Alma wrote, "she deplores the environment in which her life has been cast. And like a sad, sweet refrain through her grief for Virginia Rappe, runs a deeper, more personal grief."

Alma studied the woman tossing dramatically on the bed before her. She was slender and attractive, with masses of black curly hair, which, on closer scrutiny, showed streaks of gray. The reporter's pen flew as Maude raved on: "Virginia, you are fortunate, my dear girl! You have gone in your sweetness and in your youth where nothing can harm you." Pulling her chair closer, Alma asked the sobbing woman to explain. "It will ruin me, take from me everything that I hold dearest in my life," she moaned. "Oh, why have I drifted into this? Why didn't I cling to the things that were real and sweet? Now my name—though innocently involved—will bring sorrow to the dearest, sweetest soul on earth, my mother."

Unfortunately, there was no more to the story, at least no more than Maude Delmont could or would tell that day. Alma left the suite more puzzled than when she'd entered it. But returning the following day, she found the star witness in a far more informative mood.

"Was it murder, Maude? Did Mr. Arbuckle do it?" Alma asked.

"Of course he did it! They say he was drunk. Maybe he was, but he wasn't too drunk to dress in evening clothes and go downstairs and dine after he had ordered my friend taken away as he would a piece of debris. Virginia Rappe fought her final battle all alone, knowing that she was dying, and said nothing, but I know the truth. I know her. I'm glad she's dead.

She's better off." Maude then went on to describe how Arbuckle had dragged her friend screaming into another room. Returning much later, he'd asked them to dress Virginia and take her away. Entering the bedroom, she'd found her friend lying on the bed "almost entirely nude, her clothing torn."

The account was in direct conflict with Arbuckle's story. The comedian vehemently denied that he'd mistreated Miss Rappe. According to his story, she'd had three drinks, become hysterical, and, claiming she couldn't breathe, begun tearing off her clothes. He'd asked the other women at the party to dress her and called the hotel manager to arrange another room for her. Later, seeing no improvement, he'd summoned the hotel physician.

R. J. Boyle, assistant hotel manager, told Alma that the party had been a quiet one. "Nothing happened to cause comment until late afternoon, when a woman called down to say another woman was hysterical and tearing off her clothes." When Boyle investigated, Arbuckle admitted him and then asked for an additional room. "A small party was present, three men and four or five women. Miss Rappe was lying on a bed nearly nude and uh—uh—unconscious. There were several bottles in evidence, and I took it for granted there was nothing more serious than a drinking party."

The hotel doctor dismissed the malady as "overindulgence in alcohol." Assured that his presence was unnecessary, Arbuckle left for Hollywood early Tuesday morning. Miss Rappe was to remain in the room he'd booked for her until she felt well enough to leave. Wednesday she was reported feeling better; however, on Thursday, her condition had worsened, and she was taken to a hospital, where the diagnosis was peritonitis. She died the next day; an autopsy revealed that her condition was caused by a ruptured bladder.

From then on events moved so rapidly that Alma was hard-pressed to keep abreast of the developments. Arbuckle was back in San Francisco by Saturday morning. The man who'd been welcome anywhere was persona non grata. The St. Francis wouldn't admit him. As the perplexed comedian stood in the street trying to decide what next, the immediate problem was solved when four policemen arrived and took him to the Hall of Justice for questioning. After three hours of grilling by Brady without an attorney present, Arbuckle was brought out. Playing to the assembled press, the district attorney pointed his finger at the comedian and announced dramatically, "You, sir, are under arrest on a charge of murder." It was pandemonium—everyone talking, questioning, yelling at once. Magnesium flashed, recording forever the moment when the laughter ended.

A few days later Alma attended Virginia Rappe's funeral, the only woman present. Watching as the pallbearers carried the casket from the small chapel, she recalled a funeral march by Leo Ornstein. Alma had once heard the iconoclastic young Russian perform the work himself and felt revulsion, even horror, at the harsh discords of the savage dirge, the spasmodic outbursts and weird, shrieking staccatos that seemed a sacrilege. Now, Alma told her readers, if the sadness and the drama of Virginia Rappe's service could be translated into musical sound, the Ornstein score would be a fitting medium.

It wasn't that any possible symbol of respect and grief was lacking. On the contrary, as the undertaker proudly pointed out, the arrangements were "perfect in every detail" and "most expensive." The pearl gray casket was especially "costly," and its mantle of one thousand purple and white tiger lilies, a rare specimen of the florist's art. Alma told her readers:

> There were several other spectacular floral pieces, but not a
> suggestion of genuine human sorrow or loss raised its plaintive
> note during the obsequies. Not a tear was shed, not a head bowed.
> No friend or acquaintance stood in a sadly reminiscent mood as
> the body of Virginia Rappe passed down the aisle of the chapel.
> Instead, florists and undertakers stood in a group appraising the
> degree of commercial attained.
>
> Was Virginia Rappe's funeral tragically typical of her short
> life? Did she ever come close to the great fundamental truths of
> existence—close to humanity's infinitely warm and tender heart?

Urged on by frantic reminders from Crothers of the *Bulletin's* flagging fortunes, the desperate competition for readers, Alma's flair for melodrama soared. "Did she ever realize the supreme happiness of a woman's life, in loving and being loved to the point where nothing but love counted? Or was it all pathetically incoherent, meaningless, unsatisfying—like the wild, mocking discords of the Ornstein death march?"

But while Alma was philosophizing, some of her club women friends were mobilizing for action. A Vigilant Committee sprang into being with a new and radical feminine bill of rights. At first Alma thought it was wonderful. "The several hundred women present at the first meeting—conservative, conventional, constructive women from the clubs, the schools, the professions, from public services, the church and the home—went on record for a principle that possibly has never been voiced at any previous meeting of women," Alma informed her readers.

Despite the fact that nearly every committee voice demanded the unqualified enforcement of Prohibition, the committee itself proclaimed "the right of every woman to become intoxicated in personal safety." Alma resonated to the radical implications of the idea and with much personal satisfaction quoted the committee member appointed to sit in on the Arbuckle trial, Mrs. W. B. Hamilton, an old ally from the Simon Ruiz fight: "If a man gets drunk, it is regarded as his liberty. If a woman does the same, society, like the Romans of the Coliseum, is willing to loose the wild animals upon her. Society says. 'When a woman drinks to excess, she is playing with fire. It makes no difference what happens to her.'"

Despite the florid rhetoric, Alma agreed with the sentiments which she quoted at length in her article.

> *The outrageous case now before us offers a rare opportunity for us to show this courage of women. We will and must stand behind the girls who are crucifying themselves in revelations of their private lives on the witness stand. We must recognize their heroism in assisting to bring about justice at terrific cost to themselves. We are not throwing our arms around that type of girl and making her believe that she is doing the right thing, but we are giving credit where credit is due, and are giving her our genuine admiration for her stamina in tearing aside the veil from her often disgraceful private life in order to better serve the ends of public justice.*

Mrs. Hamilton and the other members of the Vigilant Committee were themselves especially anxious to service those same ends and assured the district attorney's office that they were more than willing to sit on the jury however personally distasteful the case might be—and here the emphasis was strong—*in order to secure a fair trial.*

Unfortunately, as Alma was soon to discover, the trial was anything but fair.

First the highly verbal Maude Delmont suddenly became unavailable. As Alma investigated the background of Brady's star witness, she began to suspect why. The woman was a shadowy figure known to hotel detectives as "Madame Black." She could always be counted on to supply pretty young women of itinerant virtue for a quick party, but often there was an unexpected price tag included. Maude's girls had a propensity for crying "Rape!" Invariably a thoughtful—and quick—gift of money ensured sudden memory loss on the part of the victim.

As it turned out, Maude had known her "dearest pal," Virginia Rappe, for all of a week. She'd met the down-and-out starlet in central California, where both women had been selling magazine subscriptions only days before the party.

Maude Delmont had made the initial charges against Arbuckle and had testified against him before the grand jury and the press. Now it appeared that the canny D.A. wasn't about to put this questionable character on the stand, where she'd be open to cross-examination by the defense. His case was built around the statements of two show girls, Alice Blake and Zey Prevon. These were the "courageous young women" so much admired by the Vigilant Committee. Alma, noting their reluctance, began to experience doubts.

On September 22, 1921, five hours before the police court hearing was to take place, the Hall of Justice filled with women. Nearly one hundred police were needed to keep some semblance of order as they shoved and elbowed one another to gain entry. When the court doors opened, they spilled in, scrambling frantically until seats, benches, and windowsills were filled. The rest sat on the floor.

Alma, seated with the press, saw a number of familiar faces, among them Mrs. Hamilton. Many people applauded as Arbuckle was brought in from his cell, a spontaneous reaction to a much beloved comedian. Instantly, Hamilton was on her feet, exhorting, "Women of America, do your duty!" The applause stopped immediately, and Alma was appalled to see some women actually spit at the defendant.

As the hearing dragged on through a record heat wave, it became obvious that the facts of the case weren't as clear-cut as Brady had maintained. The judge was as surprised by and as suspicious of the prosecution's failure to bring the vociferous Maude Delmont in to testify as was the defense. The eventual indictment of manslaughter was a severe blow to Brady, who had hoped to add a hanging to his credits.

Alma later suspected that Arbuckle would have preferred hanging. Within a few short days the image of playful innocence that had made him a star was destroyed forever. His three movies were scrapped, and his current films removed from theaters; Roscoe "Fatty" Arbuckle, once "the funniest man in the world," was suddenly the most despised.

Maybe people felt that life had moved too fast since the Great War, Alma speculated. Was Prohibition merely an effort to turn back the clock to less radical times? The same cautionary forces now condemned leisure not earned by sweat and tears as undeserved, immoral. Shutting down saloons wasn't enough. They wanted to close theaters as well. In a time of hysterical intolerance, the oversized comedian was a target made to order. A new rumor was circulating. As if rape weren't enough, Arbuckle had violated the woman with a bottle of champagne.

One lone dissenter was Minta Durfee Arbuckle. She'd immediately caught a train from New York to be at her husband's side. En route, besieged by reporters—one even pursuing her with a megaphone from a low-flying plane—she reiterated her belief in him. Alma, one of forty reporters meeting Minta's train at the San Francisco depot, admired the actress's loyalty and shuddered at the ordeal ahead of her.

On October 12, the Vigilant Committee passed a unanimous resolution proposing a permanent country-wide ban on the exhibition of Arbuckle's films. Alma was shocked by the vituperation of the women she'd so recently admired. Her own sympathy for the fat man with his round baby face was growing; she doubted him capable of the crime.

But Paramount, convinced that their former star was box office poison, fired the high-priced lawyer they'd hired to defend him. Arbuckle turned to Gavin McNab, a charismatic San Francisco attorney.

On Monday, November 21, the state produced its key witnesses, Zey Prevon and Alice Blake, who'd been kept in "protective" custody for six weeks. After much wrangling, McNab managed to get their original grand jury testimonies read into the trial record. Their stories had changed. Had Brady pressured them? Alma suspected that he had and began to regret the sensationalism of her early articles.

McNab's trump card was hotel detective George Glennon, who'd interviewed Virginia a short while after her collapse at the party. "Did Mr. Arbuckle hurt you?" he asked. "No, no, he never hurt me," she had replied.

"Then who did?"

"I don't know. I may have fallen off the bed."

Determined to learn more, Alma cornered the district attorney during the recess. "Didn't you question Glennon after the death?"

"Of course I did. I have his statement.

"Where?"

Brady met her gaze defiantly. "In a safety deposit box."

"Didn't you consider it important evidence?"

"No, I thought it of no importance, so unimportant that I'd forgotten its existence." Abruptly the man turned on his heel. Although Alma was shocked, the brazen admission only confirmed her suspicions. The whole case was built on a tissue of lies and innuendo. The life of an innocent man was being destroyed before her eyes.

Back in the courtroom, she looked at Mrs. Hamilton, who turned away. These women who'd been the friends and supporters of Mrs. Goodfellow, who'd worked so diligently with her to save Simon—these same women now wanted to make a scapegoat of Arbuckle. The issue wasn't guilt, but morality—or their concept of it. It wasn't the man they wanted to punish so much as his carefree, glamorous Hollywood life-style.

When Arbuckle took the stand in his own behalf, only twenty minutes of his four hours on the witness stand was spent in direct examination by the defense counsel. The rest was relentless cross-examination. Arbuckle withstood a battery of invective calmly, never raising his voice, never changing his story. He appeared an honest man standing up well under persecution as well as prosecution.

Alma listened, fascinated; the picture of the party as it was drawn by various witnesses disgusted her. When Virginia Rappe began tearing off her clothes and screaming that she was dying, the others helped strip her naked—men and women alike—then placed her in a tub of water cooled by party ice. One man—not Arbuckle—had actually held her upside down because someone said that was a remedy for hysteria and intoxication. They were all in varying degrees drunk, all breaking the law, but Arbuckle, she felt, clearly appeared the most humane.

The fatal flaw was his conviviality, his desire to be a good guy. He could have stopped the party, but didn't. A Greek tragedy, Alma thought, complete down to a chorus of harpies, the grim-faced, gimlet-eyed Vigilant Committee. "Surely," she summed up a story, "if the shocking events surrounding the death of Virginia Rappe accomplish no other end, they should arouse the careless to a keener discrimination."

At 4:15 on the afternoon of December 2, the jury withdrew to deliberate. By 11:00, they were eleven to one for acquittal. The holdout was Helen Hubbard, a personal friend of Brady's—a fact that McNab had somehow failed to uncover on voir dire examination—who refused to listen to any discussion and threatened to vote guilty "until hell freezes over." The jury remained sequestered for forty-four hours, appearing at last to announce a hopeless deadlock. The final vote was ten to two for acquittal; Mrs. Hubbard had persuaded one of the men to keep her company.

The jury was dismissed, and Brady announced that a second trial would take place as soon as possible. Alma saw Minta and Arbuckle exchange weary glances. It was far from over.

Within four days, Hollywood moguls made another decision. The sensational trial's effect upon box office receipts was devastating. Not only was Arbuckle on trial, but the whole film industry. Movies were still too new, too controversial; public opinion could close them down. In an effort to prove their own virtue, they sought as high as they could go. God was unavailable; in his place, the United States government would have to do.

Their appointed conscience was Postmaster General William Hays, named czar of the spontaneously created Motion Picture Producers and Distributors Association of America—the "Hays Office." Hays, a pillar of Presbyterian rectitude and chairman of the Republican National Committee, was credited with Harding's presidential victory the year before. His Calvinism rising quickly to the challenge, he took his mandate of censorship seriously. Accepting the position for three years, Hays would serve three decades.

Naturally, Alma's former friends on the Vigilant Committee were delighted. They considered Mrs. Hubbard a heroine, criticized the eleven other jurors, and congratulated the prosecution. Each, when interviewed by Alma, piously insisted, "Of course, I'm not prejudiced in any way."

It wasn't easy to find a new jury. Who had not read about or discussed the lurid case? Finally, a new trial began January 11, 1922. Much evidence was a repeat, with notable differences. Alice Blake was having trouble recalling her previous testimony, but Zey's memory was very clear. Under

McNab's cross-examination, she confirmed Alma's suspicions, admitting that she and Alice had been pressured into perjury. Despite repeated objections from Brady and his prosecution team, she told the whole story. The district attorney now tried to have his former star witness labeled hostile, but the judge ruled against him.

McNab was so confident of victory that he decided against having the exhausted Arbuckle take the stand in his defense, thereby depriving the jury of an opportunity to evaluate the defendant's testimony. "The jury has all the facts," he said in his closing statement. "It is unnecessary to weary you further. We therefore submit the case for the defense without further argument."

Alma, sensing a grave tactical error, was correct. In demonstrating confidence in his client's innocence, McNab had intentionally omitted arguments and testimony that had convinced the original jurors. So casual was his closing summation that the majority of the jury believed that the defense attorney was actually conceding defeat. They adjourned for two days and returned once again deadlocked. This time the verdict was ten to two for conviction.

The third trial commenced on March 13. Now desperate, McNab decided there would be no soft-pedaling, no taking for granted of *anything*. Zey Prevon had fled to Cuba, leaving Alice Blake to testify for the prosecution. McNab took no chances, his cross-examination so intense that the show girl collapsed on the stand—but not before disclosing Brady's threat not only to reveal the fact that she had an illegitimate child, but to have that child taken from her by declaring her an unfit mother.

This time McNab disclosed all previously withheld information regarding Virginia Rappe's past, which included two abortions. A series of witnesses described her propensity to liven up a party by tearing off her clothes. The most recent occasion had occurred on September 3, just two days before the Arbuckle party. Testimony by attending physicians revealed that Virginia had been suffering from gonorrhea, a disease that Arbuckle did not contract. Now the defendant took the stand, eloquent and sincere.

On April 12, Gavin McNab made his closing speech to the jury. As at the first trial, he went through the evidence slowly and very deliberately, point by point. The statements of George Glennon, the hotel detective, were reviewed. He'd questioned Virginia only a few hours after the party, and she had absolved Arbuckle completely. Dr. Melville Rumwell, who'd attended Virginia, testified that there were no bruises on her, that she had in no way blamed Arbuckle for her condition, that she had, in fact, told him that the two had never had intercourse. A nurse who'd attended Virginia the previous year described a history of severe bladder problems aggravated by liquor. ("Virginia cried out in pain when she urinated and frequently had to be catheterized.") This was only the beginning; McNab presented a medical history of bladder infections going back to 1907. Brady had tried desperately to suppress those statements.

The defense finally went so far as to have Virginia's bladder brought to court, where it was examined by three physicians, who confirmed what the defense had contended all along. Virginia Rappe's bladder was diseased. She had suffered from cystitis, a condition predisposing bladder rupture—particularly susceptible to liquor. It was the conclusion of all the physicians involved that, despite previous medical warnings, Virginia Rappe had become intoxicated at the party. Her severely diseased bladder had ruptured, and peritonitis had developed, eventually proving fatal.

Watching the jury file out, Alma settled back, prepared for a long stay. Glancing at her watch, she noted that it was 5:10 P.M. At 5:15, the jury returned. "Those who crowded into the courtroom to witness the closing scene of this drama will never forget the force of those brief moments into which were crowded the emotions of a lifetime," she would later write.

The verdict, written on a piece of paper, was handed to the judge who read, "We, the jury, find Roscoe Arbuckle not guilty of manslaughter."

Pandemonium broke out. Alma was screaming, cheering; so was everyone but the Vigilant Committee. Finally order was established, and the jury foreman asked permission to read a statement. It developed that the jurors had taken an immediate standing vote upon retiring. The five minutes had been spent composing a statement that their foreman read:

> *Acquittal is not enough for Roscoe Arbuckle. We feel that a great injustice has been done him. We feel also that it was only our plain duty to give him this exoneration, under the evidence, for there was not the slightest proof adduced to connect him in any way with the commission of a crime.*
>
> *The happening at the hotel was an unfortunate affair for which Arbuckle, so evidence shows, was in no way responsible.*

We wish him success, and hope that the American people will take the judgment of fourteen men and women who have sat listening for thirty-one days to the evidence, that Roscoe Arbuckle is entirely innocent and free from all blame.

The statement was signed by the jury of twelve and the two alternates. Arbuckle, who had "celebrated" his thirty-fifth birthday during the seven-month ordeal, was ecstatic. Though the trial had cost him more than $700,000 at a time when he'd lost an estimated $600,000 in income, he was certain that he would make it back.

Equally confidant, the movie moguls were smiling again. Arbuckle films were immediately returned to the screen and played to capacity audiences. Just prior to leaving for Hollywood, the comedian told Alma, "I will be able to go back to work if the public wants me. If the public doesn't want me, I'll take my medicine. But I am sure the Americans will be fair and just. I believe I am due for a comeback."

On April 18, 1922, Walter Hays made public his first major decision since becoming the official conscience of the film industry. Just six days after the jury's wholehearted acquittal, Hollywood's avenging angel banned Roscoe Arbuckle from the screen.

If Alma had been eager to go to Mexico before, now she was frantic. Shocked by the outright dishonesty of the district attorney's office and the city police force, sickened by the vindictive intolerance of her former friends, and frightened by the cynical exercise of power by many of her own newspaper colleagues, she was anxious to leave San Francisco.

The fact that during the course of the Arbuckle trial three Mexican trains had been seized by bandidos and their American passengers killed did nothing to dampen her enthusiasm. Nothing that any of the Sullivans could say would disuade her.

The whole family was on hand to see Alma off as she boarded the Daylight Limited. Soon they had her settled into a corner of the pullman car. Beside her bags and hatbox were magazines and books, a basket of fried chicken, fruit, and candy. At the last minute—when Adelaide was looking the other way—Eugene tucked a small flask into Alma's handbag. "Sometimes it comes in handy." She nodded gratefully.

The train snorted, jolted, then slowly began to move. The family hurriedly clambered off, Walter and Prescott supporting their mother, who was sobbing openly. "I'm afraid I'll never see you again," she called over her shoulder.

"You will, Mama; of course you will," Alma promised.

Eugene hung back to give her one last hug. "Take care of yourself, and write. Your mother will be very worried if you don't write."

"I promise"—Alma buried her head in his chest, lest he see her own tears. To her surprise, they were streaming down her face as she watched him leap onto the platform.

But the tears quickly dried as Alma settled down to enjoy the landscape. I'm going to Mexico, I'm going to Mexico, I'm really going to Mexico, it's finally happening, she congratulated herself as the train sped by the proud mansions of Hillsborough and Atherton. There was a brief stop at Palo Alto. Alma thought of Sam, who was teaching now at Stanford, and of Ethel Scott, but quickly banished both from her mind. This was a new adventure, she reminded herself.

Soon she was passing the orchards of the Santa Clara Valley. Spring had been late that year; the gray day was enlivened by a delicate riot of pastel blossoms as far as her eye could see. Headed toward California's heartland, she traveled across the fertile valley floor; then, finally, the train turned westward, snaking its way through the coastal mountain range briefly turned to emerald by recent rains. Within a month she knew they would resemble nothing more than gigantic dun-colored lions crouching in the distance. At last she reached the sea, on that day a pewter platter; its grayness did nothing to dampen her spirits. Alma ignored the books and magazines the family had thrust upon her and sat watching the fleeting scene until twilight.

Late that evening she reached Los Angeles and was glad that her brief time there was taken up with the fuss and bustle of changing trains, leaving her no time to think of Arbuckle or anyone connected with the film industry.

It was nearly midnight by the time Alma was settled into her berth. She'd enjoyed an elegant meal in the dining car, complete with translucent china and even finger bowls. She should have been sleepy, but excitement kept her wide awake. Switching the light back on, Alma took out John Reed's *Resurgent Mexico.* His coverage of the revolution was anything but reassuring. It seemed hours before she finally grew drowsy.

The sight to which Alma awakened early the next morning was quite different. The sky was azure—Eugene had told her the Arizona sky was like none other. Yuccas and ocotillos, desert survivors, dotted the moonscape outside. Once Alma spotted the crumbling adobe ruins of a stagecoach stop. "It used to take them fifty days to cross the country," a porter told her. "The fare was $150. This was Indian country," he explained. "Cochise fought his last battle near here, then disappeared forever into those very mountains."

Alma stared at the jagged peaks in the distance and felt a twinge of apprehension. Indian country, yes, but more recently Pancho Villa country. The train was passing near the Mexican frontier, and not only Alma but all the passengers were well aware of it. A few sips from Eugene's flask had finally put her to sleep the previous night; now it was reassuring to remember the tiny revolver he'd insisted on giving her the day before. Not, Alma reminded herself, that she was in any way frightened.

In the late afternoon the train wound its way upward, twisting through deep, red canyons, with rocky bluffs and peaks that reminded her of sugarloaves. Then at last they reached El Paso, a narrow garden of green along the Rio Grande. With the other passengers, mostly men, Alma left the car at Union Station. Once again she would have to change to another train. The depot was largely filled with doughboys in steeple-crowned campaign hats, reminding her that since the Mexican revolution, the border town had required military protection.

The new train was a distinct disappointment. Seats sagged like the jowls of a bulldog, several windows were missing, and strips of tape held what remained together. Slowly, as if the coaches were harnessed to tired mules, the train crept southward and then across the Rio Grande. The Mexican city of Cuidad Juárez was like no place she'd ever seen before. Stepping out onto the observation platform at a stop, Alma felt that she'd moved backward in time to another century. The dirt streets perilously close to the tracks seemed to be fronted only by saloons. Laughter spilled from behind slatted doors. Knots of Mexicans in pajamalike clothing and sombreros slouched against adobe walls, silently watching her. Each looked like a *pistalero* who'd cut a gringo's—or gringa's—throat with relish. Glancing back in the distance, Alma fancied she could see the United States flag flying from atop an El Paso building. For the first time, Alma thought seriously of turning back. She *wanted* to turn back, but when the train at last jolted forward, Alma jolted with it.

Mexican soldiers now occupied most of the car. Young men with crossed cartridge belts and rifles slung casually over their shoulders, they lounged about the corridors smoking and laughing. Obviously they were enjoying themselves, which apparently was not de rigueur, for whenever their potbellied officers appeared, the young men would stare out the windows as if transfixed by the sight of cacti.

The officers, portly fellows wearing many ribbons, much brass, buffed leather boots, and elaborately bored expressions under their expansive mustaches, appeared dressed for a parade. Invariably each attempted to strike up a conversation with Alma, but she had been strongly admonished by her friend and ally from the Simon Ruiz case, Alberto Mascarenas, the Mexican consul in San Francisco. It was not the custom for "nice" Mexican women to travel unchaperoned, he had reminded her. Trouble could easily arise from simple friendliness. She meticulously avoided encouraging them; the expression of world-weary boredom returned to every face.

Alma was reassured by the careless confidence on the part of her military companions. These men obviously weren't worried about bandits, although the train was now passing through the state of Chihuahua, an area that had, until very recently, been Francisco Villa's private fiefdom. According to numerous legends, "Pancho" Villa had originally been a man of ideals, a modern-day Robin Hood. People had formed long queues to receive money and food from his very hands, but later others had not been so fortunate. In one tiny town, the bandit had massacred seventy-two young boys and old men, and, because he was short of ammunition, the story went, he stood them domino fashion so that one bullet might do the job of two.

There were frequent stops. It seemed to Alma that the greatest part of the journey was spent standing still, and, if the train seemed slow in the flat country, it huffed and trembled its way up and around the sharp, steep curves. Each bend of the mountain revealed breathtaking vistas of peaks and deep rocky canyons that brought gasps to her lips—not only of admiration but fear. Was this ancient train, possibly from another century, capable of getting her all the way to Mexico City? What if she was stranded in this godforsaken place? Often Alma caught glimpses of walls and buildings pockmarked by bullet holes. At some stops in the small villages, she beheld a person bearing the "mark of Villa"—a clipped ear, a missing nose, a branded face—mute evidence of the insurrectionist's grisly sense of humor, his enjoyment of humiliation and torture.

At one small town Alma was startled by a group of Indians—warriors, she surmised, naked but for breechclouts, bodies gleaming with sweat, long tangled hair trailing, swaying with their lithe movements, eyes dark, fathomless. The soldiers had stopped their laughter and were staring, too. "Yaquis," someone said. Alma shuddered; she'd heard terrible tales of the brutality of these Indians. Only a few years before they'd wiped out whole isolated villages of settlers. Times must be changing for them to come into a town, however small. At least she hoped they were. She allowed herself a small sigh of relief when the train at last moved on.

At every stop barefooted women and children in various degrees of nakedness ran beside the train selling beer and orange juice. *"Tacos dorados,"* a small girl of about eight offered, looking upward through the open window. Alma surveyed the potato and bean taco doubtfully. The girl turned the full force of her limpid brown eyes on the gringa. "I am an orphan," she explained. Alma nodded, passed some coins down in exchange for the taco. Soon, an even smaller boy appeared. He was selling *jicama* and mangoes seasoned with chili. The food was surprisingly good.

In the station at Aguascalientes, mariachis serenaded the train. Again and again, she caught the refrain "Alma de mi Alma." How exciting! They were singing for her! It was to happen again and again as the ancient train inched its way southward toward Mexico City. Surely the government must have arranged it as a welcome. The sense of recognition and flattery did wonders to silence her misgivings and liven a long, arduous journey. There were no bandidos.

Her welcome at the Mexico City station was beyond Alma's wildest dreams. A delegation of important officials along with what looked like half the city were there to greet her. Alma was swept into a large, open touring car and paraded along the breathtaking Paseo de Reforma to the Hotel Regis in the center of town. There she was escorted to an elegant suite jammed with floral tributes, but that wasn't all. The modern bathroom was filled with bird cages. In Mexico, she was to learn, a bird in a cage was a sentimental tribute surpassing flowers.

There would be many more bird cages in the weeks that followed. The young bloods of the capital, handsome sons of the rich, were captivated by this beautiful, spirited gringa. She was escorted to balls and grand parties, where, as her Spanish rapidly improved, she discovered to her chagrin that "Alma de mi alma" was actually a popular ballad. The words meant "Soul of my soul." Many men, young and old, were only too eager to sing it just for her with a new, more personalized meaning.

The new aristocracy—the generals—besieged her as well. Shocked to hear that she'd made the long journey unattended in an ancient dilapidated train, each offered to show her the country in his own private railroad car. At first impressed, Alma quickly learned that nearly all of them had private cars. Hardly a day passed that Alma wasn't interviewed by some periodical or didn't attend a party in her honor. President Alvaro Obregon was a charming and gracious host and Alma, was a frequent guest at Chapultepec Palace.

The whole holiday was a glamorous, heady experience, one that she would remember all her life. A vivacious, totally feminine woman, Alma basked in the masculine attention but did not allow herself to be taken in by it. In Mexico, she was discovering, two plus two wasn't four at all. It was twenty-two. What mattered most was *"más grande, más prestigio, más personalidad."* The claims, the flattery, the promises were all quite delightful, but never to be taken seriously.

One man alone succeeded in capturing her imagination, if not her heart, largely because of his immense wit, talent, and perception. He was the political cartoonist José Clemente Orozco. As a journalist, Alma was amazed to see that street corner newsboys had no need to yell out the day's most sensational headlines in order to attract the attention of passersby. They had only to unfold their papers to a page that featured an Orozco cartoon. The acerbic characterizations could be devastating. Here was an artist who could make or break a budding politico. Small wonder that President Obregon held him in high esteem and, upon occasion, invited the bohemian radical to the palace.

Coffee with Orozco at the famous Casa de Azulejos introduced Alma to a whole new world. The historic residence, built in 1596 by the count of Orizaba, with its hundreds of colorful tiles, had become a popular restaurant frequented by the city's politicians. In fact, her new friend told Alma, it was to the Casa de Azulejos that Pancho Villa had come to celebrate the success of his revolution. "He may have drunk his famous cup of coffee right where you're sitting," he pointed out.

Alma smiled absently; she was contemplating their walk up the Avenida Madero. It seemed to her that she'd just passed through three stages of human evolution telescoped into a single sun-drenched moment in a few feet of stone pavement. First there had been a somber-faced peon enveloped in a serape, head and shoulders all but hidden in the depth of a large, straw sombrero, grinding his midday meal on a metate that hadn't changed since the Neolithic epoch. Then there was the resplendent edifice against which the man leaned, no doubt the townhouse of some feudal lord built during the colonial era. But this too was yet another juxtaposition; the facade had been transformed into a store, and behind plate-glass windows were displayed electric irons, refrigerators, and automatic heaters.

Through her association with Orozco, Alma discovered a whole new dimension of Mexico. Anywhere else the bohemia of the capital might have bankrupted fantasy, but within its own setting, it was a very natural expansion of popular psychology. A surrealist mood dominated the social gatherings of the intelligentsia. In this intense, irrational reality, Alma found the "something different" for which she had been searching all her life. At thirty-two, she was certain that fantasy had somehow collided with destiny, bringing her "home" at last.

She discovered the same mood of incongruous imagery evidenced in Mexico's totally distinctive folk art and began to collect it with a passion. Alma found it asserted most vigorously in the bizarre decorations of neighborhood bars, which she often amazed her escorts by preferring to the gilded bistros that lined the Reforma. These were called *pulquerías* for the *pulque,* a fiery liquor made from the fermented juice of the maguey plant, dispensed there. Invariably, the firm names were whimsical: Wise Men Who Never Never Study, The Magnificent Jewess, The Errors of Cupid, No One Will Ever Know and Who Cares Anyway?

Where else, Alma wondered, could one find a greater sense of duality than in Mexico? The extremes of night and day, birth and death, plenty and poverty, light and shadow were interwoven into every aspect of the culture.

It appeared as she delved more and more into the history of Mexico that a strange sense of macabre destiny had existed from the very beginning. The fabled Quetzalcoatl seemed to reach out to her across the centuries, a figure of romance, betrayal, illusion, and eternal mystery. *Who* was he? *What* was he?

According to the story, Quetzalcoatl descended from heaven and proceeded to introduce concepts of penitence and love, scorning the traditional rituals of blood sacrifice. The embodiment of divine love and wisdom as well as an able administrator, he united the people and ruled them as one large confederation of tribal groups.

As with the Arthurian Round Table, it was all too good to last. The high priests and warriors didn't take kindly to Quetzalcoatl's substitution of incense and flowers for human sacrifices. There had to be a way of removing him, and, of course, they eventually found it.

Quetzalcoatl was known to be vigorous, sexually potent, and endowed with a heroic penis, yet he vowed to remain celibate, sublimating his considerable energies to good works. Finally the day came—naturally it would have to be a ceremonial day with an attendant cast of thousands— when the wily priests handed Quetzalcoatl a drink laced with magic mushrooms. While under the influence of the powerful aphrodisiac, he was seduced by a beautiful woman.

Awakening later, he was consumed with guilt. In his own eyes, he had condemned himself by breaking his self-imposed vows. Leaving behind everything—palaces, kingdoms, even clothes—he arrived naked on the shores of the Caribbean. After promising to return one day, Quetzalcoatl embarked on a raft of snake skins and sailed eastward until a tremendous heat ignited the boat and, in a burst of flame, his heart arose, flying upward to finally merge with the sun.

The story of his disappearance was told and retold, a legend that refused to die. Everyone knew that one day, just as the god had been deposed in the past, so he would one day return to overthrow his adversaries and usher in a new era of peace and justice. The hope remained for hundreds of years until the early sixteenth century, when history and mythology united to produce a great tragedy.

It seemed to Alma that a sense of fate overshadowed so much of Mexican history. Poor, frightened Montezuma, the Aztec ruler, had been waiting for the other shoe to drop. From his palace rooftop, the ruler watched with apprehension as a dark shape crossed the face of the sun. The last time this had occurred had been three hundred years before. A devastating flood had followed. Montezuma was aware of this bit of history and felt certain that some similar disaster was pending.

Quetzalcoatl had promised to appear before them again in some Ce Acatl year on the day of his birth, Chiconaui Ehecatl. This celestial combination, which came up every fifty-two years, was scheduled to occur in the spring of 1519—only a few months away. This remarkable Aztec astronomical calculation has been the subject of scholarly speculation for centuries.

Only a short while after the celestial omen Montezuma received word that tall, fair, bearded men had disembarked from a "winged tower that floated across the sea." The date was April 21, 1519. The Spanish conquistadores called it Good Friday, but Montezuma knew that it was Chiconaui Ehecatl, the birthday of Quetzalcoatl in the year Ce Acatl. He considered his doom sealed. Who could fight a god? This sense of grim inevitability explained the the takeover of the mighty nation by so few men. By the time Montezuma realized that they were merely men, it was too late.

After Montezuma was tortured and killed, his nephew, Cuauhtemoc, assumed command and almost succeeded in routing Hernán Cortés and his army, but was eventually overcome and imprisoned. Determined to force the young monarch to reveal the whereabouts of the imperial Aztec treasure, Cortés had Cuauhtemoc's feet rubbed with oil and then set ablaze. When one of the prisoners who suffered the same fate turned imploringly to the young ruler, Cuauhtemoc replied, "Am I perchance reclining on a bed of roses?"

Alma's facile imagination was captivated by such stories, her idealism fired by the revolutionary heroes who followed throughout a long and bloody history: Hidalgo, Morelos, Juárez, Madero, Zapata. She fervently hoped that her host, President Obregon, a leader of the 1910–1921 revolution and the second president in this postrevolutionary period, would bring true freedom to the embattled country.

The country's heritage seemed to her a very rich layer cake: the Indian world conquered by the Spaniards, followed by three centuries as a Spanish colony, ending with political independence after a bloody war lasting from 1810 to 1821, then years of misrule, anarchy, and a loss of almost half the nation to the United States in 1847, French intervention and Maximilian's ill-fated empire, leading to the long-lived dictatorship of Porfirio Díaz, only to be overthrown by the 1910 revolution. This whole strange confection reminded Alma of the cakes made for the Feast of the Dead, macabre creations made in the shape of skulls with ghoulish features etched in icing, but there were also unexpected veins of lush sweetness.

Mexico had absorbed Alma completely. As though caught in the net of a passionate affair, she struggled for a way to remain with her love, but encountered a stone wall. Few women outside the peon class worked in Mexico; there were certainly no jobs available to gringas. She wrote a series of articles for the *New York World,* but the paper could not afford to retain her on a continuing basis. Meanwhile, Crothers at the *Bulletin* was growing impatient. If she didn't want her job, there were plenty who did. President Obregon was a gracious host, but the time had come when she could no longer accept his hospitality. Sadly, Alma departed for home, all the while promising her new friends—and most of all herself—that she would return.

Much had happened in the three months she'd been away. Prescott was a full-fledged sports reporter. Sam and Theoline had a baby son; Alma wasn't surprised to hear rumors of her former husband's infidelity. Under pressure, William Hays had removed his ban on Arbuckle films, but the damage was done. The announcement triggered a tidal wave of angry invective.

Against her will, Alma was assigned to cover a meeting of the Vigilant Committee and encountered a surprise. Mrs. W. B. Hamilton had called it. Alma thought her ears must be deceiving her when she heard the club woman challenge the others, asking, "Where is your forgiveness?"

The question was greeted by boos and shouts of derision; the display of venom was beyond Alma's comprehension. These ladies were still out for blood.

"As your representative, I attended all three trials," Hamilton reminded them, shouting now to be heard. "I know that Arbuckle could not in justice have been convicted of manslaughter on the evidence presented. Why should he be made to pay for the sins of the whole motion picture industry? He's been reinstated, why not give him a chance to make good as a man?"

Alma left the meeting with renewed respect for Hamilton, but the continued militancy of the others made it difficult for her to work with them on the civic and philanthropic projects that she was again covering for the paper. Even without this difficulty, Alma's old enthusiasm for her work was missing. The exaggerated drama and sentimentality of sob sistering had lost its appeal; she still felt guilty about the lack of objectivity in her earlier Arbuckle pieces. Alma's heart remained in Mexico; she lived and worked in a twilight zone, going through the motions of her life as if in a dream.

Then, when least expected, the call came. Adolph Ochs, owner of the *New York Times*, was in town. He'd read some of Alma's articles in the *World* and wanted to talk with her. Over lunch at the Poodle Dog, he offered her the job of California correspondent.

"You know this town well, could get to know the rest of the state quickly. You're just the writer we've been looking for."

Alma smiled ruefully. "I'm very flattered."

"Whatever the *Bulletin* is paying, we can beat it."

"Yes, I'm sure you can, but, but—"

"You don't seem very pleased."

"Oh, Mr. Ochs, of course I'm pleased. The *New York Times* is every writer's dream. None of us San Franciscans think we've really made it until we've been accepted in the East."

"So?"

"I've got to be honest with you. Yes, I do know the town well. I've lived here all my life, but that's the trouble. I'm more than ready for a change. What I want more than anything in the world is to work in Mexico."

"Mexico!" Ochs was astounded. "Well," he hesitated, carefully buttering a piece of French bread while Alma held her breath, "perhaps something might be arranged—but it would just be an assignment, not a real position like the other. I wouldn't take it if I were you, but if you're really interested. . . ."

Alma leaned forward as he explained. "I came out here to fill two spots. I had you in mind for the San Francisco one, the other—I don't know. I really wanted someone with an archeology background, maybe some Berkeley prof on sabbatical."

"Archeology! That's my passion. I practically grew up in the De Young Museum. I've read everything that I can get my hands on about Schliemann, Evans."

"That's Europe, Asia Minor," he reminded her. "I thought Mexico was your passion."

"It is!" Alma assured him. "I wrote an article on the pyramids at Teotihucan for the *World.* I've got a clip, wait till you see—"

"I have seen it. You did an excellent job. Could be that you're the one for this assignment. The new governor of one of those jungle states, something of a revolutionary, I understand, has invited a team of archeologists from the Carnegie Institution to survey some ruins there. Strange name—Chichén Itzá. My managing editor calls it 'that chicken place.' Do you think you could handle it?"

"Mr. Ochs, I know I can. When do you want me?"

"The team's leaving in February. I'll want you back in New York a week or two before to meet the Carnegie team. Can you manage that?"

"You bet I can! Oh, by the way, where am I going?"

"Damned if I know really. Those 'lost city' pieces are hot now. Everyone wants to fantasize about exotic places. Don't imagine you or anybody else ever heard of this one. It's called Yucatán."

PART II

CHAPTER · 4

The Plumed Serpent

On the train to New York, in her hotel room there, on the train again—this time to New Orleans—and now on the boat headed for Mexico, Alma had undertaken a crash course in Mayan history. There wasn't much to be found, but what there was fascinated her as nothing ever had.

Though the Aztec and Inca civilizations were the dominant ones at the time of the Spaniards arrival, it was the world of the ancient Maya that appealed the most. All that anyone knew was that the Mayan empire, consisting of who knew how many city states, had flourished for a millennium. During their ascendency, these mysterious people formulated the concept of the zero before the Arabs and devised a calendar actually more accurate than the one she'd taken for granted all her life. Then, as mysteriously as it all began, the Mayan civilization abruptly ended. When the first Europeans set foot on the ancient soil of the "New" World, most of the Mayan ceremonial centers had been gobbled up by jungle. Only the tallest buildings still towered above the dense vegetation. Who built these cities only to desert them? they had asked. The degree and extent of her curiosity and the corresponding lack of answers produced a frustration in Alma that would remain with her for the rest of her life.

The first contact between Spain and Mexico had been with a small Mayan trading party. "What—do—you—call—yourselves?" the Spanish commander had yelled after the departing dugout canoe. "Ci—u—than." Their shouted reply, meant simply, "We don't understand you." To Alma, it seemed, the echo hung in the air for centuries, perhaps explaining why the Old World not only believed it had discovered the new, but invented it.

The Spaniards had believed the words to be the answer to their question, and somehow Ciuthan had evolved into Yucatán. Years later a conquistador attempted to set the record straight, writing: "The Mayas now say their country is called 'Yucatán' and so it has that name, but in their own language they do not call it that." Unfortunately, he neglected to mention exactly what they did call it, and now no one knew.

Devout Christians that they were, the Spaniards believed that every human was descended from not just Adam and Eve but Noah and his family, the sole survivors of the great flood. Could the Indians of the New World claim such descent? Obviously not, and ergo, the Maya weren't actually human. The rationalization helped the conquistadores to justify a lot. Who could be blamed for killing or enslaving animals?

Clearly, the "animals" had to be protected from themselves. One of the most vicious of the protectors was Diego de Landa, first bishop of Yucatan, whose autos-da-fé were intended to wipe out the entire Mayan history. In service to his piety, priceless manuscripts were consigned to the flames as the superstitions and falsehoods of the devil.

Eventually, even the conquistadores complained about the extremes of de Landa's fervor; the bishop was recalled to Spain and imprisoned. With time on his hands, he did an amazing thing. De Landa attempted to replace what he'd destroyed by compiling an account of everything he'd observed about the Maya during the conquest and every story he'd since heard about them. The record constituted the bulk of what little there was to be learned about their civilization. At least Alma had been unable to find more.

De Landa recalled a story told him by an old man who said his ancestors were descended from a race that had come from the east by way of twelve paths opened through the sea. From the legend, De Landa, effecting a

180-degree turn, hypothesized that the Maya might be descended from one of the Lost Tribes of of Israel. The theory gained acceptance that grew and endured throughout the sixteenth and seventeenth centuries.

The more contact Europeans had with the magnificence of the Mayan civilization, the harder it was for them to accept the original Spanish theories as to its genesis. These people had to be transplants from their own world or at least a world with which they were familiar. As a result, the Maya had over the years been identified as descendants of Norse explorers, Phoenician traders, shipwrecked Huns, Romans, Africans, Irishmen, and even crew members from a lost fleet of Alexander the Great.

Surely the most controversial theory—and to Alma the most intriguing—dated from the sixteenth century. *When Atlantis sank, Yucatán rose.* The possibility had been introduced and reintroduced over the past four hundred years. According to legend, Atlantis had been a great land mass in the Atlantic destroyed by volcanic eruptions, earthquakes, and tidal waves. Unproved and frequently derided, the story of the sunken continent was a myth that refused to die.

Her mind awhirl with theories, Alma turned to an account by a more pragmatic investigator, John Lloyd Stephens, best known of the Mayan scholars. In addition to Stephens's contribution to the Mayan story, Alma found the saga of his expeditions fascinating. A prominent New York attorney, Stephens got himself appointed U.S. diplomatic agent to Central America. It was thought the title might come in handy in the event of an insurrection, which it did.

His companion on the journey was the English-born artist Frederick Catherwood, who'd traveled and painted extensively in the Near East. Catherwood's fascination with ancient cultures was extreme. In order to gain admission to the Mosque of Omar, where he wished to make detailed architectual drawings, he'd had himself circumcised.

Undeterred by the grudging reception they'd received from the war-torn population of Yucatán, Stephens worked for months uncovering ruins while Catherwood struggled to capture them with pen and ink. Groggy from malaria, their bodies swollen from insect bites, they continued their work until Catherwood collapsed. When the two finally staggered out of the jungle, they had the makings of what would be one of the great best-sellers of the nineteenth century. *Incidents of Travel in Central America, Chiapas and Yucatán,* a two-volume book, revealed a whole new world and introduced to general usage a word that had not appeared in any dictionary. It was "Maya."

These adventurers had explored the Yucatán Peninsula some eighty years before Alma's arrival, hacking their way through almost impenetrable jungle. In 1840, Stephens had written,

> *We sat down on the very edge of the wall, and strove in vain to fathom the mystery by which we were surrounded. In the ruined cities of Egypt, even in the long lost Petra, the stranger knows the story of the people whose vestiges he finds around him. America, say the historians, was peopled by savages; but savages never carved these stones.*

But then, Alma puzzled, who did?

The Atlantis theory was good for endless rounds of arguments aboard the ship, but actually the archeologists knew no more than Stephens. Alma found the Carnegie team, headed by Sylvanus Morley, a lively bunch. She liked them all but was particularly drawn to Ann and Earl Morris, young archeologists of about her own age, excited as she with the opportunity to explore the Mayan country for themselves. It was Ann who set Alma straight about the "chicken place," their ultimate destination. "It's Chichén Itzá. Chee-chen Eat-sa," Ann explained.

"And the meaning?"

"Mouth of the Well of the Itzas. Itzas were the people who lived there long ago. Some say their name meant wizard."

"Mouth of the well of the wizard"—Alma savored the words deliberately. They sounded wonderful and mysterious. "Why has it taken so long for archeologists to come here?"

"There was a man, one Edward Thompson. Apparently *he* subscribes to the Atlantis theory. Thompson went down in 1885 with his wife and baby and never came back."

"Never came back! You mean he died down there?"

"No, he's very much alive. His wife and children returned to the States years ago; but they say Thompson's kind of gone native, has a Maya family, lives in a splendid old hacienda—well, we'll soon see for ourselves."

"Did he learn anything—anything new?"

"He sent back lots of intriguing reports. The Carnegie's been dying to send someone down to investigate for years."

"So why haven't they?"

"The Mexican government never wanted us, but now this new revolutionary governor, Felipe Carrillo Puerto—he appears quite different."

Alma's spine tingled at the reference, an unexplicable frisson. During her holiday in Mexico City, she'd heard a lot about Yucatán's new leader. Though he enjoyed a close friendship with President Obregon, Carrillo was viewed as something of a loose cannon by the conservatives. One man, she recalled, had gone so far as to call the reform governor "the devil with green eyes."

The team had made the final leg of the journey by tramp freighter from New Orleans, where they watched in amazement as forty frightened cows neatly tagged for Yucatán were herded on deck. All available space was to be shared with these bovine companions. It was cows to the right, cows to the left, but mostly cows to the windward.

A night and a day and another night and another day and yet another night passed—hot, dull, malodorous hours that seemed all the slower because of Alma's eagerness to reach their destination. Then finally a morning when the tremendous silence of stopped engines was punctured by hammering at the cabin door—"Breakfast served"—then a terrific blast on the whistle. Alma dressed quickly and hurried out on deck. Before her was a dazzling stretch of beach, green coconut palms against a bright blue sky, and a long line of pink and blue buildings that made up the port of Progreso, Yucatán.

The Carnegie party soon disembarked and boarded a train for Mérida, the state capital. Although their car was labeled first class, it resembled a poultry show. Alma suspected that no self-respecting Yucatecan traveled without an accompaniment of live fowls. She saw chickens in baskets, turkeys in sacks, geese tied in family bed linen. And then there were the pigs.

Relieved as she was to at last reach Mérida, Alma was certain she would have loved it on sight anyway. As the hub of the giant "thumb" that comprises the Yucatán Peninsula, Mérida had a special flavor, a feeling unlike any other city in Mexico. She was thrilled by the sights glimpsed from the *Fortinga*—Spanish for "Ford"—which took her from the station to the Gran Hotel, where the party would be staying. It was an elegant hostelry with a massive doorway, exquisite grillwork, and a sweeping stairway. Alma's room had a balcony looking out onto a pretty park.

She was not to meet the "devil with green eyes" that night. The governor had been detained by official business, his representative apologized, before outlining their agenda. A sight-seeing tour of Mérida had been planned for the following day, but on the next day, the party would be the governor's guests at a ribbon-cutting ceremony honoring the new road that he'd had constructed through the jungle to the ruins of Chichén Itzá, where they would remain for the duration of their survey expedition.

The others nodded approvingly, but Alma stepped forward. She was determined to have time alone with the controversial Felipe Carrillo Puerto. "May I see the governor tomorrow?"

"I doubt it, Señorita. His Excellency is very busy. Many important projects claim his attention, but of course you will see him at the ceremony."

"I represent the *New York Times*," she reminded him, "the *New York Times*. Many in the United States believe your governor to be a Bolshevik. My readers are most interested in learning more of his policy and future plans. Surely some time can be found for me to speak with him alone— perhaps an hour? Certainly if *you* were to arrange it yourself?" Recalling their effect upon Senator Inman, she leveled the full force of her enormous blue eyes on him.

"I shall do my utmost, Señorita."

The following day as the others assembled for their city tour, Alma fumed. "It's hopeless," Morley told her. "Mexicans are so polite, they can't bear to say 'no,' especially to a woman. He never had any intention of arranging an appointment. You'd better come with us; you don't want to miss Mérida. It may be the only chance we'll have to see the city."

Alma hesitated. She did want to see Mérida very much, but not so much as she wanted to interview Felipe Carrillo Puerto. Writing archeology stories was fine—better than fine, a dream assignment. Ancient civilizations had fascinated her from childhood; more than that, the myths and legends surrounding the Maya awakened a penchant for the bizarre and the mysterious that lay just beneath her facade of lively sociability. Still, Alma wanted more. Proud, adventurous, idealistic, she identified with the social reformer and felt instinctively that writing about his cause would further her own.

Just then a bellman rushed in. The cars and drivers were waiting outside
for them. She followed the group out to the curb. Everyone was getting
in. There was one seat left.

"I'm going to stay. I'm sure the representative will have some word for
me today." Alma forced a confident smile. Drivers were cranking up their
vintage *Fortingas.* She waved them out of sight and returned to the hotel.
Settling herself in the lobby, Alma ordered coffee and began a postcard to
her mother.

Twenty minutes later the governor's representative appeared, breathless. "Señorita Reed, I feared you might have gone! His Excellency has
agreed to an interview. His car is waiting outside. I shall take you to the
palace at once."

Alma, five feet, seven inches tall, had already become accustomed to
towering over the rather diminutive Yucatecans. So the man who now rose
to greet her was a distinct surprise. Felipe Carrillo Puerto was big, athletic
looking, over six feet tall. His hair was light brown. The fabled green eyes
had an intensity she had never before experienced.

It was *amor calido,* a "romance of the steam," and it began at that
moment. Both would strive earnestly to overcome it.

Alma sat down, her composure regained as she pulled a notebook and
pencil from her bag. She began the interview with questions about the
governor's constituency. His English, she was relieved to find, was faultless, far superior to her still-halting Spanish. Until recently, he explained,
most of Yucatán had been owned by less than one hundred families. These
genteel hacendados were, the governor believed, among the most savagely
cruel slave masters in history, reducing the Maya to a doglike servility
where a laborer would crawl to kiss the hand of an overseer who had just
lashed him till blood ran in rivulets. The hacendados had an aphorism: "The
Indians cannot hear except through their backs."

"When did it all begin?" Alma wanted to know.

"Long ago—with the Spaniards. Cortés granted Francisco de Montejo
the title *adelantado* with permission to exploit Yucatan at his own expense
in 1527, a—what do you call it—franchise, yes, a franchise. Perhaps you
saw his palace, just across the plaza. Outside you see the Montejo family
crest—a foot planted firmly on the head of a Mayan slave—repeated the

length of the building. A descendant of the family still lives there." He spoke with a detachment that Alma sensed did not come easily. "An interesting building architecturally, much of it was constructed from stones stolen from a nearby Mayan palace."

Alma shook her head, the pathos of all that he'd told her was beyond response. "I find it curious that the Maya—the first to make contact with the Spaniards—were the least in awe of them, the last to be subdued."

"Yes, that's true"—the governor was thoughtful. "Possibly it was because we'd had an opportunity to study two shipwrecked Spanish sailors and had no illusions about their godhood. We didn't have to fight fate—just men, superior weapons, and smallpox. It took four tries and more than twenty years before the Spaniards succeeded in their conquest—in contrast to only two years to overcome the Aztecs. Actually, although the conquest of the Maya was considered complete in 1547, the resistance never ended."

"It must have been terrible for your ancestors. I read about Diego de Landa on the boat coming here."

"He was only one, Señorita. The good Spanish friars," the governor's bitterness was no longer concealed, "brought all the refinements of the Inquisition with them. Interrogation techniques were brutal; the lightest sentence was one hundred lashes. Many Maya died or were crippled for life. Others—in the words of the padres—'displayed their cowardice' by committing suicide before the questioning could be completed."

As Alma's fingers raced across the paper trying to keep pace with his words, her mind raced, too, in an attempt to place them in perspective. The governor's identification was clearly with the Indians, yet a mixed lineage was obvious from his appearance. Who was this man really? Pausing at last, she looked up to see him smiling at her.

"Surely as beautiful a woman as yourself has no wish to hear of such things."

"I wish to hear about you. I mean," Alma quickly amended, "I'd like to hear about your reforms."

"Perhaps you'd like to see some of them?"

"Of course! But can you spare the time?"

"I can think of no better use for it." The governor was on his feet, summarily ordering his car and the cancellation of the day's appointments.

While driving through Mérida and its environs, Alma learned that Obregon's revolutionary soldiers had given Yucatán its first honest election since the conquest. As a result, Felipe Carrillo had been swept into office, 60,765 votes to 400. Immediately embarking on a vigorous program of social reform, the new governor organized Feminist Leagues and placed women in governmental positions. He legalized birth control and then established the first family planning clinics on the western hemisphere. How could Alma not have been impressed? But she wondered, too, about his landslide victory that could only have been possible during a time of immense social upheaval. How long would the rich and powerful allow the governor's new policies to go unchallenged?

The Leagues of Resistance, an underground guerrilla movement originally organized by Felipe Carrillo against the hacendados, had been turned into night schools for adults. That was only the beginning. He'd built schools and more schools and still more schools. He'd seized the uncultivated land from the huge haciendas and distributed it among the Maya. He'd built a model prison embodying ideas so advanced that New York State had sent a commission to study them. Next, Carrillo had turned his attention to the native arts and crafts that had been suppressed by Spanish overlords and encouraged cottage industries to produce them. He built highways from the villages to the cities so farmers might get their produce to market quickly. The latest accomplishment was the completion of a highway from Mérida to Chichén Itzá, enabling the Maya—as well as the outside world—to more easily view, and, so understand, their great heritage.

"But what about that heritage?" Alma pressed him. "What do you really know about it—what does anybody know? No one that I've talked to seems able to explain who the Maya really were, nor do the books. It's said that they built great cities without metal cutting tools, without wheelbarrows or draft animals, but then they seem to have just walked away. Why?"

"Why, indeed"—the governor shrugged his massive shoulders. "Here we have a saying, perhaps you've heard it—¿quien sabe?"

Alma caught the mischievous gleam in his eyes and laughed. She'd heard the expression a bit too often in Mexico. "Who knows—that's the best you can do?"

"I'm afraid so. Perhaps you and the others from the Carnegie Institution will one day be able to tell me. In the meantime, possibly you'd like to drive out to Kanasin, a model village just completed—it's not too far from here."

Alma nodded happily; she wouldn't have cared if it was on the other side of the earth. Her copious notes dutifully recorded one more of the governor's many modern innovations. The people of Kanasin were clean and well fed, and appeared industrious. It was obvious that they adored their benefactor. Alma was unaccountably reminded of the legendary god, Quetzalcoatl, whose strange story had captured her imagination in Mexico City.

Felipe Carrillo glanced at his pocket watch, exclaiming, "You must be famished! I know North Americans are often bewildered and frustrated by our dining hours."

When Alma smiled at him appreciatively, he suggested, "We'll return at once to Mérida. There's an excellent European restaurant that I believe you'll like."

"I'm sure I would, but why don't we eat here in Kanasin? Isn't that a cafe?" She pointed to a white stucco building with a thatched roof.

"The food is very simple here, not what you're accustomed to at all."

"All the more reason for me to try it."

The governor was smiling broadly as they entered the cafe. All eyes were on Alma, watching her with admiring curiosity. He said a few words in Mayan to the owner, who rushed to greet them.

The man soon returned with a tray of hot tortillas, flat corn cakes patted thin as cardboard and filled sandwich-style with venison. It was new to Alma, but her enthusiasm was unfeigned; she found the food delicious. Taking a sip of the dark native beer that had been brought to her, she smiled delightedly at her host. As they ate, their conversation returned to the conversion of the Maya to Christianity.

At first, Carrillo thought, their cyclical view of time might have facilitated the transition. "There's comfort to be found in a circular world in which history and prophesy intertwine in recurring patterns, events repeating themselves in the same orderly fashion as planets: 'This too shall pass.' All things good and bad have their appointed times to end—if only so that they may be repeated later."

"What a windfall for the missionaries," Alma speculated. "At last, raw material with which to work, subjects to mold into paragons of propriety unrealized anywhere else. A zealot's fantasy come true!"

He nodded, all the while watching the play of expressions on her face. "The introduction of Christianity produced a far greater crisis than the devastation of political systems or even warfare. Nothing in our history could have prepared us for their determination to obliterate our entire culture."

Alma, watching him as well, was having difficulty concentrating on his words. I'm here for an interview, she reminded herself and forged on. "Surely there was nothing unusual about a victorious army introducing a new god. It must have happened many times. Wouldn't it have been prudent, even desirable, to accept a victor's god?"

"Indeed. I doubt that the Maya realized at first what was happening. The child, Jesus, was appealing enough. Some thought the Mother Mary vaguely reminiscent of our Ixchel. The sticking point was the jealous nature of the head god. Accepting this new personage as the one and only sacred being was not the same as accepting him as one of a pantheon. The idea that divinity was concentrated in a remote, singular figure to the exclusion of all the more familiar and intimate deities was incomprehensible. We believe that a sacred umbilical cord links heaven and earth. Nourishment flows in both directions, sustaining men and gods. The Catholic Church's ban on Mayan ritual cut this essential cord, placing the entire cosmos in jeopardy. The culture shock that resulted from this assault on the whole nature of our universe is difficult to imagine. Too late, the once-willing converts discovered that the missionaries who'd so patiently explained the exemplary qualities of their god could be as cruel and implacable as the soldiers."

Alma had stopped eating; her gaze followed him intently. "Your English is perfect, Your Excellency. I can follow you easily. Part of what you were saying—you weren't talking past tense. You're talking of *now,* the present."

"Please, not 'Your excellency'; call me Felipe."

"Then tell me, Felipe, do the old gods still exist?"

"Yes, despite the early brutality of the church, despite today's nominal homage to Catholicism, many of the old, secret rituals are still performed, and other quite public ceremonies take place regularly at planting time. What occurred over the years is a blending of the two, but, make no mistake, the old gods are very much alive."

The drive back to town was made late in the afternoon. Along this road, the flat countryside was planted in orderly rows as far as Alma could see. The plant's long, sharp bayonet leaves reminded her of cactus.

"It's sisal, henequen," Felipe explained. "The leaves, processed and dried into a fiber from which rope is made, have been both a curse and a blessing to us."

Alma looked at him, puzzled. "I think I need another history lesson if I'm ever to understand your amazing country."

"Very well, but I promise this is the last. When Mexico finally achieved independence from Spain, great feudal empires sprang up employing hundreds of Maya who were tricked into virtual slavery. The hacendados, who took pride in their direct lineage back to the conquistadores, realized that the only way to keep workers on their plantations was to entice them into debt. When this method didn't net a large enough labor force, a new state constitution was passed compelling the Indians who didn't pay taxes in money to pay them in work. The hacendados and their puppet politicians soon learned that once the Indians owed money, they could be kept so deeply mired that they could never buy their way out.

"However"—Felipe sighed—"the world was rapidly changing and Yucatán with it. The United States and Europe needed rope for shipping. Here was a handy source of supply. The hacendados discovered wealth beyond their most avaricious dreams. Ignoring the rest of Mexico as not worth bothering with, they turned to Europe for cultural standards. Children were educated on the Continent and, while the Maya worked the land, the hacendados enjoyed a perpetual party in Paris. A way of life developed, a nobility of style as well as birth, that required that one's wealth be produced by the labor of the lower orders. It would cost the Creoles dearly."

"Are you talking about the Caste War?" Alma asked, remembering the bloody account in the Stephens book.

"Ah, you've done some homework."

"A little—all that I could. There's so little to be found," she lamented, already planning to rectify the lack.

"The inevitable revolt came in 1847. Valladolid, the most isolated and vulnerable of the Yucatán cities—and the stronghold of the most arrogant Creoles—fell to the Maya forces. But when Mérida was threatened, your country intervened; Washington sent one thousand handpicked troops, 'military advisers,' they were called. The tide of battle turned, making possible merciless reprisals against the Maya. Men, women, children, whatever their economic or political beliefs, were slaughtered. Others were sold to Cuba as slaves. The lucky ones escaped into the jungles of Quintana Roo, which still remains a virtual no-man's-land."

"Did nothing change then?" Alma wanted to know.

"An estimated three hundred thousand people—half the population of Yucatán—were killed, but the hacendados immediately returned to their old ways, growing richer and richer while their Mayan peasants barely survived. The haughty Creoles had changed not at all. So anxious were they to establish their superiority by setting themselves apart that they passed a law decreeing that women of mixed blood could wear only *huipals,* Indian dresses. Working men on the haciendas were arbitrarily flogged by their overseers, then put in stocks overnight so as not to miss a day's work. Were they to lay their grievances before the owner of the hacienda, their only redress was to receive a double beating for daring to protest. If they attempted to lodge a complaint before a judge as, by law, they had a right to do, he was very likely the friend or relative of the planter or perhaps a planter himself with servants on his own plantation treated the same way."

"There was nothing that anyone could do?"

"Many of us tried, but it wasn't until the revolution that was sweeping the rest of Mexico finally reached Yucatán in 1917 that the old ways were challenged."

"Why, that's barely six years ago! You're responsible for all these reforms, aren't you?"

"I've done what I could, but there's much remaining to be done."

That night, back at the Gran Hotel, Alma wrote in her journal: *"He is a miracle of goodness and beauty."*

The day had begun with a train ride to Dzitas, where a huge crowd awaited the archeological team. It was all part of a grand ceremony honoring the newly constructed road to Chichén Itzá. There were many speeches, native dances, feasting, and still more speeches. Hundreds of people, most of them Maya, had come from all over the state to be present at the historic ribbon cutting. There was no way the small village could accommodate them all. Makeshift tents were set up for the dignitaries. As for the others, the lucky ones discovered distant relatives in Dzitas. Some strung up hammocks in the nearby forest, and for many, the party lasted all night.

To Alma, the formalities seemed endless. When the following day began with more speeches, she felt ready to explode. Fortunately, the breakfast banquet was blessedly short, the ribbon-cutting ceremony already anti-climatic after the rhetoric of the previous day. The time had finally come to proceed down the new road to the sacred city, Chichén Itzá.

Felipe Carrillo Puerto was justly proud of his new road, but Alma and her party suppressed both smiles and shudders when they were confronted with the caravan of ancient vehicles commandeered to transport them to the site. Dubiously, they surveyed the cars: unbelievably patched tires, broken lights, and broken windows. They hesitated, each looking doubt-fully at the others, but the governor, Alma realized, was looking at her. "Perhaps we should be on our way," she murmured to Morley. "Shall I ride in this one?" Without waiting for a reply, Alma clambered in beside the driver of the nearest car. The others followed suit until each car was crammed.

It took nearly ten minutes of spirited cranking before Alma's car was galvanized into action. As it jolted down the road, the jungle closed in around them. Distance ceased to exist, as strangely contorted trees, tower-ing plants, feathery ferns, and spongy fungus all crowded together. Then, the last corner turned and instead of another vista of unchanging forest, a clear straight road led for another mile or so to a sight of breathtaking grandeur. A great white pyramid towered high above the forest, capped by a temple. There was a moment of stunned silence, followed by excited gasps, and then the crew were pummeling one another deliriously.

Chichén Itzá, the end of the road at last, Alma realized, shivering with anticipation at being so near to her goal. This was what the conquistadores had seen four hundred years before. No wonder they had written letters filled with superlatives, a vain attempt to describe the indescribable. Would she—could she—do better? Alma wondered. Could she bring to people who would never see Chichén Itzá for themselves a sense of its beauty, its wonder?

The only way to stop the car was to kill the engine and coast to a stop, but finally her vehicle and the others before and behind her were still and members of the party scrambling out, each hurrying off in a different direction. Alma paused uncertainly, looking up at the tall pyramid.

"Would you like to climb El Castillo?" Felipe had left the other officials who'd been riding with him in the lead car and now stood at her side.

"El Castillo—so that's what it's called—not a Mayan name at all."

"No," he agreed. "The name was supplied by the conquistador Montejo.

Because the structure was so big, he assumed that it had to be a castle and requisitioned it for his own use. We of the Maya know it by its true name, the Temple of Kukulkan."

"Ku-kul-kan"—Alma savored the unfamiliar word.

"Yes"—he nodded. "The Plumed Serpent."

"Why, I know about the Plumed Serpent! I heard of him in Mexico City, but I thought his name was Quetzalcoatl."

"You are right; it is the same god, but here he is known as Kukulkan."

There were many stairs—364, Alma would later learn—and they were in ruinous condition, but that wasn't the worst of it. Instead of constructing a step deep enough to accommodate a normal foot, the Maya had made each so shallow that one had to climb sideways like a crab—at least that's how Alma was doing it—and they had made the risers so high that it was difficult for Alma to keep her chin out of the way of her knees. Trying desperately not to look down, she pulled herself up, hugging the steps so tightly with the soles of her feet, digging her toes in so violently, that by the time she reached the top, her outraged muscles felt as if they would never unkink themselves.

Once the last step had been negotiated, Alma sank gratefully to the stone floor, her heart pounding. It would be a simple matter, she reflected, for a high priest to remove that throbbing organ. Hers felt ready to leap from her chest of its own volition. A wave of revulsion swept over her as she thought of hundreds, perhaps thousands, of sacrificial victims who'd climbed those very stairs only to be arched backward across the stone altar, their heaving chests sliced open with an obsidian blade, a fountain of blood, and then the heart ripped out before their still living eyes.

Why, she wondered, would a supposedly peaceful deity demand such tribute? Kukulkan/Quetzalcoatl had descended from heaven to introduce the concept of love and peace. The embodiment of divine benevolence and wisdom, he'd been an able administrator uniting his people and ruling them well. Her mind again turned to the man beside her. He, too, seemed mythic, an Arthurian figure, idealistic, intent on unity, already something of a god to the masses he had helped to free. How would Felipe's story end? she wondered. Kukulkan, try as he might, could not suppress his virility, and ultimately, it was his desire for a woman that proved his downfall. Alma glanced with veiled curiosity at the man lounging beside her, only to discover that he was watching her with open admiration.

She did not look away, but met his eyes directly. "You are married?"

"Indeed, yes."

"And you no doubt have many children?"

"I have four."

Hardly a handicap in Mexico, Alma reflected. In her travels she'd met a number of politicians who flaunted their mistresses openly. Did Felipe's idealism extend into his private life? Such an attractive man must have many temptations. She resolved not be one of them.

"If Kukulkan was so good, why the sacrifices here—why this temple?"

"Some blame the Toltecs, a warrior race from the northwest for introducing the practice of sacrifice to the Maya. Somehow, in the process of conquest and assimilation, Kukulkan—a peaceful god—evolved into a rapacious taskmaster who demanded blood sacrifices in return for the sun's fertilizing rays. But now"—he smiled at her—"I believe that Kukulkan will be changing once again. *You* will fulfill his plan. You were sent here to tell the world about the glorious past of the Maya."

"Is that really good?" she asked, at last voicing a question that had concerned her throughout the trip. "My being here on this expedition is a reporter's dream, but you know what the final result will be. The archeologists are one thing—meticulous scientists, most of them; but eventually there will be tourists. Yucatán can't help but change."

"Yucatán *must* change; the dependence on sisal must end. Tourism will be our industry, an industry without smokestacks."

"I suppose"—Alma paused, uncertain—"but there's such a sense of power about Chichén Itzá. I almost believe what you said the other day about the old gods—that they never left. The sense of them seems to permeate Chichén Itzá. It's as if they're right here now, as if they still watch." She paused uncertainly, her voice dropped almost to a whisper. "Aren't you afraid . . ."

"You mean the curse? No need to blush. Of course, I'm aware of it. I've heard the old *brujas* talk, the witch women, but many of them—well, let's say it—they're ignorant. They live in the past and yet forget it. They have forgotten that Chichén Itzá was not only a ceremonial center but a commercial one. Ek Chuah, our god of trade, was greatly venerated. He would very much approve of tourists and, most particularly, the trade they will bring to our artisans."

Alma looked about at the monuments of cold stone and lost memories, trying to imagine what it must once have been.

As though reading her thoughts, Felipe conjured up the ancient scene. The site thronged with vendors hawking sandals, weavings, condiments, vegetables, and rare stones. There were cages of hairless dogs, chattering monkeys, and brightly plumed birds talking Mayan. Other areas were set aside for feather merchants, goldsmiths, healers, scribes, and storytellers.

"Too bad none of those storytellers is around to tell us what really happened here," Alma quietly lamented. "Why did they build this great city—this fantastic city—only to desert it and then why"—Alma was almost whispering now—"did they come back hundreds of hears later and rebuild it only to leave again?"

"Perhaps one day *you,* little *peregrina,* will discover the answer to that riddle."

"Peregrina?"

"Pilgrim—is that not what you are?—a pilgrim who will all too soon return to your own far-off land?"

"Yes, yes," she assured him, her voice rising, ignoring the challenge in his eyes. "I will be returning home soon, just as soon as this survey expedition is over."

CHAPTER · 5

The Cenote's Secret

In 1923, except for the temple, there were only shapeless mounds with an occasional glimpse of cut stone to suggest the ancient grandeur of Chichén Itzá. Many, perhaps hundreds, of these untouched mounds, large and small, had been completely engulfed by ruthless undergrowth. When the roof and walls of a building collapsed, seedlings quickly took root in the tumbled mass of mortar, earth, and stone. The same climate that enabled beans to sprout through a new cement walk was a forcing house for the great trees that sprang from the mounds. Insidious roots pushed relentlessly through the crevasses between the stones, distorting and finally demolishing what remained.

Alma marveled at the ease with which the Mayan guides slashed pathways through tangles of trees and dense undergrowth with a great, lethal-looking knife—a machete, she was told, a blade that served many needs in Central America from kitchen utensil to weapon of war or revolution.

She soon learned one of the first laws of the jungle, for humans at least:

Never put your hand in a place where you can't see. Tarantulas, centipedes, and scorpions as well as coral snakes and rattlesnakes might well be lurking in any dark or hidden recess. It was a lesson she would carry with her always. Nothing would ever induce Alma to slip her hand under a cushion or to grub around in a dark closet. Shaking out her shoes became automatic on rising in the morning, a habit that persisted even years later at San Francisco's Fairmont Hotel.

Edward Thompson's hacienda was quickly established as base camp, and Alma was quartered there with the rest. It was a curious blend of pomp and squalor. Built in the 1700's, some traces of colonial splendor remained, though, for the most part, the building was dilapidated and all too rapidly falling into ruin. For Alma, what counted was her discovery of the library of rare books the archeologist had accumulated over the years.

The *sala,* an architectural survivor of the great halls of European castles, served as their main dining room. The *sala* was large, high ceilinged, and full of echoes, and Alma found it impossible to converse with anyone but her immediate neighbor across the table. Ordinary chitchat degenerated into shouting matches: "Better—did you say better? Better or butter?"

Alma slowly came to know her host, Don Eduardo—as Thompson was known to everyone. She was as much intrigued by the pioneer archeologist as he was charmed by her. Now well into his sixties, Thompson was accustomed to having the site to himself. The invasion of noisy young people with their new ideas was at best disconcerting. But Alma—lovely Alma with her winsome ways and eagerness to listen—well *she* was different.

Scarcely a day had passed before he introduced her to the sacred *cenote,* which gave the site its greatest significance. The life-sustaining power of water was all important to the Maya, he explained; the *cenote,* a natural well, a gift from the gods. Unfortunately, sometimes it had been necessary to propitiate those gods, and human beings—most frequently women— were hurled into the well. Occasionally, according to legend, a victim returned to the surface; such a survivor brought not only blessings but prophetic messages from the gods.

One intended sacrifice, this time a male, had become a legend. Hunac Ceel was an ambitious commoner from the city state of Mayapán. Impatient with the manner in which matters were going with the Triple Alliance, an organization of city states comprising Chichén Itzá, Uxmal and Mayapán, he determined to put a stop to the growing prominence of the former. Perhaps his own political future was an even greater incentive. Hunac Ceel's opportunity came when the leaders of Mayapán organized a pilgrimage to the sacred *cenote* at Chichén Itzá. The occasion was to be celebrated by flinging a number of people into the well in the urgent hope that at least one might return to the surface with a message from the gods concerning Mayapán's administration.

Collective sighs of disappointment arose from the crowd gathered around the well as victim after victim was cast into the water. The surface remained ominously still; not one person emerged from the depth. Suddenly, Hunac Ceel bounded forward and dove into the *cenote*. There was a stunned silence as the crowd waited.

The volunteer victim emerged. "I have spoken to the gods," he cried out. The people listened, speechless, as Hunac Ceel revealed the divine message. The gods had decreed that he was to be not only Lord of Mayapán, but ruler of the entire Yucatán Peninsula.

Alma had listened with her usual interest to the story of this consummate risk taker. "What happened to him?" she asked when Don Eduardo paused.

"What could the priests do with a man so divinely inspired but fulfill his destiny? A supreme opportunist perhaps, but still a prudent man, Hunac Ceel left nothing to chance. Just as he'd prepared himself for the plunge by learning to swim, now he insured Mayapán's supremacy by importing Mexican mercenaries. These men, *ah canuls,* they were called, were expert archers—a skill until then unknown to the Maya. The combination of Hunac Cell's sagacity and force was formidable. The Cocom dynasty he founded lasted for two hundred and fifty years."

"You mean it's true—it really happened?" Alma looked at him in surprise.

Thompson shrugged. "Many believe it to be. In fact, your friend, the governor, is the direct descendant of Nachi Cocom, the last Mayan king."

Alma was even more incredulous. "Surely you're joking?"

"Not at all. Hunac Ceel may or may not be a mythical character, but Nachi Cocum, the last ruler of a shattered Mayan confederation, the last holdout against the Spaniards, was very real, and Yucatán's present governor is directly related to him. I'm surprised he didn't tell you."

· · ·

As the days passed, Felipe visited Chichén Itzá with increasing frequency. Whatever his excuse, Alma knew he was coming to see her. Most of the others were aware of it as well. She was flattered, embarrassed, pleased, and frightened. It was an impossible situation. The only solution was to avoid the governor completely. She made every possible excuse to be absent, often retreating into the jungle for hours when she saw his official car approaching. It was all very difficult. There was so much that Alma was learning about Felipe, things that made her admire him all the more. The fact of his own prominent lineage, for instance. How easy it would have been in the course of his little history lesson to drop in the part played by his own illustrious ancestor. How many men could have resisted the opportunity? There were other more telling details of the governor's background that caused her to respect him even more. Like herself, Felipe was self-educated. His mentor had been the Cura of Valladolid, who'd taken a liking to the earnest, hardworking seventeen-year-old and introduced him to the French rationalists. It awakened Felipe to the possibility of a changed order—release from material, intellectual, and spiritual bondage—and it set him on a course of liberating action.

As the owner of a one-boy transportation service for the hauling of sisal hemp, Felipe had had occasion to visit many haciendas throughout the length and breadth of the state, learning firsthand the terrible wrongs committed against the helpless people he claimed as his own. This total identification with the Maya intrigued Alma. Obviously there'd been a conscious choice involved. Felipe might be descended from Mayan royalty, but his appearance made it obvious that European blood mingled with Indian. The scenario was easy to imagine: a powerful Creole grandee, possibly descended from the conquistadores, and a pretty Mayan girl— willing or unwilling, it would have made little difference. Many Yucatecans of mixed blood were proud of their European connection; Felipe obviously was not. Clearly, he'd elected to ignore it. Disregarding the Creole good looks that might have gained him access to high places, he preferred to be known as a man of the people.

Felipe's decision to cast his lot with the Maya came in his teens. Once during this time he'd intervened on behalf of a woman being beaten by an overseer and was imprisoned for it. Another time, Felipe translated the entire Mexican constitution into Maya so that his people might know their rights. For this he was imprisoned for an even longer period.

In an action that was a precursor of the Mexican revolution, Felipe fought alongside Emiliano Zapata and never forgot his crusading battle cry, "Tierra y Libertad"—"Land and Liberty." He had represented Yucatán in the National Chamber of Deputies in the years before his election to the office of governor and made several trips to the United States, where he lectured to a variety of audiences, among them the Rand School of New York. Somehow, he'd managed to include among this friends and correspondents Franklin Roosevelt, Herbert Hoover, and Samuel Gompers, president of the American Federation of Labor.

The Leagues of Resistance that Felipe had mentioned to her in passing had been a rallying point to the people during the chaotic years of the revolutionary ebb and flow. Each was a local organization responding to community needs, a political unit, a grange, a forum, and a cooperative educational and recreational center in one; each was a new idea, typical of Felipe's progressive social thinking. His Feminist Leagues, led by dedicated women, many of them schoolteachers, had successfully combatted illiteracy and intemperance. Systematically, they'd introduced hygiene, modern child-care techniques, and birth control into the social fabric. It was totally unprecedented in Yucatán, where the Indians had been rooted like trees to the soil—property of their respective masters, allowed to marry only members of their own hacienda.

After the fall of the Díaz dictatorship in 1910, during Madero's presidency and the Huerta reaction, Yucatán, remote and isolated as it was, continued under the suppression of the feudal system imposed by powerful landowners. But, throughout it all, Felipe had, under the banner "Land and Liberty," organized and developed his Leagues. These units, ultimately operating in almost every town and village in Yucatán, managed to each send representatives to a worker's congress, at which a program for emancipation was drawn up and a plan developed for the gradual restoration of the communal village lands stolen from the Maya under the Díaz dictatorship. Naturally, the hacendados, enraged not only by the loss of a few acres from their thousands but, more significantly, by the freeing of their slaves, had not been idle. Seizing the opportunity afforded by President Carranza's retreat from his military pledges in 1918, they opened warfare against the recently freed serfs, selecting as their special targets the local leaders of the new "socialist" organizations. Hundreds were killed—their homes destroyed, their meager funds confiscated. During this period, Felipe had barely escaped with his life. The next president, Alvaro Obregon, had ended this reign of terror and, under the protection of the federally appointed governor of Yucatán, Felipe had returned to complete his work. His election as governor, the first honest political competition to be held in Yucatán, had taken place in 1921—less than two years before Alma's visit.

It was difficult to keep thoughts of such a man out of her mind, and Felipe's frequent presence did nothing to ease her confusion. It was obvious that he had no intention of allowing her to either forget or avoid him. Alma tried hard to keep busy, exploring the site and recording the finds of the archeologists. She was fascinated by Don Eduardo and often sought him out for interviews. The more questions she asked, the harder she had to concentrate and the less time there was to think about Felipe. At least that was her theory. Actually, the swift passage of time brought pain rather than relief. She dreaded the thought of leaving.

Thompson did prove an interesting source. His own life was rich with story material. While still a student at Worcester Polytecnic Institute, she learned, he'd written an article entitled "Atlantis Not a Myth," which appeared in *Popular Science Monthly.* His premise that the mysterious Maya civilization on the Yucatán Peninsula might be an offshoot of the lost continent of Atlantis won friends in high places.

Stephen Salisbury, one of the founders of the American Antiquarian Society, and Charles O. Bowditch, the guiding light of the Peabody Museum, whose functions reminded Alma very much of Hunac Ceel's high priests, had agreed that Thompson was the very man to investigate and catalogue Yucatán, an area that had long intrigued both. In one clever coup, they insured their protégé both a free hand and a salary by using their political influence to get him appointed U.S. consul to Yucatán and Campeche. In 1885, Thompson—at twenty-five, the youngest consul in United States history—set out with his wife and baby daughter to explore Yucatán. It was an adventure that would occupy the next forty years of his life.

Five years later, Thompson was able to send a vast array of temple molds for display at the 1890 Chicago World's Fair. Allison V. Armour, the meat-packing magnate, was so impressed that he made the young archeologist a cash gift intended for the purchase of the Chichén Itzá ruins. Acting quickly, Thompson also acquired nearly one hundred square miles of land, which included a Spanish plantation house and untold ruins, for approximately seventy-five dollars. At that time, the outpost area was accessible only by jungle footpath. On the night Thompson took possession of the place, he stumbled over the remains of the last inhabitant of his new hacienda, who'd been murdered by insurrectionists.

"What a life you've had"—Alma sighed, looking admiringly at the man before her.

He hesitated. "There's something more—something no one knows. . . ."

"Tell me—will you tell me?" Alma leaned forward eagerly. She had sensed that there was more, something slightly mysterious, about Thompson. Though always polite, seemingly affable, he had appeared somewhat guarded. Occasionally it seemed to her that he'd actually avoided the technical questions of the other archeologists.

"I shouldn't have mentioned it—I shall have to think about it."

"But tomorrow is my last day here—"

"Yes, I'm quite aware of that, but I do need time. Meet me tomorrow at the *cenote*. Come at day's end. We will be alone. Perhaps I will have something of interest to tell you—a real, as I think you young reporters call it, 'scoop.' "

The following morning seemed interminable. At midday when the group met in the sala for lunch, Alma studied Thompson's face but could read nothing. The rest of the afternoon passed even more slowly. Around 5:00, the team activities began to wind down. A party had been planned to commemorate the last day of the Chichén Itzá survey.

"Aren't you about ready to knock off, Alma?"—Sylvanus Morley had spied her heading toward the *cenote,* notebook in hand. "The mariachis will be tuning up. What do you bet the governor's already waiting for you at the hacienda. You don't want to disappoint him."

She ignored his teasing. "I'll be along shortly—don't wait." She hurried down a narrow path, hoping no one would follow.

Alma found Thompson seated on a small granite platform, the remains of a temple. Below him was the large pool of lusterless green water. In all her visits here, Alma's initial sense of its malevolence had never abated. She couldn't help but see the *cenote* as a gaping wound in the heart of the surrounding forest.

Iguanas crawled from beneath the rocks to blink at her with vacant eyes as she seated herself beside him. "What I have to tell you, my dear—my story—is really a confession," he began. "You must be patient, you must hear the whole thing in order to understand how it first came to me, for the story is uniquely mine and only I know all of it."

Alma relaxed with an inward sigh. Surely with a buildup like this, he planned to tell her everything. She leaned against the crumbling wall. The sun, a glow of purple and gold, was beginning to set.

"You have to know that when I first came here all I heard were stories— legends—about the *cenote*. After a time it seemed that my very dreams were haunted. I could see it all as if I'd been there, had actually seen those girls sacrificed. It must have gone something like this . . ."

Alma hung on his every word as the archeologist's dramatic account summoned a lovely sad-eyed phantom out of the *cenote*'s depth. As the tale took shape, she readily saw a flawless young beauty emerge from the small sanctuary that crowned El Castillo. The victim wore a bridal wreath of white *tulipanes* as the black-masked priests led her from the sculptured chamber. Her descent from the great stairway was announced by the beating of the death drum, the shrill screeching of a reed whistle, the plaintive notes of a high-pitched flute. Below in solemn procession were the nobles and priests. Trembling, quite helpless, the maiden joined them in their march along the sacred road. They paused on the pool's edge, the ominous music increasing in volume as the maiden was lifted to the granite platform with its sculptured entrance.

Alma saw it all, almost unaware of Thompson's narration. The nobles and priests forming a circle around the *cenote*'s rim, their voices raised in frenzied supplication as they threw their precious jewels and vessels of smoking incense into the dark green water; then came the moment of appeasement to the offended deity, the moment of supreme sacrifice.

The maiden had been mercifully drugged with *balche,* the sacred nectar. Her entire life had been a preparation for this hour. She believed that her symbolic marriage to Chac, the water god, in the depth of the sacred *cenote,* would save her people from the anger of the deity vented in some form of disaster. She had been assured that the *cenote* was only a doorway to immortal happiness. But the urge to live and love proved stronger than a drug or faith, and a shriek of despair pierced the forest as she was hurled headlong into the yawning water pit.

Alma sat silently, spellbound by the vision. Aware of her fascination, Thompson smiled. "You feel it, too; it's real for you as well."

"Yes," she agreed. "It's difficult to believe that it's just a legend."

"But it isn't just a legend. It's all quite true—every bit of it is true."

"How can you know that?"

"Because I, too, have descended into the well."

"What are you saying!"

"The more I thought about the myth, the more real it became to me. I determined to master the Mayan tongue. Then, as time passed, I became the friend and confidant of the *H'Menens.*"

Alma shook her head. "The *H'Menes?*"

"Mayan wise men. They taught me everything, and eventually, after many trials, inducted me into the Sh'Toi Brothers, a secret society that somehow escaped notice of the Spaniards and survived all these years. Eventually they even trusted me enough to confirm the legend of the *cenote.* The sacrificial ceremony had been performed for centuries, they said, whenever pestilence, famine, or military defeat threatened them. Eventually, they even pointed out the part of the *cenote* beneath which Chac had his palace."

"His palace!" A wave of doubt swept over Alma as she surveyed the drop of some seventy-five feet to the murky surface of the pool. She smiled, "The king's 'palace' must be very grand indeed, a palace of mud. Is that where the mermaids live?"

Thompson smiled back indulgently. "I can well understand your skepticism, my dear. That's how everyone reacted. I, too, assumed the *H'Menes* were merely colorful storytellers, but eventually in my studies I came upon proof of a sort."

"Proof? What kind of proof?" Alma leaned back against the rock, her arms crossed unconsciously in the classic "show me" stance.

"I'd begun by then to study the history of the country. Whenever possible, I collected rare manuscripts—you've seen some of them. One day I came across a copy of a letter, a very detailed descriptive letter, that had been sent in 1579 to King Charles V from the mayor of a nearby city, Valladolid. Old people had told him stories of their youth. They spoke of young women who'd been sacrificed—thrown into this very well. The descriptions were vivid and intimate. They had the ring of truth. It was obvious that the mayor had believed them and so, I must confess, did I. The more I thought about it, the more credulous I became, and then there was something else . . ."

"What more could there be?"

"Quite a bit, my dear, quite a bit. If the nobles were willing to make the supreme sacrifice of human life—if that part was true—then what about the other part?"

Alma was mystified. "What other part?"

"Why, the gold, of course—the gold, the jewels—the treasure."

As Alma listened, it seemed to her that Hunac Ceel and Edward Thompson were kindred spirits cut from the same cloth. There was the legendary hero diving into the Well of Sacrifice in search of fame and fortune, a drama repeated by the visionary archeologist hoping to extract a bit of the same.

It remained only for Thompson to take the plunge. As the archeologist's story unfolded, he explained to Alma how he'd consulted a dredging expert, who'd advised that exploration was impossible without strong windlasses and heavy-duty dredging equipment. When he queried other experts he was told "No person can go down into the unknown depth of that great water pit and expect to come out alive. If you want to commit suicide, why not seek a less shocking way of doing it?"

Unable to find financial support for such an undertaking, Don Eduardo went to Boston and studied diving from a pioneer expert, Captain Ephraim Nickerson. Next he enlisted the aid of Nicholas, a Greek sponge diver then living in the Bahamas, persuading him to come to Yucatán. Soon the two of them had acquired a primitive pontoon boat and added an air pump.

Nicholas sent for an assistant, and the two expatriot Greeks set about teaching a chosen gang of Maya how to manage the pump and send the steady current of air upon which Thompson's life was dependent through the tube, as well as read and answer signals sent from below. The diving suit that Thompson designed for himself was made of waterproof canvas with a large copper helmet weighing more than thirty pounds and equipped with plate glass goggle-eyes and air valves near the ears, lead necklaces nearly half as heavy as the helmets and canvas shoes with thick wrought-iron soles.

Alma shook her head, trying to imagine the picture that Don Eduardo had described. "You were brave, incredibly brave."

"I was incredibly determined," he recalled. "With the speaking tube, air hose, and lifeline carefully adjusted, Nicholas helped me to waddle to the ladder that led down into the water."

Alma shivered. "The whole idea is absolutely terrifying."

"But also thrilling"—Don Eduardo assured her, "—the idea of being the only living being who'd ever reached the bottom alive and expected to return the same way."

"Except for Hunac Ceel," she reminded him, smiling.

"Except for Hunac Ceel," he agreed. "As I stepped on the first rung of the ladder, each of the pumping gang, my faithful native boys, left his place in turn and with a very solemn face shook hands with me and then went back to wait for the signal. It wasn't difficult to read their thoughts. They were bidding me a last farewell, never expecting to see me again. Then, releasing my hold on the ladder, I sank like a bag of lead down into the water."

Thompson went on to relate how, feeling only slightly more secure than the sacrificial victims, he descended through some thirty-five feet of water into the ooze. Alma marveled at the display of courage she considered fully on a par with that of Hunac Ceel's. Several of these early dives, she learned, were nearly fatal, and one had resulted in a ruptured eardrum.

The *cenote* at its widest point measured some 187 feet across. The limestone wall dropped about 75 feet from the tree-fringed rim to the surface of the pool. And, beneath approximately 36 feet of water, was a mud bed 30 feet deep, a deposit sufficiently consistent to sustain tree branches and roots of considerable size. About 18 feet of this was so compact that it held large rocks, fallen columns, and wall stones.

"During the first ten feet of descent, the light rays changed from yellow to green and then to purplish black. After that I was in total darkness. Sharp pains shot through my ears, because of the increasing air pressure. When I gulped and opened the air valves in my helmet, a sound like 'pht! pht!' came from each ear, and then the pain ceased. Several times this process had to be repeated before I stood on the bottom. I noted another curious sensation on my way down. I felt as if I were rapidly losing weight until, as I stood on the flat end of a big stone column that had fallen from the old ruined shrine above, I seemed to have no weight at all. I fancied that I was more like a bubble than a man burdened by heavy weights."

Though Thompson had acquired a submarine flashlight, it was useless in this gruel-like combination of deep water and mud. All exploration had to be accomplished in a darkness that was blacker than Stygian. For weeks, Thompson made daily descents. Once he floated up to the surface without warning and struck the bottom of the pontoon with a loud thump. His

terrified helpers ran off screaming, certain that it was Chac rising in righteous anger at this invasion of his inner sanctum. Load after load of mud
was brought up and examined, always with the concern that, despite his
mapping efforts, excavation of an area might be duplicated. Hours of heartbreaking anxiety and backbreaking effort netted nothing more than the
sedimentary collection of centuries of jungle decay.

Then, late in 1903, two nearly white balls turned up in the muck. Thompson pounced on them, felt them, smelled them, tore one open, and touched
a match to its heart. As a long spiral of sweet-scented smoke curled
upward, he recalled the words of one of the *H'Men:* "In ancient times, our
fathers burned sacred resin, and by the fragrant smoke their prayers were
wafted upward to their gods whose home was in the sun."

Thompson described how he had shouted and danced like a child, realizing that the two small balls were copal, which the Maya used for incense.
For him, it was the scent of victory. He knew now that he was close. A
few days later, he raised the skeletons of three women. Soon after, some
gold discs were uncovered, then jade, precious ornaments, jewelry—hundreds of artifacts of all kinds.

Alma had sat speechless as Don Eduardo's story unfolded. It was amazing, surely too amazing to be true. "But"—she broke in at last—"that was
twenty years ago—why did you never tell anyone?"

"If word had gotten out, the site would have been overrun with bandits,
officials, anybody, everybody. Somehow, I think possibly because of religious fear, my assistants remained silent. For myself, I believed—I still
believe—that the land was mine, the risk was mine, the treasure, too, was
mine to do with as I pleased."

Alma caught her breath. "What did you do with it?"

"Sent it piece by piece out of the country by diplomatic pouch to my
benefactors at the Peabody Museum."

"Do you mean"—Alma's voice dropped to a whisper—"that you stole
those things from Mexico and just packed them off to Boston?"

"I'd hardly call it stealing; it was my land. I simply sent the treasure away
for safekeeping. What would you have done?"

Alma shook her head. This trusting man had just handed her the greatest
story of her life; she was absolutely speechless.

CHAPTER · 6

Descent into Hell

A lma wondered more than once that night, why did everything have to have a price tag? Fortune had provided her with one of the great archeological stories of the century, but if she printed it a man's reputation might well be ruined, the work of a lifetime discredited.

Fortune had also provided her with the man of her dreams, a veritable soul mate, but if she succumbed to his advances, the outcome was a back-street melodrama. Alma had no illusions regarding the constancy of Latin lovers. Why shouldn't his passions be kindled briefly by a bright and stylish North American, particularly when she shared so many of his visions? But if Felipe's feelings went deeper than a passing fancy, even if he truly loved her, where could it lead? Divorce was unthinkable in this Latin land.

The party was a jolly affair, the archeologists excited by their finds, the dignitaries pleased by the enthusiasm of their guests. Felipe was present, sans wife as usual. At first Alma tried to avoid him, but soon abandoned the effort. He was constantly at her side, claiming too many dances. To refuse their generous host would have been impossible, even if she'd wanted to.

Don Eduardo was jovial. He looked often at Alma, smiled frequently. Perhaps, she speculated, his disclosure had removed a burden the veteran archeologist had carried for years. During the course of the evening, he announced to the Yucatologists—a term he'd recently coined for the visiting team—that he would return with them the following day to Mérida. There were two other sites that he and the governor had agreed must be viewed. Don Eduardo would be their "director general."

The following day Alma politely refused the seat offered her in the governor's limousine, pleading that she still had much to discuss with Thompson. It was true. Fortunately the other passengers in the *Fortinga* spoke no English, so she and the archeologist were able to speak freely.

"I'm deeply honored by your confidence, Don Eduardo, but you know I *am* a reporter, my duty is to the *Times,*" she reminded him.

"Yes, yes, I realize all that. I thought a long time before I told you my secret."

"Then you *are* aware of the possible consequences of my story?" she asked, vastly relieved by his air of calm confidence.

Thompson smiled, shrugging expansively. "The consequences may be fantastic. Oh, I realize there will be talk. Some may resent the fact that I kept my discoveries a secret, that I sent them out of the country. What is that compared to the revelation that such treasures exist? Now people everywhere will understand and appreciate the glories of the Maya heritage. The treasures of one of the greatest civilizations the world has ever known have been hidden in the basement far too long."

Alma frowned. "I'm concerned about that; the treasures *have* been hidden a long, long time. Apparently the Peabody wants it that way. Suppose they refuse to let me see them? I can't write about something that I haven't seen for myself."

Don Eduardo stroked his beard, frowning thoughtfully. Obviously the possibility hadn't occurred to him. "Very well then," he conceded. "I shall have to put my 'confession' in writing. Give me your notebook, your pencil." He wrote quickly, a few brief paragraphs, then signed his name with a flourish. "They can hardly ignore this, but should they try, a word from the Mexican ambassador should suffice."

With a relieved sigh, Alma took the paper gratefully, slipping it into her purse. One problem dealt with, for the time being at least, but the other . . .

That evening Felipe Carrillo Puerto was again their host at a splendid banquet. Alma found herself placed at his right. Afterward they all retired briefly to change their clothes and pack a few things, then reassembled. Once again the twenty Yucatologists were back in their *Fortingas,* this time en route to the Estación Peninsular, where at midnight they boarded a luxurious Pullman car. Trailing behind was the banquet orchestra. Alma suppressed a smile at the tribute. She'd come to realize that absolutely nothing was done in Yucatán without a musical accompaniment.

In the morning, she rolled over in her upper berth and pulled the window curtain. Outside was the village of Muna. After a breakfast of tropical fruits, the group left the train. More *Fortingas,* these much the worse for wear but brightly polished, were waiting to take them the remaining ten miles to Uxmal. This road, unlike the one approaching Chichén Itzá, was very rough. Alma, now sharing a car with Thompson and the governor, thought she'd be jolted out of her skin.

"I know it's bad," Felipe acknowledged, "but only months ago it was navigable only by *volan.*"

Alma winced, thinking of the two-wheeled native cart and trying to imagine the Empress Carlota, who'd made the trip some sixty years before, bouncing over these same potholes wearing a corset and hoopskirt.

Uxmal, once they reached it, was worth the discomfort. Alma could think of nothing more strangely startling than the lofty pyramids and stately terraced buildings towering before her on every side. The mystery inherent in the abandoned site impressed her more than the spectacle itself. From where did this tremendous artistry come? What was the impetus for such magnificence? she wondered. Why was the city abandoned? All that Alma could know for certain was that before her stood the remains of an achievement of civilization that had been centuries in the molding. Here was proof that a colossal culture was born, flourished, then vanished, yet its rise and fall had left no written record.

Flanked by Don Eduardo and Felipe, Alma approached the tallest structure, an immense pyramid. "It's called the Temple of the Magician," the governor told her.

"Or the Temple of the Dwarf," Thompson added.

"Dwarf!" Alma's curiousity was piqued.

"That's the legend," Thompson explained. "A most magical dwarf is said to have built the pyramid, built all of Uxmal, in fact."

"After defeating the former ruler in a series of feats that remind one of Hercules," Felipe added. "Obviously the dwarf lacked the physical attributes of the Greek hero, but he was more than Hercules's equal in luck and cunning."

They'd reached the pyramid, and Alma surveyed the distance to the top. "The climb isn't as bad as it looks," Felipe assured her. "Around on the other side there's an iron chain that was installed when the Empress Carlota came here on her grand tour. We'll go up that way."

With outward unconcern and inward misgivings, Alma clung to the heavy chain, inwardly blessing Carlota as she began her ascent up the precipitous stone steps of the pyramid's eastern face, the remains of what was once an imposing staircase, seventy feet wide and over one hundred feet high. The men, she noted self-consciously, did not resort to the chain.

The summit reached, Alma surveyed the panorama spread before them. The former inhabitant might well have been, or at least felt like, a magician. From this eminence, he could keep constant vigil over everything taking place on the vast encircling plain below. At a glance, her eye identified some of the principal buildings of the Uxmal group, at least those her increasingly practiced companions had identified for her. Directly beneath was the Temple of the Nuns, its great quadrangle enclosed by beautifully sculptured walls. To the west, the House of the Tortoise, named for its long frieze of that creature. To the right, in the distance, she could make out the double-terraced structure called the House of the Doves because the conquistadores thought it resembled an enormous dovecote. The House of the Old Woman was off to the left and on all sides were nameless mounds, overgrown and awaiting only the implements of the excavator to reveal their long-concealed marvels.

"And that building?" Alma pointed toward the south. "Surely that must have been a great palace."

"Indeed, it was," Thompson agreed. "It's generally regarded as the most extensive and magnificent ruin in Latin America."

"And its name?"

"The Palace of the Governor," Felipe told her. "Perhaps you would care to explore it more closely."

The descent from the Temple of the Magicians was actually more terrifying than the ascent. Alma decided to try it backward, very slowly, her eyes always on the step before her, never looking down. By the time her trembling legs reached the ground, she'd learned the true meaning of the phrase "One step at a time."

"Was it really a governor's palace?" she asked as they approached the building.

"Perhaps not; that's merely the name the Spaniards gave it," Thompson answered her. "You know, 'being this grand, it must have belonged to the governor.'" He gave Felipe a sidewise grin. "My own theory is that it's purpose had something to do with astronomy. I've spent much time at this site, and it's my feeling that all the buildings were designed to reflect the configuration of the heavens. Astronomy is at the very center of Mayan culture, and I believe that each temple in this group was dedicated to one of the zodiacal signs, and its position relative to other temples corresponds with the relative position of zodiacal asterism."

Alma paused from her hurried note taking. "But wouldn't that mean that the topography of the entire city would have to be studied and arranged before a temple was erected? It seems to me that otherwise there might not have been room to complete the whole celestial scheme. But how could they do that without telescopes?"

"My dear, it isn't only telescopes that they lacked," Thompson reminded her. "We're talking about Stone Age people. They had no cutting tools, at least not as we know them. This whole building, this whole city, was done stone on stone, with no wheels, no draft animals."

Alma surveyed the building before her in wonder. It stood on three ranges of stone-walled terraces. The first was six hundred feet long and five feet high. The second terrace, standing fifteen feet above, was topped by a broad platform, around which extended a row of low stone pillars. The third was reached by a flight of steps some one hundred feet broad. The facade, a stone frieze, resembled nothing more than a bolt of sheer lace. How did they do it? she wondered. Studying the edifice before her, it was apparent that, as at Chichén Itzá, the serpent motif was predominant. The effect was massive, grand, a little heartless, "Who were these people?" she considered aloud.

"¿Quien sabe?"—Thompson shrugged. The too-familiar answer.

As Alma and Felipe continued up the stairs, Thompson drifted off to join

Morley's group over by the Temple of the Nuns. "There are legends," the governor said. "Some of us feel that grains of truth are found in myth."

Weary of climbing, Alma sank down on a stone parapet. Leaning back against one of the many elephant-nosed masks of Chac, the rain god, she looked up at Felipe invitingly: "Tell me a story."

"Ah, yes"—and Felipe paused—"tradition has it that the dwarf-magician was a very wise ruler who set in motion a government that thrived for hundreds of years. Part of its success was due to the Triple Alliance with Chichén Itzá and Mayapán, which he is said to have founded. The Triple Alliance was all well and good until love entered the picture and a triangle resulted."

"Oh, dear." Alma shuddered; this was getting too close to home.

"Princess Sac-Nicte of Mayapán was beautiful. Canek, the young king of Chichén Itzá, handsome. When they met by chance, it was love at first sight. Unfortunately, there was one major drawback; the lovely daughter of Hunac Ceel was already engaged to the king of Uxmal."

"Was that the same Hunac Ceel who dove into the sacred well?"

"The very same. Perhaps Sac-Nicte pleaded with him, but such an ambitious man would have little sympathy with romantic preference. As the daughter of a king, hers was a marriage of state. The agreement had been made; a slight to the king of Uxmal was unthinkable. The wedding plans continued. At last the day came when Hunac Ceel brought his daughter to Uxmal for the nuptial ceremony. People bearing lavish gifts flocked to the great city from all corners of the Triple Alliance. Then a murmur arose. Where was King Canek's tribute? Where, for that matter, was King Canek?

"The three-day marriage ceremony began—one day and then another of festivities. Princess Sac-Nicte walked through the rituals as though in a trance. Then, on the third day, King Canek arrived with a large army and literally swept her off her feet. In the confusion, the lovers disappeared, leaving the three armies to fight it out among themselves. While Sac-Nicte and Canek were settling into married life in what is now known as Guatemala, the army of Chichén Itzá was devastated by the combined forces of Uxmal and Mayapán. The survivors are said to have abandoned Chichén Itzá, scattering into fragments which would one day rally to overthrow the descendants of Hunac Ceel."

Alma sighed. "A lovely story—a little like Helen of Troy. It seems appropriate that Uxmal, which looks a lot like pictures I've seen of the Acropolis, would be a ghost town haunted by parallels to both Hercules and Helen. But the legends make about as much sense as what we know about Uxmal. Obviously, it, too, was abandoned and that's about as likely as walking away and leaving the Empire State Building. Don Eduardo says the name, Uxmal, means 'thrice built,' but why was it built even once?"

"I've wondered the same. There's almost no water in the area. Yucatán is one vast limestone slab with rivers running underground. In some places the rock has caved in—that's what causes the *cenotes*—but you will find none of them at Uxmal. Here the Mayan builders carved giant reservoirs, but surely there were years when there was no rain."

Alma ran her fingers tentatively over Chac's snout. It was easy to understand the omnipresence of the elephant-nosed rain god. His mask was everywhere at Uxmal. It protruded from friezes, filled in corners, and clung to spaces above doorways. The Chac features—sneering, half-open mouth exposing jutting fangs, horns, globular eyes, and snoutlike nose— were designed to be awesome. And they were. Nearly a thousand years had passed since Uxmal had been abandoned, but here, in this land still totally dependent on rain for its agricultural survival, the spirit of Chac felt very much alive.

Back at Muna, Alma determined to avoid Felipe in their final outing. At Morley's request, the group was going to visit the caves of Loltun, some hundred miles south of Mérida. Boarding the train at dawn, she slipped past the governor, who was discussing last-minute logistics with Thompson, and joined Ann and Earl Morris. Seating herself across from the couple, she carefully placed all their assorted gear in the empty seat beside her. Later, when the governor came looking for her, the car had quickly filled. There was no place for him. She saw the fleeting look of disappointment and felt a twinge of guilt. He had been so wonderful, but that was just the trouble; he was so wonderful and so unavailable. Alma kept telling herself that her imminent departure was the best thing for both of them. Fond as she was of Yucatán, she would never return.

Slowly the train wound its way through the low hills of the Puuc country, at last reaching the village of Oxkutzcab, where the party was warmly greeted by the *presidente municipal,* the full membership of the local Liga de Resistencia, and scores of schoolchildren, all to the familiar accompaniment of mariachis. At the station, the "Feministas," in colorfully embroidered *huipils,* stood before a background of triangular red banners, dispensing cool beverages from flower-bedecked tables.

After a few words of official welcome and the governor's response, both spoken in Mayan, Oxkutzcab's entire population, preceded by the musicians, escorted them to several waiting trucks, their beds covered with mattresses—*plataformas*—vehicles ordinarily used to transport *henequen* from the haciendas. They climbed aboard in the wave of festive enthusiasm that envelops a group at the start of a novel and potentially exciting adventure, but as they bounced from rut to rut some of the enthusiasm faded. Alma smiled at her complaints on the previous day's trip to Uxmal. This ordeal was far worse. Finally they jolted to a stop at a weather-beaten caretaker's lodge, where a small group of *chicleros* waited.

Felipe warmly greeted their leader, Nacho, an old *compañero,* then introduced him to the archeologists as *un buen colaborador.* Alma studied the stocky Mayan, trying to imagine this genial-seeming man with his broad smile and warm handshake fighting beside Felipe. A small camera was suspended from a chain around Nacho's neck. Cameras had been issued to him and other *chicleros* by Felipe for the purpose of photographing unknown Mayan ruins concealed in the lush vegetation of the chicle-producing region. For the delivery of each picture of an undiscovered site, they received fifty pesos.

"This is a time-saver for us and lucrative for the men," Felipe explained, "and, maybe equally important, it helps to instill in them a deeper pride in their Mayan ancestors." He went on to describe to the group the hardships faced by the *chicleros,* whose lives were pathetically short. Not only was there danger of wild animals and poisonous snakes, but often the men, high above the ground, slashed too deeply into the trunks of the tall zapidilla trees, the source of the sap for manufacture of chewing gum. The miscalculation was fatal, sending them hurtling to the jungle floor with the falling tree tops.

An excursion to Loltun as the governor's "special assistants" was a treat to the *chicleros,* who leaped happily onto the *plataformas,* scarcely aware of the bouncing and heaving motions that were almost unbearable to the Yucatecologists.

As *director general,* Don Eduardo was an authoritative and entertaining guide; his anecdotes helped some to forget their queasy stomachs as they bounced along. At last, as they approached their goal, Loltun's deeply shadowed mouth camouflaged by a defensive barricade of heavy boulders, he recalled his first impression of the interior. "It was like entering an enormous tomb—truly a place of death."

Alma fully appreciated his description once she'd descended the rough stone steps to the damp floor of the cavern. Wasn't this the embodiment of the nether world, the dismal abode of disembodied spirits she'd pictured as a girl reading the *Aeneid?* Trying to penetrate the openings to the black spaces that Don Eduardo explained expanded to still larger and more awesome chambers, pierced here and there with patches of light as distant as stars in the night sky, she fought a profound sense of terror and desolation.

The party inched cautiously along a narrow ledge in single file. *Chicleros,* clad in white cotton *camisas,* lit the way with torches, while another group, carrying ropes and tackle for emergency use, formed a rear guard. Mingled voices speaking Mayan, Spanish, and English echoed through the vast silence, eerily suggesting the futile moans of lost souls.

Guided through long corridors that connected the grottoes, they emerged at last in a high-domed gallery hung with stalactites. Some of the more massive forms were a dull gray stained with reddish brown, rust coated by centuries of dripping water. Others, more delicately shaped, were pure white, their crystalline tips sparkling like multifaceted brilliants in the torchlight.

Amid what had first appeared to be unrelieved bleakness, they discovered other objects exquisitely fashioned by nature's artistry. Don Eduardo pointed out his personal selection as the "prize exhibit in Loltun's subterranean museum." It was a pearly white stalagmite, a cylindrical pedestal with a fluted base, the rounded crown of the column resembling tightly closed petals of a snow white blossom. At its center was a chalicelike cavity. He explained that not a single drop entered the chalice from the cavern's ceiling, yet it was always filled with cold, clear water, which, as they could see, overflowed down the sides of the pedestal. "The curious phenomenon," Alma later wrote, "resulted from an interior reservoir and a natural syphon within the walls." Her long suit may not have been hydraulic engineering.

The spectacle of Lotun, its magnitude—Thompson believed it extended

for miles beneath Yucatán's limestone crust—captivated Alma's imagination, as she observed traces of ancient people and their handiwork for
which the cavern served as a repository. Don Eduardo had previously
located numerous signs of prehistoric occupancy, notably extensive deposits of shards. There were also troughs, hollowed-out boulders, placed
where they received water that percolated, drop by drop, through roof
openings. Now he called their attention to a broad band of hierogylphics
carved on a smooth section of a vertical wall. Moss had grown over the
inscriptions, but they were still faintly visible. Morley interpreted some
rock carvings as the conventional formula design for mummification, but
conceded that no proof had yet been found to indicate that America's
pre-Columbians interred their dead in the Egyptian manner.

In the midst of their discussion of the "mummy" symbols, the group was
suddenly plunged into total darkness as the torches were simultaneously
and unaccountably extinguished. Some *chicleros* stood as if petrified with
fear, while others ran blindly into the darkness. Clearly the Maya had
interpreted the sudden light failure as a sign of impending disaster. Her
heart pounding, Alma felt growing panic as she recalled similar crises at
other archeological sites where native laborers believed their deities possessed power to destroy those who desecrated their temples. Recent
newspapers had been full of stories of awful vengeance thought to have
befallen the violators of King Tut-Ankhamen's tomb. With growing exposure to Maya history and fable, Alma's pragmatism was increasingly diluted
by a recognition of metaphysical factors. Now, fanned by the awful panic
about her, a dreadful thought occurred to her. Perhaps Loltun *was* cursed.

The Indians of the region were known to hold the cave in dread, rarely
visiting the place and then only in groups. Why wouldn't they read evil
omens, a superstitious warning that their worst fears had been realized, in
this mysterious blackout? The already incendiary situation threatened to
leap completely out of control when someone shrieked: *"Estamos per-
dido!*... We are lost.... We cannot find the trail!" In the rising commotion,
Don Eduardo's slightly nasal voice, pleading in Mayan for calmness, was
barely audible. His pleas went unheeded. Alma felt herself consumed by
the blackness, the sense of doom and desolation. Was Loltun indeed a
tomb, her tomb?

Then, out of the darkness, she recognized another voice. The words
were Mayan, the commanding tone one that she had never heard. It was

Felipe. The howling ceased, and every Maya present stood at attention. He wielded a flashlight like an imperial scepter, swiftly passing its beam back and forth across the faces of the now-demoralized "auxiliary corps," while his voice continued to resound with accelerated power and tempo. Felipe's commands were answered with immediate action. Guides came forward to relight their torches from matches that he supplied. Nacho with two of his *chicleros* left with Don Eduardo in search of the trail.

Alma marveled at the silent speed and precision with which all orders were carried out. It occurred to her that the implicit obedience of the Maya might be less a result of their fear of the governor's official authority than a recognition of tribal leadership inherent in his royal lineage; it had seemed almost mystical. He was beside her now, an arm around her still-trembling shoulders. After a day spent trying to avoid even a glance at Felipe, it was all Alma could do to avoid throwing her arms around him.

After what seemed like hours of uncomfortable suspense, Nacho returned to announce that Don Eduardo had located the passage from which they had inadvertently strayed in the confusing maze of chambers and tunnels.

"What caused the torches to go out?" Ann Morris asked.

"Probably just a strong air current blowing through some overhead opening," Felipe suggested.

"Tell me what you said that made them so obedient," Alma urged as they began to slowly retrace their way.

Felipe merely laughed. "I don't think you'd care to know that." Her hand was in his now as they began their ascent from the abyss. Alma did not withdraw it.

Alma was crying and didn't care who knew it. The shores of Yucatán were fading from view. She would never see them or Felipe ever again.

She and Felipe had spent the previous night, all of it, talking. Both had openly confessed their feelings. It was love on his part as well, Alma now felt certain, but his sincerity only made the situation more difficult. Even though the depth of their love had been acknowledged by both, Alma was adamant. It would be impossible to stay in Yucatán and keep their love a secret; scandal was inevitable. "It doesn't matter," Felipe insisted. "I want the whole world to know how I feel about you."

Alma shook her head wearily. It would be political suicide for the governor of the state, a married father of four, to openly flaunt an affair. In a Latin country, a discreet mistress was one thing, a high profile Norte Americana like herself quite another. Besides, she had no desire to be a mistress. She had a life of her own to live, a promising career; Alma had no intention of forfeiting it, not even for Felipe.

At last she rose to her feet, tugging at Felipe's arms until he stood facing her. "Look outside; it's nearly dawn. The train leaves in a few hours. I haven't begun to pack."

"Don't worry about that; just take a few things for the boat and leave the rest here. When you return, they'll be waiting for you—just where will be my little surprise." When her gentle fingers sought to silence his lips, Felipe continued to hold her, still talking. "I realize that you must return to the *Times* to handle the *cenote* matter. It will be a big story, bigger than you realize. You will have a jaguar by the tail. That's your job and you must do it, but surely a month will suffice—travel time, time at your paper, time at the Peabody—then back here to Mérida, to me."

Alma was sobbing now. "No, Felipe. *¡No es possible!* I shall never return. This is our good-bye. What we say later at the train will be for others." She found herself literally pushing him from the room, aware that his eyes, too, were wet with tears.

Alma had walked through the official leave-taking as though in a trance. The train ride to Progreso had been a low-grade nightmare as she struggled to make normal conversation. Ann Morris and several of the others surrounded her, tactful, affectionate buffers against the inevitable stresses of departure. Alma's bags were lined up and checked in, her papers in readiness. A comfortable corner seat was found for her. When Ann realized that what Alma wanted most was to be alone, she ran interference.

Now at last the party was on board the Ward Line steamer headed homeward. Alma turned from the rail, relieved that she had a job to do. Felipe had been right; she did have a jaguar by the tail. The *cenote* was a hot potato. Besides Sylvanus Morley, exploration director, the big guns on board included Dr. Charles Merriam, president of the Carnegie Institution; Dr. Marshall Saville, head of the Museum of the American Indian, and, most significantly, Dr. H. G. Spinden, a representative of the Peabody Museum. The men for the most part had been helpful and considerate, answering her many questions, explaining their finds and conclusions, but there remained the inescapable fact that they were highly esteemed archeologists, she merely a "girl" reporter. Their old-boy network was a closed corporation. It was unlikely that Spinden would take kindly to the bomb she was about to drop. How would his colleagues react?

Alma worked over the story for several hours in her tiny stateroom. Once the ship docked in Havana, she went immediately to the cable office.

Soon the return: "STORY UNBELIEVABLE. CORROBORATION ESSENTIAL. GET QUOTE FROM TEAM. SEND NEWS RELEASE. FULL STORY MUST FOLLOW EXAMINATION OF PEABODY TREASURE."

Alma returned to the ship and went directly to Merriam's cabin, tapping softly at the door. The archeologist's smile quickly faded as she explained the situation. "The story is preposterous!" he fairly roared. "You're suggesting that not only does a vast amount of treasure exist, but that it was stolen by an archeologist, secreted out of the country in diplomatic pouches, and then deliberately hidden by one of the most distinguished museums in the United States."

"I have Thompson's word for it," Alma reminded him. "Why would he lie?"

"No one will believe you."

"I have his confession in writing—would you care to read it?"

Merriam's hands were trembling with agitation. "Get Saville and Spinden in here."

"Very well, sir, but remember the ship leaves Havana in four hours." She paused to control the slight quaver in her voice. "I intend to cable my paper before we leave. It's the greatest archeological story to come out of this hemisphere. Surely you agree that an official comment should be included?"

The story, datelined "HAVANA, March 1," was understated, each word carefully chosen. It read:

> What is conceded to be the most important find of archeological objects ever made in America was revealed yesterday at Mérida by Edward H. Thompson, owner of the hacienda at Chichén Itzá, Yucatán, in which the famous Maya ruins are located.
>
> The discovery, which had been kept secret, includes priceless turquoise masks, jade carvings, gold ornaments and numerous other objects which throw new light on the ancient Maya

*civilization. The objects, now privately held in the Peabody
Museum, Boston, were found in the sacred* cenote *near the
ruins.*

*Among the most important individual objects found is a
sacrificial knife with an ebony handle in the form of two twined
serpents biting the flint blade. Fragments of textiles of hitherto
unknown weaves, solidified masses of copal embalming human
hearts and beautiful jade ornaments are among the treasures.
The gold ornaments include breast shields, pendants, bells,
earrings and other rings.*

*At the conclusion of their trip, Dr. J. C. Merriam, President of
the Carnegie Institution, and Professor Marshall H. Saville, head
of the Museum of the American Indian, pronounced this
discovery to be the most important source of information in
unraveling the story of the Mayas now available to science. . . ."*

This was certainly not the story Alma had wanted to write nor intended
to write, but for the time being it would have to serve the purpose.
Conspicuously absent was any comment from Spinden, who professed to
know nothing about the treasure stashed in his museum's basement.

Now there was nothing left to do but wait out the remainder of the trip.
Spinden scarcely spoke to Alma, and some of the others viewed her with
obvious suspicion. "They think I'm some kind of traitor," she complained
to Ann.

"Well, it *is* going to be embarrassing to the whole archeological community—particularly if the treasure is as vast as you claim."

"*I* claim! It's Thompson who stole it."

"Poor man, his career will be ruined."

"Perhaps not; at least he didn't seem to think so. I've thought a lot about
it these past few days. Actually, there's a pretty good case for what he did.
Don Eduardo bought the property fair and square and actually owned the
cenote—so you could say he owned the contents, too. He took all the risk
as well, and seriously impaired his hearing in the process. But"—Alma
hesitated, then reluctantly continued—"the fact remains, the treasure has
been kept a secret all these years. It's been one long conspiracy between
him and the Peabody."

"Maybe Don Eduardo thought that if he told the Mexican authorities, that bandit dictator Díaz would steal it for his own collection," Ann suggested.

"I suppose he did think something of the sort, but don't you see—it's the Elgin marbles all over again. These are Mexican treasures, and they belong *in* Mexico. They should be returned to a museum there."

"Well, I wish you luck persuading the Peabody of that."

As it turned out, Alma needed more than luck to persuade the Peabody Museum even to show her the treasure. Despite the pressure from the *New York Times,* officials denied her claim. Eventually, it was necessary to show Thompson's signed confession to the Mexican consulate general. When Alma finally paid her call on the museum, she was flanked by representatives of the Mexican government.

Spinden, who was on hand, studied Thompson's written "confession" critically. The message was all too clear. Finally, he had no choice but to admit the party to the museum vaults. The *cenote*'s magnificent contents were all there—exactly as Don Eduardo had described—yet still beyond Alma's wildest dreams. It was a treasure that would, even in 1923, be valued at two million dollars.

Alma was curious to see the sacrificial snake knife that had so impressed Don Eduardo. The eight-inch handle was of polished ebony carved in the form of two entwined serpents biting a flint blade. The discovery was made in three sections—one scoop bringing up the blade, with a missing piece near the point, the next scoop producing the handle. Days later, to the intense joy of the scientist, the tiny missing piece rewarded their careful examination of the mud. Spinden handed the knife to Alma, who held it carefully, her finger testing the blade while her mind relived the afternoon at Chichén Itzá when Thompson had revealed his great secret.

Melting slightly as he became aware of the young woman's genuine reverence for the artifacts before her, the museum official pointed out what he considered the most significant find. Called a votive *atlatl,* this ceremonial spear thrower was a device that made it possible to send a spear twice the usual distance. For this reason it became an emblem of power and, as such, is pictured in ancient sculptures throughout the American continent. Quetzalcoatl is depicted in Aztec art as holding one, and the emblem has turned up in such diverse areas as Alaska, Peru, and Arkansas.

Alma was eager to write the full story, the *Times* more than eager to print it. Her subsequent article was headlined "THE GREATEST AR-

CHEOLOGICAL ADVENTURE ON THE AMERICAN CONTINENT."
Other publications in the United States and Europe immediately picked up
the story. There were repercussions in the United States Congress and in
the courts of Mexico. The Mexican government lost no time in initiating
a lawsuit against the Peabody Museum, demanding the return of the entire
collection of ancient objects or two million dollars in damages.

Felipe's letters and telegrams had begun to arrive in New York even before
Alma did. They tugged at her heartstrings, awakening memories she was
struggling to bury. His words were full of hope and encouragement. He had
found a way for them to be together forever; she must have confidence.
Alma felt anything but confident; instead, there was a sinister, recurring
premonition. She knew she must forget this man, that she must not see
him again.

Often Alma recalled Felipe's welcoming speech to the Carnegie team,
"The ghosts of the Maya have been waiting for you," he told them.
"Through your knowledge and patient research, you can rescue from
oblivion the story of the builders of our magnificent cities, the epic of the
Mayan civilization, its beginnings, its glory, and its night of doom. The story
that you wrest from buried stones will serve the descendants of the Mayan
ghosts, the long-suffering, exploited Maya of Yucatán, as a guide and a
warning, but above all, as an inspiration to build anew, to reclaim their
ancient birthright."

To Alma, it seemed that it was *his* spirit that was calling her, tempting
her with forbidden thoughts of what their life together might have been if
only circumstances had been different. In desperation, she went to see her
benefactor, Adolph Ochs, and pleaded with him to send her to Turkey. "Let
me interview Kemal Pasha," she pleaded.

"No dice," Ochs shook his head. "You wanted to be our woman in
Mexico, and that's what you are. I'm proud of the way you've managed to
put that 'chicken place' on the map. There must be dozens of other great
Mexico stories, and they've got your name on them. I'd like to see your
series on the expedition wrapped up this week. I've decided to put you on
permanent staff. The sooner you're back down there, the better."

In less than a month, Alma was standing on the deck of another Ward
Line steamer as the now familiar shoreline of Progreso came into view.

Headed her way was a launch decorated with floral arches and salutations written in flowers. On board were the inevitable mariachis playing love songs. Alma's cheeks burned as she saw other passengers eyeing her curiously. She was both relieved and saddened to note that Felipe was not on the launch.

It was his secretary who leaped aboard with a huge bouquet and a letter from Felipe begging her to disembark. "A small group of hacendados threatened trouble. Nothing serious," the aide hastened to explain, "but His Excellency felt it prudent to remain temporarily in Mérida. He begs Señorita Reed to join him there."

Alma shook her head. "You must tell His Excellency that my plans are made. I'm not disembarking; I shall continue to Veracruz and go from there by land to Mexico City. I'll never return to Mérida."

Reluctantly, Felipe's delegate reboarded the launch. Tears stung Alma's eyes as she watched the boat's diminishing silhouette. "You've turned down a good man." A voice cut into her melancholy revery. Turning, startled, she confronted the ship's captain, Angus Blackaddder.

"It's no secret, you know. The whole of Yucatán—the whole of Mexico's talking."

Alma sighed. "That's what I hoped to avoid."

"Impossible. Everything the governor does is common gossip."

"I was afraid of that. I don't want to hurt him politically."

"You haven't, at least not yet. There's nothing the Meridians relish more than a good romance."

"You said, 'yet.' How do you think people would react if I remained?"

"North Americans aren't too popular around here. It's no secret that International Harvester sets the price on the henequen, but you're a bit different, a heroine to many. People have heard about what you did for that Mexican lad back in the States and now the *cenote* thing has everybody talking. Who could blame Carrillo for losing his head? If you returned to him—well, that's anybody's guess. This is a Catholic country. The man's very much married, you know."

"I know very well—it's not only how the people feel, it's how *I* feel. I'm divorced, but that was very different. No one was really hurt. This is—oh, my poor parents—" Alma stammered, struggling to express her feelings. "I was also raised a Catholic." She hesitated a moment, then asked, "Tell me, what do *you* think?"

"I think the governor deserves some happiness. He's not had an easy life, for all the good he's done for others. He was a boy when he married. The woman he chose then—"

Alma shrugged. "Who really knows what they want when they marry? Life is a mine field. It is the same for everyone. The wrong choice and then a lifetime of disillusionment, of disappointment. Hasn't it always been that way?"

"Felipe's case is a bit different."

"Different? Really? I think not, except for him it's a little easier. He's a Latin. If his wife no longer suits him, he can take a mistress, and no one will think the less of him."

"He needs a partner, someone who can share his goals, work by his side. He needs a woman who understands the world, not a simple peasant."

Alma shook her head. "Don't you think I've thought of all this? Sometimes, as we talked, it truly seemed that our hearts, our very souls, were entwined, that we were part of one another, sharing the same thoughts, the same vision—but I know it is impossible. Felipe's an idealist, but also a politician. He made a choice to negate the European part of himself. He will make the same kind of choice when he puts me behind him."

"Perhaps, perhaps"—Blackadder puffed on his pipe, studying her pale face, the hands with their long tapering fingers pressed against the rail of the ship, "—perhaps not. Forgive me; this conversation has strayed too close to home."

"Much too close to home."

They stood for a moment in silence as the coastline blended to a thin green line, then disappeared altogether. Finally Blackadder spoke again. "I suppose you've heard many times of his reforms, but did anyone tell you about the Yaquis?"

"The Yaquis!" Alma shivered involuntarily, recalling the barbarous appearing Indians she'd glimpsed a few months before in Northern Mexico.

"Yes, they're a wild bunch," the captain agreed, "but they're human— something many tend to forget."

Alma listened as Blackadder told her of the times he'd transported Yaqui prisoners from Veracruz to Progreso. The fiercely independent Yaquis, pursuing a tribal life that had served them well for centuries, were viewed suspiciously by the old dictator, Díaz, who thought they set a bad example. His method of "civilizing" was to condemn the Indians to virtual slavery for the rest of their lives. Uprooted from their ancestral lands in Sonora, the Yaquis were shipped to the southeastern tropics. Blackadder described excruciating scenes on the docks, when husbands and wives, children and parents, were separated and forced like cattle into the cargo holds of waiting vessels for transportation to the henequen plantations. "If plantation life was bad for the native Maya, who were at least familiar with the country, imagine how terrible it must have been for these freeborn newcomers suddenly deprived of their heritage, alienated from all rights or claims of birth. Your man changed all that. When he came into power, the Yaquis were freed and allowed to go home."

"He's *not* my man!" Alma's voice softened. "But I'm very glad to hear your story. Felipe never told me about the Yaquis; there are so many wonderful things that he's done but never mentioned—things I learned merely by chance. I already know how good he is. Perhaps the governor is the best man in the world—he's certainly the best for me, but"—she straightened her shoulders—"I've a new life in Mexico City."

Alma meant it, too. The capital was as exciting as she'd remembered. Nothing, she would later conclude, could ever equal the radiance of Mexico's postrevolutionary epoch. It was a golden time, a time without precedent or possibility of return. She felt as if she were watching a a huge century plant—the vigorous agave so symbolic of Mexico—burst suddenly into splendorous blossom, filling the scene with joyous reverberations of its release from darkness to the sun. Alma thought it metaphorically glorious, the last vestiges of the fight for independence from Spain having ended just one hundred years before.

With a certain irony she addressed herself professionally to a search for the burial place of Cortés, which a group of the "oldest families," men who counted their descent from the conquistadores, professed to know. During an Independence Day celebration, one hundred years earlier, hatred of the conquerer of Mexico took the form of a plot to steal his ashes. When the government refused to intervene, violation of Cortés's elaborate coffin was averted by family members. The remains were spirited away and interred, but where? Actually, certain members of Mexico City's elitist Spanish Club had confided to Alma that they knew.

She had just decided that ferreting out this secret was a first priority and a way to avoid thoughts of Felipe, when Felipe appeared. She greeted his arrival with tears. "You've no right to follow me this way. I can't stand it, I really can't stand it! How can I forget you, how can I get on with my life when you refuse to leave me alone?"

Felipe merely smiled at her histrionics. Taking her in his arms, he stroked her hair gently, soothingly, as Eugene had long ago. "But I thought you loved me. I could have sworn you told me that."

"What does that have to do with anything!" Alma wailed. Her conflicting emotions were simply too much for her.

"I should think it would have everything to do with it. I've come to ask you to marry me."

"Oh, so now you've murdered your wife. I'm not amused." Alma, trying to control her sobs, reached gratefully for his proffered handkerchief.

"My former wife is very well, thank you. I can't say in all honesty that she sends you her regards, but she is alive and well, I assure you."

"Former wife! That's impossible. Nobody gets divorced in Mexico."

"Why be a governor if you can't enact laws? I have caused the passage of an act legalizing divorce, and I was the very first to make use of it."

The following month was idyllic. Alma had made friends in Mexico City on her previous visit. Felipe Carrillo was a national hero—the most popular man in Mexico, some said, possibly in line for the presidency. There were glorious days and evenings of sight-seeing, dancing, and dinner parties with some of the most illustrious names in the country. But, as before, Alma was also attracted to the bohemian side. She and Felipe enjoyed the company of the thriving art colony whose members drew sketches on the walls and tablecloths of their favorite cafes as payment for ever-mounting bills. Sometimes it was fun to forsake European cuisine and wine in favor of tacos and pulque, to dance the *jarabe* and *sandunga* rather than the waltz. These people were less impressed by Felipe's reputation, and he could relax and be himself.

But eventually Felipe had to return to his duties in Yucatán. This time, overwhelmed by his ardor and trying desperately to overcome her misgivings, Alma agreed to follow. Felipe had announced an all American Press Congress to be held in Mérida; she would join him there. Alma began the journey with two hundred other correspondents traveling by train to Veracruz, where they boarded the battleship *Jalisco* for the final leg of the trip. The voyage was a rough one, incredibly rough. When she became seasick, the chef's faithful remedy—red hot pepper—wasn't much help. Retreating at last to her cabin, she fell into a troubled sleep. Alma dreamed of Felipe, a terrible dream in which he was standing on a mountain that suddenly collapsed.

Awakening in terror, she sat straight up in bed, her heart pounding. Slowly Alma became aware of music, the strange and lovely strains of a melody she'd never heard before. The music was so compelling that she forced herself from bed and flung on a robe. Clinging desperately to various pieces of furniture to maintain her balance, she staggered to the door. Standing just outside was Alphonso, a popular Yucatecan singer who was a particular favorite of Felipe's, with a group of mariachis that she'd seen perform often in Mérida. The men had roped themselves into position just outside her door. Though she had to cling to the doorjamb for support and assorted unsecured objects were sliding crazily around them, Alma listened intently to the song, which she now realized had been written for her.

> *Wanderer of the clear and divine eyes*
> *And cheeks aflame with the redness of the sky,*
> *Little woman of the red lips,*
> *And hair radiant as the sun,*
> *Traveler who left your own scenes—*
> *The fir trees and the snow, the virginal snow—*
> *And came to find refuge in the palm groves,*
> *Under the sky of my land,*
> *My tropic land,*
> *The little singing birds of my fields,*
> *Offer their voices in singing to you—*
> *And they look at you*
> *And the flowers of perfumed nectars*
> *Caress you and kiss you on lips and temples,*
> *When you leave my palm groves and my land,*
> *Traveler of the enchanting face,*
> *Don't forget—don't forget—my land,*
> *Don't forget—don't forget—my love.*

When they finished, she was crying but was no longer ill. The melody, so beautiful, had a quality of sorrow. Unaccountably, a sense of fear mingled with delight as Alma thanked the men. The song, "La Peregrina," they explained, had been composed for her at the request of the governor. The words were written by the popular Yucatecan poet Luis Rosada de la Vega. Ricardo Palmerín, also of Yucatán, had composed the music. Alma perceived the haunting melody as not only a paean of Felipe's love, but also as the distilled mourning of an oppressed people crying out through the centuries. The two men were the most popular writer-composer team in the country. Alphonso and the mariachis had been smuggled on board as a surprise. Their instructions were to play for her at midnight and that they had done—despite the raging storm. She would hear the song often over the years, but never without the memory of that first occasion.

There were parties and balls and fiestas in Mérida; Felipe was not only hosting the Press Congress, he was celebrating his engagement. There were solemn moments, too. One day Alma and the other journalists accompanied Felipe to an *ejido* ceremony at the village of Suma five kilometers from Mérida. As usual, an orchestra greeted the delegation, and a reception committee composed of some fifty leading citizens escorted the group from the railroad station.

Walking four abreast, they passed under a cardboard arch adorned with Mayan symbols and fresh flowers. At the end of the unpaved street leading to the village plaza, their little procession broke rank in front of a low wooden building where the *presidente municipal,* in white cotton shirt and trousers respectfully holding his sombrero over his heart, came forward to meet the governor and his visitors. Two hundred campesinos, Suma's entire male population, most attired like their representative, crowded into the plaza around the table where the governor signed the document returning to their communal possession the public lands of which Suma had been robbed.

Nearby were Mayan women in white cotton *huipals* gaily embroidered with flowers at the neck and around the hem of the loose one-piece garment. Many held infants wrapped in rebozos, while older children stood beside them or squatted at their feet. Other women, carrying banners, arranged themselves in semimilitary formation facing the official group. These newly enfranchised members of the Feminist League watched the proceedings with a proud proprietary air, for many had, as agitators, helped bring about the necessary measures that hastened federal legislation.

Speeches, music, fireworks, a banquet, and dancing to the national *jarana* followed, marking Suma's celebration of its great day, the most memorable since 1847, when the grandparents of these townsfolk had gathered at the same spot to assume their roles in the War of the Castes, a bloody uprising of the Maya against their Spanish Creole masters. Now at last, and without bloodshed, the *ejido* was returning the land that was their birthright.

Concluding the ceremony, Felipe urged the townspeople: "Use your freedom to become better citizens, never basely to revenge yourselves on some individual who was himself a victim of the wretched order that is gone forever. Forget the past, except as a lesson for your future guidance. Hate corruption, hate vice, hate cruelty, hate the institutions that breed them, but not the individuals caught up in their meshes. Destroy the worn-out forms, expose the fallacy of ancient doctrines that have been used to enslave men, and a better day will dawn for all."

Through it all, Alma was treated with the grave respect that she imagined was reserved for first ladies. At moments she was flattered, delighted; at others, apprehensive. Alma knew that Felipe hoped to create a modern state, capable of setting collective goals while promoting private property. Yucatán was actually a laboratory. The idea of working at his side, of possibly playing a part in the magnificent venture, was a dream come true to her.

After they returned to Mérida, the other journalists went home, but Alma stayed on another month. Felipe had acquired a small but exquisite home, which he named Villa Aurora. Now they were busy searching for pre-Columbian art and antique furniture with which to furnish it, their days taken up with plans for the life they would share. At a ceremony at Chichén Itzá, Alma was given a new name and a Mayan identity. The name was *Pixan-Halal—Pixan* meaning Alma, or soul; *Halal* the Mayan word for a kind of reed growing along the water's edge.

The times required circumspection; unmarried women were chaperoned. Rarely were engaged couples seen holding hands. But Felipe was forty-eight; Alma, whether she admitted it or not, was thirty-four. Both were audacious, impatient of convention. Many stories were told of them.

One was that Felipe had the temple at the top of the pyramid of Kukulkan filled with flower petals, and there the couple made love.

In October, Alma said good-bye to Felipe. This would be their last farewell, she promised. She was returning home to prepare for their wedding, which would take place on January 14 in San Francisco, and to spend time with her family. He would join her shortly before Christmas.

At first Eugene and Adelaide were appalled by this new development in their daughter's life, but, as time passed and they sensed the deep, all-abiding love that Alma felt and experienced the change in her personality, the new softness, the sudden enthusiasm for family life, their resistance began to melt. The union was unconventional, yes, but what else could they expect from Alma? If this man was responsible for the changes their daughter now exhibited—the gentle openness, the optimism—maybe he was all right after all.

Felipe wrote every day. Alma's time was filled with exciting plans. Her marriage to Sam Reed had been a civil ceremony; they had made a point of underplaying it—no fuss for that "modern" couple. Now Alma was eager to make a splash. Their divorces made a church wedding impossible, but that didn't mean that she and Felipe couldn't have a reception. Alma wanted a large party so that everybody could meet and know this wonderful man who had sacrificed so much in order to marry her. She wanted parties, showers, all the things that had never seemed important before.

Alma was busy making lists when Crothers called from the *Bulletin.* His message took her totally by surprise. "Things look pretty bad in Mexico," he told her. "De la Huerta has broken with the president. Looks like another revolution could break out any day."

Alma was shocked. Adolfo de la Huerta, secretary of the treasury in Obregon's government, had been his staunch ally for years. In fact, many assumed the president would designate him as his successor when his mandatory six-year term expired—a president was not allowed to directly succeed himself. As it turned out, de la Huerta had been bypassed in favor of General Elías Calles. Now, it appeared that his response, possibly rebellion, threatened the survival of the Mexican government.

Hopping a cable car down to the *Bulletin,* Alma set up a vigil next to the telegraph machine, the only immediate source of international news. ιt appeared that Obregon faced challenges left and right, from restless campesinos, from the church, from army dissidents, from the remnants of the ancien régime as well as from the United States, which, like the Mexican oligarchy, missed the economic concessions of the old Porfirio Díaz dictatorship. Fighting had broken out, and local grievances provided the basis for much of it. This might very well be the opportunity that Yucatecan henequen planters were looking for to overthrow Felipe, who was known to be loyal to the now-beleaguered president.

Felipe's letters abruptly ceased. Alma's attempts to reach him by cable were fruitless. She was informed that communications with Yucatán had been severed. There was no way of knowing that her worst fears were correct; Felipe was in serious trouble. The de la Huerta forces, forming an alliance with the hacendados, replaced the federal garrison with a contingent of their own troops from northern Mexico. These men, armed with the latest equipment, were commanded by Colonel Ricardo Broca, who'd sworn to kill the governor.

Felipe had always urged peace. Now, however, he wrestled with those principles but was painfully aware that his civilian working-class militia, grossly underarmed, was no match for the well-equipped army backed by the planters. The time had come for Felipe to arm his people or lose everything he had accomplished. Agreeing at last, he sent an agent to obtain guns and ammunition in New Orleans.

According to false rumors circulated by the hacendados, Obregon had been shot and de la Huerta proclaimed the new president. Colonel Broca persuaded de la Huerta to offer a $250,000 reward for Felipe, dead or alive. The governor's many friends convinced him that his only hope for survival lay in flight. There seemed no other course. Gathering three of his brothers and six chief lieutenants, he left Mérida in the dead of night, making for the coast. The plan was to board a ship for Cuba, where they would acquire arms and then return.

As they traveled, faithful Mayan supporters left their villages in great numbers, armed with machetes, offering to fight the enemy. Felipe forbade them to do so, reminding them that machetes were no match for machine guns. They must wait until he returned with arms.

At last reaching the coast, the party waded out to a launch, which was to carry them to a larger boat. It was said later that Felipe held his hat above his head while wading. He had placed a photograph of Alma inside. The men settled into the launch, believing themselves at last on the way to safety, but, pretending that the boat's engine was disabled, the man in charge signaled to shore and a squad of soldiers came into view. Felipe's party wanted to shoot it out, but he ordered them to hold their fire, realizing they were hopelessly outnumbered. Their party was marched back to Mérida and lodged in Felipe's own model prison.

On the evening of January 2, an attorney was admitted to Felipe's cell. "I represent an influential group who promise that you may leave the country in safety in return for one hundred and twenty-five thousand dollars." Felipe noted with irony that it was half the sum that had been posted for his death. When he scorned the offer, it was summarily announced that he and his party would be brought before a court-martial.

As he faced the court, Felipe was told to make his plea, but refused. "I am governor of the state—I do not recognize your court. You are outsiders, and I will be judged only by my people." But soon Felipe's concern for his supporters required that he acknowledge the hopelessness of the situation, and he tried desperately to save the others, insisting that they were merely loyal soldiers doing their duty. "Cut me to bits," he urged, "but spare my brothers and friends."

The plea was ignored; they were returned to their cells. During the night, Felipe was taunted by a group of soldiers who positioned themselves outside his window and began to sing a whiny parody of "La Peregrina." At dawn the party was led out of the prison and herded onto an autobus, which took them through the darkened streets of Mérida to the cemetery, where the ten men were lined up against a wall.

A squad of nervous riflemen, obviously unhappy with their assignment, were moved in for the kill. Ignoring the arrogant, bribe-taking Colonel Broca, who commanded the contingent, Felipe walked slowly and with great dignity toward the soldiers. Approaching one of them, he handed him the ring that was to have been Alma's wedding band. "Here, please see that *Pixan-Halal* gets it," he said; the soldier nodded.

Returning to the wall, Felipe bade good-bye to his brothers and friends. Colonel Broca gave the order to fire. The first volley was directed over the heads of the men against the wall, bullets shattering plaster. In a rage, Broca screamed to the riflemen in the second rank to cut down the soldiers of the firing squad. Standing over the bodies of their comrades, the second squad executed the ten men, who stood with their backs against the wall.

Felipe's supporters pondered the problem of getting word to Alma.

Finally they wrote a cable, and one man swam out to an English ship with the request that the message be sent. When the wire addressed to "PIXAN-HALAL, SAN FRANCISCO" finally reached Alma, she had already been notified by the *New York Times*.

On January 13, 1924, the day before her proposed wedding, a short item appeared in the *San Francisco Chronicle:*

> *Mrs. Alma Sullivan Reed of this city, fiancée of Governor Felipe Carrillo Puerto of Yucatán, yesterday received from officials of that Mexican state now in New York, confirmation of his assassination at the hands of rebels. The communication received by her declared that Governor Puerto, his three brothers and several members of his family had met death from the revolutionaries. The governor, Mrs. Reed said, had come to be known as the Abraham Lincoln of Mexico, by reason of his efforts to free the Indian slaves and improve their conditions in the southern republic.*

CHAPTER · 7

A Betrayal?

Felipe Carrillo Puerto had been governor of Yucatán just twenty-two months when his term and his life were ended when he was forty-nine years old.

How, Alma asked herself again and again, could such a thing have happened? In the days that followed, her thoughts turned often to President Obregon, her gallant host of the previous year. With such a witty, spellbinding speaker and raconteur, one tended to forget that the former general's astounding visual memory had enabled him to size up a potential battlefield at a glance, and then months later position his forces to take full advantage of the terrain.

Alma had come to suspect that Obregon studied opposing commanders—and political opponents—just as effectively so that he might anticipate their tactics. That previous summer in Mexico City, she had come to view the president as a consummate political organizer and negotiator. Tending as he did to distrust idealists, Obregon was at most a quasi-liberal, supportive of only the most moderate forms of political freedom, the most anemic versions of agrarian reform and trade unionism.

Obregon and his predecessor, Venustiano Carranza, had risen to prominence during the Mexican revolution by besting Pancho Villa and Emiliano Zapata. Alma found herself reconstructing past events. Villa, she knew, was a brawler and a rapist, capable of gunning down a man he'd warmly embraced only moments before. His army, for the most part bandits and army deserters, adored Villa equally for his macho image and the loot he made available to them.

Zapata she recognized as a true patriot, the stuff from which legends were woven. And it was this man whom Carranza and Obregon had conspired to lure to his death. Approaching the counsel table to negotiate surrender terms, Zapata had heard a bugle call sound three times in his honor. As the sound faded, a soldier fired a salvo into his body at point-blank.

After that it had been easy to deal with Villa. Carranza and Obregon bought him off with a twenty-six thousand–acre hacienda in Chihuahua, where the former revolutionary guerrilla lived in feudal luxury for three years. Then, only the previous summer, Villa had been shot and killed most mysteriously while driving home from a rendezvous with one of his mistresses. There had been a lot of talk in Mexico City; Alma now recalled it vividly.

The next chapter of a decade-long holocaust was a duel between the winners, Carranza and Obregon. The former's term as president was to end in 1920; Obregon fully expected to succeed him. When Carranza reneged, open warfare erupted between the two. On May 21, 1920, Carranza was shot by one of his rival's officers, clearing the way for Alvaro Obregon to become president in September of that year.

A hard-eyed survivor, Obregon was not one to be seduced by his own patriotic rhetoric. The revolution had made him a wealthy man, with a chick-pea farm in Sonora employing fifteen hundred workers. He also had a lucrative government contract to supply railroad ties for the newly nationalized trains. Promised reforms were conveniently forgotten by a leader who'd discovered distinct advantages in maintaining the status quo.

Obregon had ordered some five hundred generals to Mexico City and placed them in prestigious, but for the most part meaningless, posts. "No Mexican general can withstand a cannonball of fifty thousand pesos," Obregon joked, realizing that to leave these men in the provinces was to invite banditry on a far greater scale.

Obregon's term of office was drawing to a close after more than three years of such pragmatic compromises when antagonists rallied behind Adolfo de la Huerta, triggering yet another uprising. Local grievances provided the basis for much of the fighting and Yucatecan henequen planters had taken advantage of the uprising to attack Felipe.

Why, Alma asked herself again and again during those fateful weeks of December, had President Obregon not come to Felipe's assistance? Why had he held back crucial ammunition and troop reinforcements? And, more critically, why had he refused to ransom his loyal governor from the rebels?

Was it possible that the president had found Felipe a potential competitor and so politically expendable? Obregon was, Felipe had confided to her, under intense diplomatic pressure from the United States on behalf of cordage interests—interests known to favor the henequen oligarchy. Yucatán was the acknowledged social laboratory for the Mexican revolution. As its instigator, Felipe was the man of the hour. Had Obregon viewed the visionary whose social innovations clearly dazzled international observers as a rival to be eliminated?

Presidential condolences followed Felipe's death. Alma read and discarded them. In the final analysis, the machinations behind her lover's death were of little importance. What mattered was that he was forever lost to her. Despite the strong objections of Eugene and Adelaide, she was determined to return to Yucatán. A desire beyond her control drove Alma to see the place where Felipe had died and to visit his grave.

In the early months of 1924, the de la Huerta forces fought on, threatening to destroy the Mexican government. Alma took a train to New Orleans, where she would wait for the end of the insurrection. Her plan was to sail from the port at the first opportunity.

One day, while waiting in New Orleans, out of the depth of her grief she wrote a letter to Felipe's mother, a woman who had, the previous summer, defied convention by welcoming her into the family.

March 25, 1924
Noble Mother of My Felipe:

When I contemplate your agony of sorrow I feel that I have no right to my own grief, adored mother of Felipe Carrillo. Day and night my heart's compassion is with you in your crushing sorrow. There is no consolation that I can offer you, only God knows why the unspeakable suffering has come to you. But, perhaps it will be a slight satisfaction for you to know that the memory of Felipe shall be perpetuated. The day will come when all of his ideals and principles will be vindicated. His greatest desire in life was service to humanity, and his wish will reach a glorious fulfillment. He will become the real hero of the modern Mexico. His name will be honored as the savior of his people. His cruel murder has not interrupted his work, it will but furnish the impetus that martydom must always give to a noble cause. The world shall know of his greatness, of his nobility of heart and mind, and the murder of your wonderful sons, Felipe, Benjamen, Edsio and Alfredo shall be recorded as the blackest stain in the pages of Mexican history.

Each day something is done as a tribute to his sacred memory. My own poor life has been dedicated to this holy obligation. Somehow I have found the strength to tell the people of my country about his struggles and achievements and character through the public press. Splendid articles are appearing almost daily. I'm enclosing one as an example. I'm working now with the American Federation of Labor to have a magnificant monument erected to his memory in the city of Mexico. This work will take me to Washington tomorrow, but my permanent mailing address is in care of Señor Arturo Elias, Mexican Consulate General, New Orleans.

Around my neck I wear an ancient little copper bell found in the sacred cenote *in Chichén Itzá. It is set in the red triangle of the Partida Socialista. Felipe gave it to me and on the back he had inscribed these words in lingua Maya:* "ma tubzic mayaob chixpan pixom." *I will* not!

My greatest desire is to be near you and to go with you to that consecrated spot where rest our hopes and our dreams and our love. I shall come to you in Yucatán as soon as possible. Until that day in the near future, I am with you in spirit and in unswerving devotion to Elvira, to the other brothers and sisters, to his children, and to all the dear ones, my heart goes out in understanding and sympathy. Hasta pronto y siempre con todo cariño y la simpática de mi Alma.

Alma M. S. Reed

The bloody struggle claimed some seven thousand lives, but with most military units behind him and with weapons supplied by the United States, acting to protect its oil interests, Obregon succeeded in putting down the de la Huerta rebellion.

Now at last Alma made her lonely pilgrimage to Mérida. Many people came forward to reminisce. One was a young medical student, Prospero Martinez Carrillo (no relation to Felipe). "I wanted to become a doctor," he explained to her, "but I'm the oldest of six children. There was no way that my father could afford to send me to school. Someone suggested that I apply to the governor to ask his help. When I got to his office, the president of the Socialist League was also waiting. After a while the governor came out and apologized. He was just too busy; he couldn't see us that day. When I got up, I felt like crying. It had taken all my courage to come that day; I knew I'd never come back. Maybe somehow the governor realized that. It seemed like magic—suddenly he was gesturing to me, just me, to come into his office. I explained my situation to him, and he agreed to give me thirty pesos a month until my education was completed.

"As you can imagine, the governor became my hero. Whenever possible, I followed him about. Once I was in the shadows outside your window while he was there with two guitarists serenading you. Another time, after you'd returned to your home, I was in a cafe sitting nearby the governor when the mariachis began to play "La Peregrina." I saw the tears in his eyes. He missed you very much."

The poet, Rosada de la Vega, who'd composed the lyrics to the song, also visited Alma. "Felipe spoke to me of his feelings for you and the song wrote itself; the words were really his."

The composer, Ricardo Palmerín, recalled that, fearful lest the melody not be completed in time to serenade Alma on the *Jalisco,* Felipe had posted a guard to insure that no one interrupted his work. Then, on one moonlight night, the two of them, Alma and Palmerín, visited the cemetery together. It was midnight when they reached the tomb and, as they'd hoped, they were quite alone. As Alma placed a bouquet of white roses on the grave, Palmerín softly strummed his guitar and serenaded her with the song that he'd written in her honor.

Don Eduardo also made a point of seeking Alma out. She was relieved to see that he bore her no rancor. Alma had learned the previous summer that, following publication of her article, a lien had been placed on his property and litigation begun. Now he described how the de la Huerta forces had burned his hacienda. The most tragic loss was Thompson's priceless library, the fruit of a life of study.

Alma thought that she had no tears left to give; she was wrong.

The tenor of life, Alma quickly realized, was already changing in Yucatán. Felipe's most influential supporters were being systematically removed from power and replaced by more malleable men. Yucatán's contrasting loss of vigor and purpose was dramatized for her by the arrival of a thick envelope, which had followed her there. It was a copy of an article written by Ernest Gruening for *Century Magazine.* Dr. Gruening, author of *Mexican Heritage,* who would later become territorial governor of Alaska and sub-secretary of the interior, was an ardent admirer of Felipe.

"Felipe Carrillo Puerto would have dominated his surroundings anywhere," he had written.

> *His was a leadership almost unknown in this day and belonging rather to a legendary age. Straight, handsome, with keen, yet kindly eyes, cleancut features and a sparkling smile that could capture a child's faith or rivet the hearts of a vast multitude, taller by a head than most of his countrymen, he was truly a god among them; in any civilized society a high-spirited, brave, and gallant gentleman. Never was the heritage of nobility that he believed to be his more fervently held as a high obligation, more worthily executed as a sacred trust. Yet he was a democrat to the core, a leader, a teacher, a big brother, rather than a ruler. He lived simply, and gave no thought to pomp, to personal power or its prerequisites. A great vision, shrewd realism, intuitive sympathy, a loving sentimentality, a militant idealism and extraordinary physical energy combined with a really winning*

personality—these were the qualities which enabled him, virtually single-handed to achieve a revolution."

The eulogy, titled "A Maya Idyl," went on for several pages, at last concluding, "Like a great comet, he came out of age-long darkness, lifting man's eyes and hearts, a fiery token of cycles reaching into the vast unknown, a vision unforgettable. He was a cosmic figure. He linked in his single person the far-flung epic of the great American race and the undying epic of man's quest for freedom."

Once again Alma was reminded of Kukulkan and wondered if for a little while she had dwelt in a kind of Mayan Camelot. Her feelings were ambivalent. Mixed with happy pride that this objective statesman shared her vision of Felipe was a nagging sense of guilt. Gruening, too, saw Felipe as larger than life, a legendary figure. If such a thing were true, could she have somehow played a role in his final downfall?

Kukulkan had fallen from grace because of a woman, his need for a woman. There were rumors that Felipe, on his flight to her, had carried with him a substantial part of the state treasury. It was a story spread by the hacendados that few believed, but Alma was nonetheless deeply grieved. The tale was a blatant lie, yet this linkage of herself to the governor's murder set Alma on a twisted pathway of doubt. Was it possible that Felipe's love for her, his excitement about their forthcoming life together, had made him less cautious, less cognizant of the political dangers surrounding him? Felipe had always walked a tightrope. Had she unwittingly caused him to lose his balance?

Of course, there were many theories. When Felipe had opened the capital of the vanished Itzaes to scientists and tourists, the witch women had warned him that the gods would demand a living sacrifice for this disturbance of their altars. He'd only smiled at their warnings. There were whispers that because the governor had not killed some animal and offered it as a sacrifice for the sacred stones that he had caused to be removed from Chichén Itzá, the gods had sent him a cruel *destino*.

The fact remained however that Felipe was gone, and Alma knew that she would have to get on with her own life, to find a new purpose for living. The Carnegie Institution had received permission from the Mexican government to excavate Yucatán; and, despite Alma's damaging article, had made it clear that she would be welcome in their party. Alma declined; there were too many painful associations with Felipe. Disappointed, Ochs urged her to at least remain in Mexico to write on other subjects, but again she refused. Some day Alma might return to seek out the hundreds of hidden cities that dotted her beloved Mexico. She would see.

On the last day of her stay, Alma took a taxi to the cemetery. Bidding the driver wait, she approached the bullet-riddled wall slowly. There was a number of other mourners present who watched as she touched the still blood-stained wall.

"La Peregrina," some whispered. "It is La Peregrina. She has come back to him." Quietly they followed Alma inside and stood beside her at the grave site. The concluding words of song echoed in her brain as she placed a single rose on the tomb.

> *When you leave my palm groves and my land,*
> *Traveler of the enchanting face,*
> *Don't forget—don't forget—my land,*
> *Don't forget—don't forget—my love.*

I will not forget, I will not forget, she promised silently.

PART III

CHAPTER · 8

Dido's Legacy

"Yes, I've got a slot available, but you won't want it—no one else has," Adolph Ochs informed Alma.

She leaned forward, a half smile of anticipation lighting her still wan face. Ochs shook his head. "I wouldn't send you on this one. You've had enough trouble, you don't need a curse to contend with."

"A curse! What in the world are you talking about?"

Ochs leaned back in his tufted leather chair, arms folded behind his head. "What do you know about Carthage?"

"Carthage . . ." Alma echoed the words softly, her mind slipping back across the years to her girlhood in San Francisco, the hours spent in her father's library. "I adored *Salammbo* as a teenager; I suppose I still love it."

"*Salammbo?*"

"Yes, Flaubert's novel. My sisters thought I was crazy because I preferred it to *Madame Bovary. Salammbo* was about ancient Carthage. The

Aeneid, too—how many hours I spent on that epic! Sometimes it seemed more real than what was going on in my own life." She smiled ruefully; those weren't the happiest of days.

"But you've read nothing recent?"

"No, I'm afraid not."

"Well, of course, you've been out of the country, but there's been lots of talk about the Prorok expedition."

Alma frowned, her memory piqued by the name. "Prorok—yes, it's Count Prorok, isn't it? Some of the Carnegie people were discussing him last year. A Polish nobleman attempting to excavate in North Africa?"

"That's the one. Count Byron Kuhn de Prorok. Rather a flamboyant young man with a pretty American wife. It appears that he inherited problems, nothing but problems—big ones. Everybody's dying on him. They say the place is cursed."

"That's ridiculous."

"Of course, it's ridiculous; but the truth is those people are dead, just as dead as if it weren't."

"Is he on to anything—I mean archeologically speaking?"

"Sounds like it. Before all the problems started, he had plans for some kind of new venture—underwater archeology. He claims there are galley ships filled with priceless Greek statues sunk off the Tunisian coast. The story has another twist. He has this lost Atlantis theory; he believes it to be located some place in North Africa. Once Carthage has been excavated, he plans to pursue that."

Alma's pulse quickened, but her voice was casual as she asked, "Is there clearance for a reporter?"

"Yes, as a matter of fact, before all the trouble started, he was looking for a writer to be part of the team—someone to keep an official journal, possibly help him with a book."

"And the *Times?*"

"Yes, we'd send someone. Frankly, I've tried to interest some of the men, but no one wants to take it on."

"Don't ask any further. I'll take it, I *want* it."

"It's dangerous, Alma. The 'curse' thing is nonsense, of course—though you and I know it's the sort of rubbish that sells papers—but the fact remains de Prorok is the only one left from the original expedition. People are getting killed."

"I'm not afraid," she assured him and meant it. Some of Alma's skepticism had been feigned. She gave far more credence to curses than she would ever let on to Ochs. But what did it matter? Felipe's assassination had made her a fatalist. If her own death reunited them, she could only welcome it; but, if instead, she was to live on without him, there must be some purpose to her life. Images of Carthage had stirred her imagination since girlhood. This new development only made the ancient city more beguiling.

Alma spent the rest of the afternoon in the *Times* library researching. First of all there was Carthage itself, an ancient city on the northern shore of Africa located on a peninsula extending from the modern city of Tunis. Tradition had the original city founded by Dido in the ninth century B.C. Its people were Phoenicians, natives of Canaan in the lowlands of Palestine, who'd been driven out by the Jewish invasion. The city-state had grown and prospered until it enjoyed virtual supremacy over the western Mediterranean. Rome challenged that control in a series of three wars—the Punic Wars—beginning in the third century B.C. Though Hannibal, one of the greatest military strategists the world has ever known, was commander of the Carthaginian legions, Rome was the ultimate victor. In 146 B.C., Scipio Africanus the Younger finally razed the city, destroying everything and everybody in sight. A dreary picture.

Lost for a time in dreams and conjecture, Alma finally forcibly returned her thoughts to the present. Putting aside the well-worn encyclopedia, she turned to the newspaper files, only to discover that one scientist after another had met with an untimely death while searching out the secrets of the site. The dark mystery only increased the intensity of the assignment's appeal. Even if it hadn't, the prospect of double pay—salary from the expedition as well as the *Times*—was incentive enough. At thirty-four, Alma had begun to fear that money would always be a problem. Unfortunately, her apprehensions were warranted.

The following morning she cabled de Prorok for confirmation, secured a hefty advance from Ochs, and booked passage on the *S.S. Cleveland.*

Her companions on the cruise were old friends: Salammbo and Dido. Alma readily admired Queen Dido, who first appeared in the *Aeneid* as a recent widow. Resourceful and independent, she determined to carve out a new life for herself and the Phoenician refugee subjects who'd followed her. Charmed, Iarbas, the local Berber chieftain, agreed to give Dido all the land that a bull hide could enclose. He envisioned himself as part of the package, but reckoned without her cunning. Dido cut the hide into strips, stretching it around a hill. She rejected Iarbas's marriage suit and set about building a city on the strategically located hilltop site.

There, according to the *Aeneid,* she reigned "looking like the goddess, Diana, energetic and happy, until Aeneas, a god in face and shoulders," arrived. Dido reflected, "Were I not sick to the heart of bridal torch and chamber, to this temptation alone I might happily yield."

Though Aeneas had vowed to found a city in Italy, Dido's beauty and passion caused him to forget his purpose. During a storm, the two took shelter in a cave. "Primeval earth and Juno, the bridesmaid, gave the sign, fires flashed and high in the air, witnessing the union, nymphs cried aloud on the mountain top." The scene was almost too much for Alma. How could any couple resist *that,* she wondered. It was easy for her to envision Dido as a contemporary woman who wanted it all: a soul mate and a "career"— just as easy to see Dido as herself. Wasn't that exactly what she had desired, had even achieved for a few glorious months?

Obviously the ancient queen believed in a single standard for the sexes, a highly controversial view in Alma's time. Careless, confident Dido envisioned Aeneas as a key factor in her projected city-state and didn't care who knew it. Outraged, Iarbas complained of the "woman, a vagrant who built a small city on my territory, renting a coastal strip to cultivate under conditions of tenure dictated by me, then rejected my marriage suit and accepted Aeneas as her joint ruler."

Eventually, Aeneas's sense of duty overcame him. He'd sworn to the gods to found a colony elsewhere, and left Carthage and Dido to do so. Distraught, the queen ordered a great funeral pyre to be built from her lover's discarded possessions, and from its summit stabbed herself with his sword—but not before cursing him and all his descendants:

> *Then do you, O [Cartheginians] pursue his seed with your hatred for all ages to come . . . let no kindness nor truce be between the nations. Arise, some avenger, out of our dust, to follow the [Trojan] setlers with firebrand steal . . . shore to shore, wave to wave, sword to sword, let their battles go down to their children's children.*

The curse—of course this was its origin, Alma decided. At the very least it provided Virgil with a rationalization for the three wars that ultimately destroyed Carthage.

Archeologists were, she knew, attempting to link the Dido legend with Tanit, the moon goddess and supreme deity of Carthage. The search had extricated from a melding of myth and fact the certainty that a woman had always represented the genius of Carthage. The moon, too, swayed the city-state's destiny, entwining from earliest times a triple thread of mystery, tragedy, and doom.

Returning to her girlhood favorite, Alma found in Gustave Flaubert's striking portrayal of the first Punic War a sense of the bizarre and sinister influence of the moon on Carthaginian life. His exotic heroine, Salammbo, daughter of a king, sister of Hannibal, who interpreted the spirit of ancient Carthage for the modern world, passed many nocturnal hours on the terrace of her palace with a priest of Tanit, who explained: "The souls of the dead resolve themselves into the moon as do their corpses into the earth. Their tears compose the humidity. It is the dark abode of mires, wrecks, and tempests."

Salammbo's vulnerability to the moon's influence was palpable. When it waned, she grew weak, languishing for the entire day only to revive in the evening. During an eclipse, she nearly died. Her deification of the feminine principle in life had been a spiritual exaltation. Captured once again by Flaubert's spell, Alma saw the rich pageantry and barbaric splendor of ancient Carthage alive before her eyes. Archeologists might hypothesize where and, to some degree, how a people lived, but only the imagination could call to life the feel of sleek animal skins, the glitter of jewels, the magic of charms, the clash of swords, the scent of perfume. Could scientists ever reveal how the Carthaginians *felt* about the great and small events of their lives? Regretfully, she doubted it.

Returning once again to history, Alma refreshed her memory of the famous Hannibal, read how he'd been taken as a boy to the temple of Tanit by his father, Hamilcar. The youth had sworn a holy oath of enmity to Rome. He would avenge Hamilcar's defeat in the first Punic War. Scarcely had Hannibal reached manhood when he launched the second war, setting off with one hundred thousand men and forty elephants on a sneak attack. Fighting mountain tribesmen, landslides, snow, and hunger, he crossed the

Alps in one of the greatest military maneuvers of all times and descended to the sunny plains of Piedmont minus half his men. With this ragged remnant, Hannibal carried out his onslaught on the Italian peninsula. There he remained for fifteen years, living off the land, marching, besieging, fighting, but despite this remarkable performance, Rome, the ultimate prize, remained beyond his grasp. Jealous and fearful, the wealthy oligarchy who then ruled Carthage abandoned Hannibal as they had his father. He died, long years later, a fugitive exile in Asia Minor, his country having negotiated its second peace with Rome.

Hannibal's ultimate defeat marked the beginning of the end for Carthage. Without realizing it, she had run her course. Instead, it was business as usual—better than usual: love, laughter, spices, incense, gambling, wine. Nothing portended the Great Silence that would follow.

To visiting Cato, the extreme sensual indulgence signaled the city's patent vulnerability. Returning to Rome, he took up the cry: *"Carthage must be destroyed!"* These words came to be not only the opinion of one man, but the rallying cry of a nation. Coldly, ruthlessly, aging Carthage was to be put to death.

After landing an army in Africa, capturing cities, and ravaging whole provinces, the Romans sent an emissary demanding as the price of peace that their enemies surrender all weapons and all ships. Carthage submitted—wasn't tribute less costly than defense? Then came the further demand: "Move out, every soul of you; build a new city if you will—anywhere—provided it be at least ten miles from the sea."

Alma remembered the drama, how as a young girl she'd wanted to cheer at what came next, identifying fully with the survivor spirit of Carthage. The extremity of the Roman demand resulted in one last heroic burst of new resolve. Carthage, her back against the wall, went mad with courage. People forged new weapons out of anything, built new ships out of reserve supplies, and defied the implacable Romans.

The siege began. While the enemy hemmed in the massively fortified city of nearly one million inhabitants, famine and pestilence stalked the land. Although starving and decimated by disease, the Carthaginians showed desperate valor. Swimming out to the Roman ships, they set them aflame. They repulsed attacks by hurling huge stones; the women, it was said, cut off their hair to provide thongs for the catapults. It was magnificent, but it was futile. They continued their inspired resistance for nearly three years, but in the spring of 146 B.C., the legions of Scipio Africanus the Younger poured over the innermost wall and stormed the Forum. The carnage lasted six days and nights, as the Romans forced their way to the Acropolis, a distance of only several hundred yards. Byrsa Heights, the hill first acquired hundreds of years before by Queen Dido, was still held by fifty thousand wretched men and women and nine hundred Roman deserters. With them remained King Hasdrubal, his wife, and their two children.

Although he'd protested that the sun would never see him survive Carthage, Hasdrubal abandoned his army and surrendered to Scipio. Finding themselves deserted by their commander, the Carthaginians threw open the gates of Byrsa and were granted amnesty—slavery in the galleys or in Rome. The Roman deserters retired to the Temple of Eschmoun. When attacked, they set fire to the great structure and perished there in preference to a worse death. While flames swept through the temple, Hasdrubal's wife appeared on the roof dressed in her royal robes. Her children were at her side. Facing the hill of Junon where her husband sat at the feet of Scipio, she cried:

> *For you, Roman, the gods have no cause of indignation, since you exercise the right of war. But upon Hasdrubal, betrayer of his country and temples, of me and his children, may the gods of Carthage take vengeance and you be their instrument!*
>
> Turning toward Hasdrubal, she said, *"Wretch, traitor, most effeminate of men, this fire will entomb me and my children. In them you will die this instant. Ah, what punishment you will receive from him at whose feet you are now sitting!*

Drawing a dagger, she slowly and deliberately stabbed each of her children and threw them one by one into the burning temple, leaping after them into the flames, the ultimate sacrifice to the honor of Carthage.

The Senate, as the keystone of Roman policy, had decreed that the once proud capital should be annihilated—condemned to eternal desolation. Commissioners were appointed to exact the penalty for outraged Roman pride. The city was set ablaze by soldiers and then, as a last gesture of defiance, by the Carthaginians themselves. Flames raged for seventeen days. After the looting, after the destruction, came the final obscenity—the sowing of the land with salt—and after that the silence.

Overlooking the wreck of the city, Scipio Africanus the Younger, the supreme Roman commander, reflected a moment on the complexity of human affairs and then called down the wrath of the gods upon any who would attempt to reconstruct the ruins in any way.

There were some fifty lines in the curse. Stripped of redundancy, Carthage's doom was pronounced:

> *God of Death and War, bring infernal terrors on this accursed city of Carthage and against the army and its people. We curse with the utmost might of our being these people and this army. We curse whoever occupied these palaces, whoever worked in these fields, whoever lived upon this soil. And we implore that they be deprived forever of light from above.*
>
> *By all the laws of the highest malediction, let them be torn to bits! Let them be stricken down if they even speak its forbidden name! Hellas, our mother, and Jupiter, hear me!* (At these words he touched the earth, beat his breast and looked toward the Acropolis.) *Eternal silence and desolation must remain here! Accursed be those who return! Doubly accursed are those who try to resurrect these ruins!*

Scipio's curse voiced the suppressed hatred that Carthage had evoked for more than one hundred and twenty years. His words vibrated with frenzied exultation at the annihilation of the most dreaded enemy and the arrival of the long-delayed hour of vengeance. In it raged the leaping flames of a passion that had smoldered through the gruesome course of three wars— the fiendish cruelties, the broken truces, and the terror carried to the very gates of Rome.

Scipio would live to curse the power that destroyed Carthage. Like Hannibal, he died in misery and in exile, and, ironically, his end came in the same year as Hannibal's. An uncharacteristically ungrateful people forgot his brilliant victory over their most formidable enemy. Scipio's passing was so obscure that the site of his tomb was unknown and, to this day, has not been located.

Alma had assumed this to be the end, but it wasn't. Her studies indicated that hardly twenty years passed before Gaius Gracchus, a political reformer and leader of a powerful faction, decided that needy Romans should be given an opportunity to colonize the area formerly occupied by Carthage. Gaius was a courageous man who reminded her of Felipe. Though the same agrarian reforms had literally been the death of his older brother, Gaius, undaunted, pushed his views through the highly conservative Senate. What had once been Carthage was deeded to six thousand settlers. It was a personal coup for Gaius, a vindication of his brother's ideals.

Angrily, the conservatives accused the visionary tribune of sacrilege for daring to establish a colony on cursed land. By chance or design, the gods appeared to show displeasure. First a standard symbolizing the new colony was caught in a violent wind and torn apart. Then entrails of sacrificial animals were dispersed by a tempest and scattered beyond the limits of the proposed new city. The new community's milestones were uprooted and deposited far away—supposedly the act of wolves. Ultimately the colony was abandoned, Gaius assassinated.

Alma put the history book aside with a weary sigh. Gaius's failed dreams hit far too close to home. She would wait for Count de Prorok to fill her in on the remainder of Carthage's catastrophic past.

Dapper, debonair—he wore a pith helmet *and* a necktie—Count Byron Kuhn de Prorok was unlike any archeologist that Alma had ever heard of, much less met. At twenty-seven, he was young to be assuming the responsibility for such a large undertaking, but at first appeared totally undaunted by the run of bad luck he'd had. Unsure what to make of de Prorok, Alma was nonetheless touched that he'd taken time from the dig to meet her ship himself.

Barking orders at the Arabs lounging about the dock, de Prorok had her bags loaded into his roadster in short order. Alma thought of Felipe. He had been efficient, too, but never high-handed. Once she'd seen him stop his car to assist a small party of laborers who were attempting to load a massive Mayan statue onto a truck. I *must* stop comparing every man I meet to Felipe, she reminded herself. Not for the first time.

"Your cable took me by surprise," de Prorok admitted as they roared off. "I never thought they'd send a woman. You're a brave girl to come out here."

"Then you really believe in the curse?" Alma studied him curiously.

"Truly, I don't know what to believe—so much has happened, so many accidents."

Alma wasn't surprised, not if everyone drove like de Prorok. Fortunately his flashy roadster was highly maneuverable. Somehow at the last second he invariably managed to avoid the camels, cars, and carriages that clogged the narrow streets.

"Curse or no curse, Carthage appears to have been rebuilt," she commented, nodding at the bustling city whizzing past them. "I thought Gaius Gracchi was the last man to attempt it."

"Not quite and not exactly," de Prorok explained. "Some years later Julius Caesar camped here; he was on his way to wipe out Pompey. That night in his dreams he solved Rome's pressing unemployment problems. Upon awakening, he recorded in his journal: 'Carthage must be rebuilt.' Some historians insist that Caesar passed the night on the spot where Scipio leveled his dire threats against anyone who should even dream of restoring the city. In any event, he was murdered before the plan could be executed. His heir, Augustus, found the memorandum and built a new city, the precursor of modern Tunis."

Alma smiled, recalling Eugene and his numerous land development schemes. Scipio Africanus, for all his melodrama, must have reckoned without the realtors of his day. The peninsula "only a day's sail from Sicily" had too good a potential to ignore. So, capitalizing on the name, perhaps to lure adventurous tourists, a new resort city arose, cousin to the many springing up along the North African coast. But not *quite* on the site— canny imperial realtors would be quick to remind everyone of that.

Alma felt tingles of excitement as de Prorok pulled his car to a stop on the slopes of a hill and explained, "This is Byrsa Hill, Dido's hill. Notice that great gash"—he gestured with his pipe. "You might say archeology began there."

She frowned doubtfully. "Archeology? How long ago, two thousand years?"

"You're close, almost two thousand. At a point when Nero's extravagances were at their height and his treasury at its lowest, an adviser suggested that he send one hundred men to Carthage to search for Queen Dido's treasure."

"You'd think he'd assume that Scipio's legionnaires had carried off everything in sight."

"Perhaps he was desperate; we know he was mad. Anyway, he dispatched the men with orders to dig for three months."

"Did they find anything?"

"No, but when they returned to Rome with the news, Nero fell into a rage and ordered them back, this time accompanied by the centurion guard. If they couldn't produce the treasure in one month, they were to be crucified."

De Prorok gestured again, "Look, you can still see just how hard they worked. Day and night, they bored frantically into that rocky hillside, all the while knowing that each hour brought them closer to death. Ultimately there was nothing to show for their efforts but an enormous hole. Nero kept his word; they were crucified near the ruins of Dido's temple. Back in Rome, the ill-advised adviser met the same fate."

"Scipio's curse strikes again?"

"Well"—de Prorok puffed thoughtfully on his pipe—"that's what people said, and it wasn't the end."

"There's more? This may be the most dismal story I've ever heard."

"I agree, but I'm afraid there *is* more—past and present history. Carthage has the dubious distinction of being the city where the greatest number of Christian saints were martyred, three hundred and sixty, among them St. Cyprian, Saturnus, Salsa, Felicitas, Perpetua. During the period between the Byzantine Empire and the rise of Islam, it's thought that more than five million people died in the struggle for the city. Then, in 698, Carthage was leveled to dust for a second time."

Alma sighed, wondering if there was not some perspective to be found for her own grief in this monumental mosaic of misery. "It's unbelievable."

"My dear, it's all quite true. This time the destroyer was Hassan, governor of Egypt, another mad man. Somehow he managed to fill both of the city's two great harbors, completely obliterating the ancient haven of the Carthaginian fleet, which once nearly conquered the world—two of the greatest fill operations of all time. It wasn't until the beginning of the nineteenth century that the sites of the original ports were located. The discoveries were made by an Italian, Count Camillo Borgia, first excavator of Carthage—"

"Not counting Nero's expedition, of course"—Alma smiled, responding to his enthusiasm. She sensed that if anything could ease her through the terrible loss of not only Felipe but the grand dreams they'd shared, it might be this assignment. "Did he have any luck?"

"Hardly. Borgia proved another casualty. While searching for the location of the naval harbor, he was overcome by poisonous marsh gases. The poor fellow died miserably, near the spot where St. Louis, king of France, perished as a victim of the plague—some say Scipio's curse—while leading a crusade. Count Borgia's maps and manuscripts were lost to science."

Alma shook her head, a half smile on her lips. "What draws us here? What drew you?"

"The challenge, I suppose. People who profess to know about such things kept saying that nothing remained. I couldn't believe that. And what about you? What would cause a pretty young woman to defy death?"

She shook her head ruefully, wondering how much to tell him. Might her sorrow not be easier to bear if no one knew about it? Appearing "normal" would be a challenge, something to live up to. "There were many reasons," she said after a slight hesitation. "One is the mystery. It seemed to me that everything we know about the Carthaginians was learned from the Romans. Isn't that a bit like expecting an objective view of Ireland from an Englishman?"

It was de Prorok's turn to smile. "Yes, something of the sort appealed to me as well. I can see you're going to be an asset to the expedition."

"Mr. Ochs, my boss, said something about underwater archeology. I'm really fascinated with the idea. Borgia's example isn't very heartening, but I'd like to try it."

De Prorok looked doubtful. The troubles didn't end with Borgia. Christian Falbe, a Danish explorer, was the next martyr to Carthage—to science. In 1887, while swimming along the course of the submerged seawall, he was caught in a whirlpool and drowned."

"But surely," Alma argued, "that was just an unfortunate accident. Weren't they merely a collection of unfortunate accidents?"—she hesitated, suddenly uncertain, uncomfortable. "Or are we accepting the reality of the curse?"

"Centuries of them? Well, possibly, but it does tend to give one pause when the casualties are friends rather than historical figures. When I arrived here in 1920, I joined Jules Renault, a French archeologist, quite distinguished actually, and an eminent authority on Carthage. He'd recently excavated an immense Roman cistern, a marvelous find. Renault insisted on camping in it for closer research, a fatal mistake. The dampness brought on pneumonia. I was with him at the last—I'll never forget it. Just before he died, he whispered to me, 'I suppose the curse has me at last."

"Wow, that is scary! But surely you've had *some* success; that was four years ago."

"Yes," de Prorok allowed. "Falbe's death wasn't in vain. He'd followed the seawall for four miles, and his maps of the later Roman city are the most authentic ever made. The late Prince de Walbeck and I were able to use them when we flew over the area, the first time that submarine ruins have ever been photographed from the air and their position recorded."

Alma hardly dared ask: "The *late* Prince de Walbeck?"

De Prorok shook his head sadly. "A most marvelous man, war hero, you know—and invaluable here on the site. He was leaving for a brief holiday, speeding to catch a homeward-bound French liner when his car overturned. All the photographs we'd taken from the plane of the flying ace, Peletin d'Oisy, were burned with him." The count's voice broke; he struggled to regain his composure. "You must forgive me, it was a very great loss. Only the day before he'd received a double decoration from the French government, one for his heroism throughout the war and the other for his achievements here at Carthage."

Alma felt a wave of sympathy. "Are you—are you really the only one left?"

"Yes, of the current expedition sponsored by the French Services des Antiquities, I alone remain."

Alma's home was a palace, which she shared with the count and Pere Delattre, an elderly French monk, stationed in Africa as a member of the White Fathers Mission. De Prorok's wife, Alice, flitted in and out of their lives like a bright butterfly. She divided her time between Carthage and Paris and was full of plans for cultural events—operas and symphonies— that she hoped to have performed in Carthage. These would, she believed, infuse members of the international set with the necessary enthusiasm to underwrite the remainder of the expedition. Alma quickly discovered that dwindling funds posed more of a threat than the curse.

Despite the shadow of financial crisis, life was pleasant at the Palais Hamilcar—the name de Prorok had given to the elegant palace built several hundred years before by a Mohammedan prince. Located on a hilly promontory with breathtaking views of both sea and ruins, the ground was said to have been the site of Salammbo's palace. Located in Megara, a suburb of Carthage, it was—de Prorok hastened to point out—outside the sphere of Scipio's curse. One thing was certain, the palace had been built over Roman ruins. The cistern still housed their water supply. Alma was suffused with reverence every time she thought of this everyday link with the long-ago past.

The building serving as their garage was also an ancient cistern, which reminded her of a giant horizontal wine cask with an end removed. Watching de Prorok's car roar up the drive and disappear into the antique masonry, she was struck by the marvels inherent in the daily business of archeology, the juxtaposition of ancient and modern that after a time became almost commonplace.

In the courtyard, an exquisite example of Arabian faience, marble columns still stood and an ancient fountain played cheerily. That wasn't all. The thirst for excavation never ended. On one afternoon, Pere Delattre discovered a Vandal tomb in a fine state of preservation. Inside was a spectacular emerald necklace, which he, with a bow to Jehovah, donated to Tunis's rapidly growing museum.

Mosaic floors and crumbling tombs seemed to crop up everywhere, and Alma, de Prorok, and Delattre spent much time attempting to classify them. Because their conclusions didn't always match, dinner conversations were lively affairs, reminding Alma of evenings around the Sullivan table. Perhaps, too, she was a little homesick.

Though something of a snob, de Prorok was witty, urbane, and totally devoted to his work. For the most part, Alma liked and admired both him and his high-spirited American countess, but her particular favorite was Father Delattre. Long white hair and a flowing beard lent the priest a decidedly patriarchal appearance, yet his vigorous mind and indefatigable constitution was a constant inspiration.

With whatever time remained after satisfying his ecclesiastical duties, Delattre patiently and insistently delved into the past. And, yes, somehow he'd managed to defy the curse. "Perhaps it's because I pray a lot," he'd once told Alma, only half joking.

A devoted antiquarian on all levels, Delattre's particular passion was the early church. The greatest wish of the last great saint of Africa, Cardinal Lavigerie, had been to restore the Christian ruins of Carthage, and it was into the hands of the "White Father," Delattre, that his task had been committed more than forty years before. Older ruins were sought with much fanfare and had met with disasters great and small; but Delattre, working quietly on his own, had located some twenty-four basilicas. The priest's only reimbursement for his labors had been a yearly stipend of fifteen hundred francs from the Institut des Antiquities, which rarely covered supplies and equipment. Now, his work halted by a cutback in even that amount, he was assisting de Prorok.

"Few people realize the great significance of Africa to Christianity," the missionary priest pointed out to Alma. "Carthage was the center of Latin thought for several centuries. Crucial issues of the early church were decided right here. If you want to see today what the first Christian basilicas were like, don't look for them in Rome, where they were either destroyed or built over, but in the area surrounding Carthage, where little has changed since the days of St. Augustine."

Alma listened intently. That evening, she wrote a long letter to Eugene describing the Baths of Gargilius, where in A.D. 411 a great debate took place that helped to decide the doctrine of the Christian church. "Five hundred representatives gathered here," she told her father, "two hundred and sixty Christian bishops—St. Augustine among them—and two hundred and forty Donatists. Their debate raged for three days, sometimes they got so angry that some actually came to blows, but finally St. Augustine's brilliant oratory prevailed. Just to think, I'm working right at the scene of that historic encounter!"

Delattre described to Alma how once when crossing a field to visit the home of a sick Arab, he'd stooped to pick up a small piece of marble from among the cornflowers. Beneath the vivid blooms the soil was composed of marble dust, with here and there a gray mass of antique stones rising above a sea of color. The stone he'd found bore a fragment from an early Christian epitaph. As the priest searched the area, he discovered many more stones. In a few days a gang of Arabs was at work digging through some fifteen centuries of earth to finally expose another basilica.

Another day, Delattre showed Alma his collection of relics, illustrating the whole history of early Christian art. He had found some two hundred lamps with varying mystic signs of Christ, one hundred and twenty in an excellent state of preservation. In one early Christian chapel, he pointed out two crosses in bronze and a number of stone tombs with the names of early Christian martyrs inscribed on their covers.

Scores of such tombs dotted the road between the Palais Hamilcar and the Roman amphitheater lying to the north of Carthage. They explored many of them together. Often Alma noted that three nails had been placed in the coffin with the victim, leaving little doubt that these were the two spikes driven into each hand and the remaining one to impale the crossed ankles of the martyr.

As Alma walked about the site, often with a copy of *Salammbo* tucked under her arm, she half expected to see the heroine spring to life. Flaubert had, she learned, spent six years gathering information about Carthage from Latin and Greek manuscripts, and he had lived near the site for several months. Now it became apparent that he'd combined the skills of a scientific observer with the intuitive ability of a seer to create a historical novel that had some utility as a Baedeker.

Carthage, Alma learned, had been a great walled city—with triple towers and stabling for three hundred elephants and four hundred horses—occupying an area of twenty-four square miles. There were two excellent harbors, one mercantile, one naval. Sloping upward from these basins were markets, offices, courts, theaters, temples, dwellings—some structures seven stories high. The temples were so rich in gold, jewel ornaments, and art bought or pilfered from the Eastern world that they surpassed anything that had been gathered together before or since.

Near the old metropolis rose the sheer precipes of Cape Carthage fronting the Mediterranean. It was on these heights that Alma helped to excavate an ancient tomb that for nearly three thousand years had escaped the destruction wrought by Carthage's many conquerors. Alma was constantly aware of a distinctly Egyptian influence that reminded her of displays that Eugene had pointed out to her years before at the De Young Museum in San Francisco. Like the Egyptians, the ancient Carthaginians were mummified and entombed with their personal ornaments and utensils along with votive tablets, inscriptions, and sacred images. At the tomb entrances, grinning masks had been placed to frighten away evil spirits.

Excavating the tombs was perilous work, often done with the aid of ropes and other tackle, for below them was a drop of some three hundred feet to the waters of the bay. Once a landslide occurred, delaying the expedition for several days.

Alma would never forget the excitement of discovering her first tomb. She and de Prorok were so keyed up that they worked all night with the aid of electric arc lights. At one point the young count was very nearly cut in two by a slab of rock which crashed down as he was reaching for a delicate seventh century B.C. vase resting beside a Carthaginian skull.

Among the most interesting discoveries were the elegant mosaic floors, intact after so many centuries. It was fascinating to watch the emergence of these eternal stone pictures as inch by delicate inch the earth was removed. Fishing scenes, hunting scenes, fighting scenes, chariot races, home life, animals, and flowers appeared in vivid red, blue, green, gold, and white.

Even more moving to Alma were the minor discoveries that offered close-ups of everyday life in those long-ago days. A fisherman's tomb contained fish hooks; an actor was surrounded by comic masks made some five hundred years before Christ. In every tomb was an exquisite iridescent tear bottle created to contain the grief of friends and family.

In another area, Alma helped to unearth a complete kitchen with all its pots and pans, and, near the stove, a hoard of eighty coins. This so human link with the past was preserved as found and transferred to the open air museum that de Prorok built among the ruins. In order that no small object would be lost or overlooked in the course of excavating, de Prorok, Delattre, and Alma made it a practice to cart away all the earth they'd dug up and then pass it through sieves at the end of the day.

Near the Baths of Gargilius, they found a vaulted corridor where a chamber that may once have been the boudoir of a Carthiginian courtesan was unearthed. In addition to a great deal of iridescent glass, they found perfume bottles, tear glasses, bracelets of gold, bronze mirrors, ivory hairpins, nail scissors, and little ivory sticks that Delattre said were used to apply black paint to the eyelids. Many of the perfume bottles had been melted by the conquerors' fire into abstract forms that sparkled with jewel-like radiance when discovered in the darkness.

Not so far away was found what may have been the first recorded advertisement. On a well-made lamp, Delattre deciphered for Alma: "PLEASE BUY OUR LAMPS—THEY ARE CHEAP—THEY ARE THE BEST."

Alma found many dolls and doll houses, toys of all kinds. She was touched by the sight of children's milk bottles, made centuries before Christ; many of them painted with the droll semblance of a merry face. These charming relics made the discovery that was to follow all the more appalling.

It almost seemed that the spirits of former inhabitants had breathed their most dreadful secrets to Flaubert. The most vivid passages of *Salammbo* had been the most hideous for they described the sacrifice of children to the goddess, Tanit. It now appeared that this aspect of the novel had been true.

The Sanctuary of Tanit and her consort, Baal Hammon, was accidentally discovered one night by de Prorok when a robber was found digging on a hillside near the supposed site of the city gates. He fled, but his enterprise led to an amazing discovery. Hundreds of urns were uncovered, each of which contained the sacrificial bones of children ranging from newborn babies to boys and girls, which they judged to have been twelve years of age.

Just as had been described in the novel, it appeared that at regular intervals, accelerated in times of national stress, children were offered to appease the goddess and her consort. Continuing to excavate, they found a layer of ashes, and in it a huge, misshapen mass of metal fused by fire. Alma could visualize the horned and bull-headed image of Baal standing in constant readiness to receive his living food. Before victims were offered to him, a fire had been built between his legs and the great metal body was heated to a red-hot state. To the clamor of cymbals, the beating of drums, and the blare of musical instruments that drowned out their screams, the victims were placed in the arms of the idol, which were slowly raised with pulleys, throwing them into the burning flames.

At first it all seemed too impossible to Alma. How could human beings do such things to one another? What sort of frenzy could induce such atrocities? Then, quite by chance, her questions were answered. Alma and de Prorok were invited to be the guests of Prince M'Hamed, son of the bey of Tunis.

While seated in the prince's courtyard, they became aware of the dull booming of great drums far off in the distance. As the rabble drew closer, they could distinguish the chanting of priests and the shrill, bansheelike "lee-lee" of women on the nearby housetops—war cries, according to their host. Out of a cloud of dust had come an advancing horde forming into lines near the palace.

"They are the Aissaouas," the prince explained. "They've come to enlist my support in a holy war against French colonists."

The demonstration began, and Alma watched spellbound as men with drums on their backs braced as drummers beat a rhythm for the gyrating dancers. Faster, ever faster, they whirled, until overcome by hysteria, they fell foaming at the mouth, writhing in the dust. As the drums beat harder and faster, the chanting rose to a sustained roar. Handfuls of broken glass were presented to the delirious dancers by the priests. As a famished man might relish a few crumbs, the dancers chewed the glass. After the glass came nails, and after nails the priests gave the writhing zealots knives. The nails and knives were thrust through their flesh, and still the dancers cried for more. Finally buckets full of live scorpions were tossed into the midst of the crowd. They were consumed as eagerly as if they'd been shrimp. Alma almost doubted the integrity of her powers of observation.

The prince smiled blandly, pleased by the coincidence that had provided something different in the way of entertainment for his guests. But Alma and de Prorok exchanged looks of anguished horror. Finally they could stand it no longer, bade the prince a hearty farewell, and escaped through the palace gardens.

Later, back at the site, Alma, began to connect that wild, wanton scene with the hideous evidence daily being excavated. She wondered, was it possible that she had actually witnessed the return of Baal? And Tanit—what of Tanit? Much as Alma tended to deify the feminine principle, she could find no element of peace or mercy, no redeeming justification, for the revolting spectacle she'd observed. Could it be possible that Tanit in her darkest form had actually shown her presence? The macabre suggestion remained with Alma, haunting her in the days to come.

Within six weeks they'd dug up hundreds of bone-filled vases, sometimes as many as fifty a day. As the work progressed, their digging uncovered large stone stelae inscribed in a variety of designs. The tree of life pattern, lotus flowers, uplifted palms, and dolphins were popular subjects. Then one day a very different kind of monument was found. Gently dusting away the accumulated soil of centuries, they beheld a finely sculpted figure of a priest holding a sacrifical child.

Abbee Chabot, a recognized authority on the Phoenician language, visiting the site that day, leaned forward to decipher the message. Alma, standing beside the man, saw his face darken. Chabot hesitated, looking at the native workmen who'd stopped their digging and were watching him with interest.

"Go on, man, what does it say?" de Prorok urged eagerly.

"It's of no importance," Chabot assured him, turning away.

"But you read something; tell us what it says"—the count was insistent.

Some of the nearby workmen moved in closer, and Alma, sensing trouble, murmured, "Perhaps this should wait until later."

"That's foolishness; I want to know now," de Prorok insisted.

"Very well then. I will tell you. The inscription's a curse. It says, *'Whoever overthrows this stone shall be eternally shattered by Baal.'* Of course, these superstitions mean nothing," he added quickly, noticing that the workmen had rejoined the main force, some of whom were standing in groups muttering among themselves.

After much urging from de Prorok, the work continued. Only minutes later another stela appeared, this one contained a malediction of Tanit against "the violators of the sacred silence" of her temple. The workmen sensed something. The frightened tone of their muttering changed to one of anger. It was clear that they regarded themselves in jeopardy and blamed the archeologists. Alma recalled yet another curse experience, that of the Marquis d'Anselm and his party, believed to have been murdered by their workmen while excavating a subterranean passage between Carthage and Tunis.

The damage was done. Work that had been going so well ended abruptly. Almost immediately the workmen had thrown down their tools and walked off the site. Alma, de Prorok, Delattre, and the curator of the emergent Tanit museum continued on their own. Before the day was ended, the curator, while walking along the rim of the top of the excavation, slipped. Plummeting to the bottom of the pit, he struck his head on the very stone that had cursed them and was knocked unconscious. He quickly regained consciousness, but a pall settled over the party. No one felt like continuing.

A few days later, however, back at work again, the curator was cataloging artifacts in the museum when a bust of Tanit fell on him from a top shelf, cutting a gash in the other side of his head. Recovering consciousness for the second time, he complained to Alma, "I've had enough of Tanit, damn it!"

The next day when the team, now numbering three, returned to the excavation, they found the mutilated body of a Tunisian woman. Her hands were dismembered; the vandal had apparently wanted her rings and bracelets. It was assumed that one tomb robber had attacked another. Alma hastily rejected the thought of a sacrifice.

Forced to continue unaided, they reassured themselves that the count's efforts to get the workmen to return would eventually be successful. When a month passed and they still had no help, de Prorok made a proposal. "We've sifted everything, classified everything, gone as far as we can go unaided. Your help has been invaluable, Alma, but there's nothing more to do or write about until these Arab devils come to their senses. When their money runs out, they'll start to miss us. In the meantime, let's give them a scare, let them think we've given up. Christmas is coming; Alice wants to go to New York. Why not spend the holidays with your family in San Francisco?"

Why not indeed? Alma considered. Both the count and the *Times* had paid her well. She could afford to go home and, yes, she was a bit lonesome for her family. This would have been the first Christmas she'd ever been away, although last year had been a kind of nightmare. Alma had walked through the festivities as though in a trance. Now she could scarcely remember anything about it except her fears for Felipe, her vigil at the *Bulletin* beside the news wire.

The year that had begun so dreadfully was almost at a close. Alma found a grim satisfaction in her resilience, her ability to go on, to carve a place for herself in a new and challenging milieu. It had been easier in Carthage because no one knew her. Now it was time to go home.

Alma was used to being the interviewer; suddenly and unexpectedly, she discovered the excitement of being the interviewee.

"BURIED CITIES MEAN ROMANCE TO SAN FRANCISCO GIRL WRITER": It was an eight-column headline across the top of the Sunday, January 4, 1925, edition of the *San Francisco Examiner.* The style of Nadia Lavrova, the reporter who'd written the story, was particularly purple, but then Alma had done nothing to discourage her.

Another colorful layer of the Alma Reed legend was added with an overblown job description:

> *Alma Reed has the distinction of being the only archeological reporter in the world. Her work takes her over the five continents. She gets more exercise than a sporting editor and more excitement than a police reporter. She has become an amateur archeologist of no mean standing. And having created a job, she enjoys it to the full.*

Well, some of it was true.

Alma certainly enjoyed her new found celebrity status. She liked being an aunt, too. A growing number of nieces and nephews welcomed her arrival. It was fun to have babies to fuss over with none of the attendant responsibility. Prescott was eighteen now, both star reporter and ladies man, already affecting the raffish air that would distinguish him even in this city of eccentric charmers.

There was another new development as well. Sam Payne Reed was divorcing Theoline. According to the newspaper article, the cause was "the placement of other causes above his home interests," but everyone knew the real reason was another woman. Alma could imagine *exactly* how Theoline felt.

Then the cable came. De Prorok needed her. Work at Carthage was still temporarily on hold, but a desert expedition was planned, this one to seek the lost continent of Atlantis.

CHAPTER 9

The Road to Atlantis

Carthage, the once swaggering sea leader, insolent and unafraid, again welcomed Alma in a warm embrace.

It was springtime, the land a tender green of fields and groves, the coastline a soft pink of seaside villas, half hidden under mantles of flowers. As Alma stood atop Dido's Byrsa, the peacock sea stretched before her, a flashing sapphire where it shimmered and bubbled upward toward the sun. The old port, tranquil now, reflected only the blank sky and an occasional piping bird. At her back were mountains, violet and misty purple, cut sharply against the clear sky with an edge of pure, hard blue. In the center stood the Father of Two Horns, which once bore upon its mighty shoulders a temple of Tanit.

At noonday a hot silence lay over the land, reminding Alma that it was this very season, this very month, that had seen the smoldering ruins of the devastated city plowed under by vengeful Romans, ending forever a long history that abounded with magnificently imperious finger snappings ruthlessly backed by swords. However Alma might condemn the apparent cruelty of the Carthaginians, she could never forget that, in the end, they were few against many, their brave, arrogant spirits unsubdued.

Alma was glad to be back. Her sortie to San Francisco had been enlightening. She'd left home still something of a girl, totally devastated by Felipe's death, desperately seeking something, to fill a void that could never be filled. Crushed by the pain of her loss, the future stretched before her as a black abyss. Felipe was dead; she, sentenced to life. How to serve out her term? By chance, it seemed, the answer had come. Alma found a measure of solace for her own shattered dreams in the study of an ancient civilization. Layers of ashes buried the lives and hopes of an empire. Sifting through them brought a new perspective, a palliative for her own grief.

The Sullivans had welcomed home quite a different person. A woman now, her own personality molded, Alma's earlier defiance had softened. Eugene and Adelaide had ceased to be parents, authority figures to be pleased or flouted. She saw them now as very old friends—friends with whom she did not necessarily have to agree or disagree. In recent years, occupied with her own affairs, Alma had scarcely noticed her younger siblings grow to adulthood. Suddenly, it seemed, they were men and women. Prescott surprised her most of all. Other than journalism, they had little in common. Politically, Prescott was as conservative as Eugene!

Alma's homecoming had created a stir. Besides newspaper interviews, there were many parties. Fellow writers, school friends, and neighbors vied to entertain the international heroine who'd somehow grown up in their midst, then flown away. San Francisco was a beguiling city; its charms all the more evident after an absence. She was somebody now—professionally, at least, a big fish in a very pleasant pool, and might easily have taken her pick of jobs on any of the major metropolitan dailies. Socially, too, many doors once closed were now open to this slightly swashbuckling personality with her romantic past. Despite these attractions, Alma greeted de Prorok's cable with enthusiasm. Her destiny, she realized, was no longer in San Francisco.

The count, having rejoined Delattre at the site, welcomed her eagerly. They were busy with plans for an expedition into the Sahara and had delayed their departure until her arrival.

As they moved out, Alma realized that Carthage was merely the gateway to a vast open-air museum of ruins, which survived with much of their grandeur intact. Like some enormous prehistoric monster, the great aqueduct that had brought water to the ancient city extended for nearly two hundred miles from its source. In some places destroyed, in others as complete as the day it was finished, the extraordinary engineering achievement was unparalleled in its time.

Conquering Romans had established military strongholds against savage nomadic tribes along the northern base of the Aures Mountains. Deep in the desert, the locations of these ancient cities and fortresses were still marked by impressive ruins indicating once prosperous centers of commerce, industry, and culture rivaling those in Spain and Gaul. Many were connected by fine Roman highways, part of which were still in existence. It was the parts that were not that gave Alma trouble.

These areas had to be traversed by camel. From the beginning, she'd admired the picturesque animal, silhouetted as it frequently was against a far horizon. Riding one was something very different. Once one was astride, it was a long way to the ground. Alma's moment of truth came as the party assembled before a herd of camels. The driver, Ibn Khaldoun, prodded his beasts into sitting positions. De Prorok sprang lightly onto the saddle of the first. The driver gave a sharp command, and the animal's hindquarters rose suddenly, pitching the count forward right over the camel's nose. Fortunately, he landed on soft sand, the loss only to his dignity. As de Prorok dusted himself off, a visiting member of the party mounted the next beast. This man survived the first rise, but as the front quarters of the camel abruptly soared skyward, he lost his grip and fell backward over the creature's rump.

The Arabs thought it great fun and made no effort to conceal their amusement. Delattre put an arm around Alma. She forced a smile. "Will you pray for me?"

"For this, you will not require a prayer," he assured her. "There's a trick to mounting a camel. I'll go next. Watch me carefully. Be certain to place your feet in the stirrups. As the camel rises on his back legs, lean back as far as you can; then, when he lifts upward with his front legs, shift your weight and lean forward. There's really nothing to it."

There wasn't either—the way Delattre did it. Alma watched as he nonchalantly lifted the skirts of his cassock and easily mounted the kneeling camel. The animal rose high as the sky—Alma thought—with his back feet, then the front ones. Delattre, seated comfortably, smiled encouragingly. Ibn Khaldoun gestured to her, pointing to the next camel. "This one's for you; her name is Dido." Stepping forward, Alma tentatively patted the camel's nose. She'd heard that dogs could scent fear and hoped this wasn't true of camels as well.

Smiling weakly, Alma climbed into the high saddle, quickly wedging her feet into the stirrups. When the command came, she was ready. Gritting her teeth, she waved at the others with one hand, clung to the pummel with the other. It was a stunning triumph.

Once the rest had finally mounted, the camels moved forward with a rolling, pitching motion that reminded her of a rough sea voyage. After a time, she and Dido established a grudging working relationship, but camel would never be Alma's transportation of choice.

They were heading into the country of La Kahena, the Berber Joan of Arc. As they rode, the articulate Ibn Khaldoun, who spoke almost faultless English, regaled her with the legend. As with the French Saint Joan, voices, visions, and the gift of prophecy also guided this heroine in her struggle against foreign domination. Little was known of her parentage, but the title, La Kahena, implied that this eighth-century military leader's strength was rooted in the supernatural. She was a sorceress and the personification of patriotism.

"We are near her fortress now," Ibn Khaldoun announced. "It was originally a Roman amphitheatre, and many believe there is a tunnel that connects the ruin to the town of Selecta on the sea."

"But that's nearly twenty miles," de Prorok, who had overheard the conversation, broke in.

"True," the Arab nodded. "It is told that the tunnel was wide enough to accommodate three horsemen riding abreast."

"But what do you know about her?" Alma persisted, more interested in the woman than the tunnel.

"Only that she ruled a Berber tribe who lived in the nearby Aures range."

"And the Berbers themselves?"

This time it was de Prorok who answered. "I believe them to be the oldest of the North African peoples, descendants of the Libyans. Several tribes are fair-haired, blue-eyed, and of light complexion. You see their features portrayed on some of the earliest Egyptian sculpture. The Berber influence on early Carthage shows up in the Libyan burial customs and the name, Tanit. I think it possible, just possible, that the Berbers, through their Libyan ancestors, are descended from the Atlanteans who survived in North Africa after the submergence of their island home."

Alma had heard enough unsubstantiated Atlantis theory. "What about La Kahena," she urged, scenting a fresh story. The mere idea of a female military leader in a Moslem country was extraordinary enough, even without the supernatural angle.

"Our people say that when Carthage was destroyed, the Berbers pretended to adopt the beliefs of the Romans and to pay them allegiance. They played the same game with other conquerors, all the while clinging to old beliefs and maintaining a tribal identity. Remaining aloof from the struggles that shook all of North Africa, they sought refuge from the more ruthless invaders in the mountains fringing the desert, content to merely watch the conflict. Finally, after many wars, long and bitter ones, the Byzantine Empire was crushed, and Arabs under Hassan-en Naman gained a foothold in North Africa."

"Isn't he the one who destroyed Carthage the last time, the one who filled up the harbor?"

"Yes," de Prorok answered. "The fool finally wrested possession of it from the Byzantines, but was so fearful of losing his prize that he ordered Carthage's total destruction."

"Then he went on to loot and ravage the interior"—Ibn Khaldoun continued the savage history. "La Kahena rose to power as the Berbers prepared for resistance. In a battle at the foot of these very mountains, she repelled Hassan's attack and drove his army back to Gabes. The enemy forces numbered forty thousand, and her army had only twelve thousand men. Eighty of Hassan's bodyguards were taken prisoner, and, with one exception, La Kahena sent them back without ransom. The unreturned prisoner was Kahled, a beautiful boy whom she adopted as her son and the brother of her children." Ibn Khaldoun's abilities as a storyteller aroused Alma's envy. She would attempt to capture him as well as his legends in the article she was already constructing in her mind for the *Times*.

"Convinced that the Arabs were fighting only for plunder," he continued, "La Kahena decreed the destruction of the whole country between El Djem and Sfax. We know her words by heart: 'Our cities perpetually attract the

Saracens by our riches in gold and silver. These vile metals are not our ambition. We are happy with the simple products of the earth. Let us destroy these cities! Let us bury all the great treasures and perhaps then peace will come to us.' "

"Really!" Alma exclaimed, overcome by the enormity of the act. "Is this actually reliable?"

"A bit extreme, one might even say fanatical," de Prorok agreed, "but everything our glib camel merchant has told you is quite true. The policy was carried out with systematic zeal. City after city was destroyed in vain. Finally La Kahena made her stand here in the old Roman coliseum. The attack lasted for three years, but she remained well supplied with food obtained from mysterious sources. The enemy suffered cruelly from hunger, and it's said that La Kahena ordered her soldiers to throw them fresh fish. Perhaps subsequent expeditions will uncover the subterranean passage that our verbose friend spoke of. That would explain the abundance of fish so far inland."

Alma was fascinated by the Berber heroine and determined to write about her as she had Dido. She had always responded to courage, activism, and idealism in others, just as she had always striven to make a positive difference in the lives of those she touched. As a crusading journalist, Alma had done her best to effect social change. Later she had dreamed of taking an active part in Felipe's endeavors. Now, it appeared, her life had taken a more vicarious direction. So be it; someone had to report, and more important, interpret the lives of the brave and the noble. She turned back to Ibn Khaldoun. "But what happened to La Kahena?"

"Ah, it is very sad. There was a betrayal. La Kahena realized that all hope was gone, yet she continued to fight bravely. The day before the final battle, she imposed submission on her natural sons and the adopted Kahled and sent them to Hassan's camp, hoping to save their lives. Then she led her troops into battle, a queen to the last. The traitorous Kahlad led the enemy forces that defeated and beheaded her.

"And thus," their historian-philosopher concluded, "the freedom of North Africa, this Barbary, descended into the grave, never to rise again, not on the third morning, not on the third week, not on the third year."

. . .

As different as they might appear on the surface, Count Byron de Prorok, the dapper boulevardier, and Edward Thompson, the intrepid jungle man, were kindred spirits. Both subscribed to the Atlantis theory.

The latter had abandoned his early passion for a later obsession, the sacred *cenote,* but de Prorok's belief in and quest for the fabled lost continent was deathless. The young archeologist based his hypothesis partially upon the skeleton of an Egyptian woman that he'd uncovered beneath the Carthagenian graves and an Egyptian amulet discovered in the Temple of Tanit. The Egyptian findings predated the Carthaginian ones by some five hundred years. Thus his theory: Egypt was a colony of Hoggar.

Hoggar. Hoggar. Hoggar. It was all the count talked about. At first, Alma thought the theory farfetched, but now some of de Prorok's enthusiasm was rubbing off on her. Amidst fields of poppies and groves of olive trees, they'd come upon ruins of golden cities, many of them miraculously preserved. Seared by the blazing sun and scarred by the hands of man and ravages of times, the martyred cities of Africa lay half buried in sand. Sometimes the ruins were partially hidden by mountain mists; at others they rose miragelike from the shimmering sand. Using a two thousand–year-old Baedeker, *The Itinerary of Antoine,* their preliminary expedition followed the African coast to Leptia Magna, where they switched back into the desert past the ancient crossroads of Rhadames. The trail led through a seemingly endless series of triumphal arches, aqueducts, bridges, forums, fortresses, basilicas, palaces, and temples. Except for gigantic butterflies and an occasional Bedouin with his flock of sheep, the sites of these forgotten outposts were utterly without signs of life. Alma longed to stop, but de Prorok invariably urged them northward toward the Mediterranean.

At the apex of the great triangle, the Hoggar plateau lay in a virtually inaccessible spur of the Atlas Mountains. Myths associated the area with a continent in the Atlantic Ocean, peopled by the fabled "great, broad-eyed, sunken race" who gave the world its civilizing arts before vanishing in a dreadful cataclysm. Guided by ancient historians, local legends, and his own recent discoveries, de Prorok hoped to scientifically link Hoggar with the lost Atlantis.

"It's a project that will take twenty years," he admitted, pointing out the area to her.

"At least," Alma agreed. "Twenty years and a million dollars."

"That's my estimate, and that's why I brought you here. Our funds have almost run out, and we've barely scratched the surface. We need donations. The *Times* circulation is tremendous. Who knows what magnate will see your article and be tempted to open his purse strings."

Alma shook her head. "Do I need to remind you that most of the archeological establishment rejects the Atlantis theory as a fable? Yes, yes, I know, but"—she waved him to silence—"Plato's description of Atlantis as a vast island off the Straits of Gibraltar has been tossed about for eons. A few dissidents even think the Mexican Gulf may now cover part of it, but I'm sure a big gun like Dr. Merriam would consider what you're attempting nothing less than scientific heresy."

"That's it, that's part of your article—the controversy. That's why we came to Hoggar—so that you can write the story at its very source."

Looking about at the lush, inviting oasis, she shrugged. Well, why not? Soon Ibn Khaldoun had her typewriter unpacked, a wooden lap desk was constructed, and Alma, her back resting against a palm tree, was typing briskly, words flowing like the nearby spring.

> *"Explorations in North Africa must eventually lead to heresy,"*
> *says the distinguished young archeologist, Byron Kuhn de Prorok,*
> *in defense of his aim to locate definitely the birthplace of*
> *civilization in the mid-Sahara. "Workers in the field," he*
> *explains, "see legend substantiated at every turn and have learned*
> *to respect the stories of deluge and flood that linger in the*
> *universal memory."*
>
> *Count de Prorok's excavations at Carthage have already*
> *undermined the outer walls of history. His unearthing of an*
> *Egyptian culture that preceded the Phoenician by at least five*
> *hundred years is the starting point of the proposed investigations.*
>
> *As one of his main objectives, he hopes to prove that the*
> *Egyptians had their origin in the desolate Hoggar spur of the*
> *Atlas Mountains—the mysterious "land of fear" which has*
> *tempted few explorers and from which fewer have returned.*
> *Accepting the age-old theory that the Hoggar is the remnant of a*
> *vanished continent and the region where man first emerged from*
> *barbarism, Count de Prorok holds that the Egyptians were*
> *Atlantean colonists. Whether they came down from the Hoggar*

directly into Carthage or whether they pushed across the Sahara to the banks of the Nile and from there sent a colony to Carthage is a secret that he may eventually wrest from the shifting sands.

Alma's enthusiasm was feeding on itself as she espoused de Prorok's theory.

Many versions of the lost Atlantis have been given by ancient and modern writers. Practically every civilization of the Old and New Worlds had its tradition of a great natural catastrophe that wiped out a large portion of the human family. Generally pictured as peopled by supermen, all the myths and alleged historical accounts agree on the existence of a great land where mankind lived peacefully and happily over a long period.

The story, as related by the priests of Egypt to Solon, "wisest of the Greek," and preserved by his descendant, Plato, tells us of the disappearance of Atlantis beneath the ocean in one day and night. The archives of the temple of Sais recorded the event as the result of terrific earthquakes and volcanic eruptions and placed it at nine thousand years before Solon's time.

The Hoggar had been identified with Plato's description of the "nature and arrangement" of Atlantis. "The country," de Prorok related, "was very lofty and precipitous on the side of the sea, but the country immediately about and surrounding the city was a level plain, itself surrounded by mountains which descended toward the sea. It was smooth and even, but of an oblong shape extending on one direction three thousand stadia and going up the country from the sea through the center of the island two thousand stadia; the whole region of the island lies toward the south and is sheltered from the north. The surrounding mountains were celebrated for their number and size and beauty, in which they exceeded all that are to be seen anywere."

Count de Prorok's expedition faces its most baffling problem in the coordination of geologic and paleolithic evidence found in Southern Tunisia. The Gafsa, Tamersa and Redeyf regions have yielded up traces of pre-historic man, yet there is ample proof that these same burning sands with their fossilized remains, are a deposit of the sea and that the entire desert was once the floor of the ocean.

Tozeur, halfway between the coast and the Rhadames crossroads, has its legend of an ancient galley found embedded many feet below the surface. To the Arabs, the place is still known as Mersa-es-Sahara, or the "inland port." It is a matter of record that at or near this spot, in 1306, a caravan of one thousand camels suddenly sank into the earth. Not far away, at Nefta, a whole city lies buried and the sands are rapidly advancing to devour the present city.

But neither the earliest historians nor the latest discoveries have pierced the mystery of the Sahara itself. In his study of its vast literature, Count de Prorok has found no key to its conditions at the dawn of civilization. Was the Sahara a part of the lost Atlantis? Did it collapse and fall to the bottom of the ocean to be thrown up in another cataclysm? Or did the waters merely recede at their destruction of "the sacred island lying beneath the sun that brought forth all fair and wondrous things in infinite abundance"—leaving the bleak, towering Hoggar in a sea of sand?

Back at Palais Hamilcar, Alma discovered trouble in paradise. Of course, only she perceived it that way. The survey expedition returned to Carthage to find not only Arabs ready to work, but additional funds with which to pay them. Large donations had arrived from wealthy Americans who had read about de Prorok's problems. If money could dispel a curse, they meant to do it. De Prorok would also be receiving academic direction from Professor Francis W. Kelsey, head of the anthropology department at the University of Michigan.

The young archeologist was ecstatic and so, for a time, was Alma. Then, on May 7, 1925, Kelsey's wife arrived with three graduate students, Dr. Orna Butler, Nita Butler, and Julia Brittain. It wasn't that the women weren't *nice.* Alma wondered sometimes if their niceness wasn't a form of noblesse oblige. They came from the wealth and position that her parents had aspired to, and, more significantly, they had the formal education that Alma always dreamed of. Suddenly her own background seemed woefully inadequate. "I'm a graduate of the University of California," she told them. "Thought I'd get a little experience in the field before I hit the books again. I'm thinking of getting my doctorate at an eastern university, not sure where, possibly Barnard or Columbia."

Work resumed at Tanit's sanctuary. Soon more than one thousand urns had been found intact, or almost so. The legend on each inscription was monotonously the same, "The Goddess, Tanit, Face of Baal," to which a wish was added, and then the name of the offerer and the dedication. The inscription bore the triangle of Tanit, the mystic sign of the Carthaginians found throughout the dead city.

Mrs. Kelsey and her three assistants kept busy sifting through the bones of the sacrificial children. For a time, Alma worked with them. Despite the macabre circumstances, there was almost a quilting bee atmosphere. Listening to the other women reminisce about sorority affairs and undergraduate pranks, she found herself succumbing more and more to the temptation to embroider her original academic pedigree. She was skating on thin ice and knew it. It was only a matter of time before someone or something tripped her up. Another assignment for herself was essential.

The casual camaraderie of the earlier days had changed forever. Delattre had returned to his monastery to live, but still, whenever anything new was discovered, he came flying over the hill, in Alma's fancy an angry prophet, his robes flying in the wind, his tremendous beard waving like a flag. It seemed to her as though the "palace" had turned into a school. Alma was quartered now with the three women graduate students in a dormitory arrangement. Routines and schedules had become very important. A bulletin board minutely detailed the duties of the day, beginning with a 6:30 breakfast for those going out to the field, 7:30 for the rest. Latecomers went hungry. Lunches were consumed at the scene of work. In the evening, after sluicing off the dust of Carthage, dinner was served. Afterward the day's work was evaluated, dimensions checked, photographs of the previous day viewed, and finds classified. Alma missed the old rousing arguments.

Having lost her job as journal keeper to Kelsey's assistant, Professor Peterson, she was piqued, but she missed the money even more. Alma had thoroughly mined the field of Carthage for the *Times*. Clearly it was time to move on, but where?

. . .

"Eugene, Eugene! Oh, my goodness! Will you look at this?"

Eugene glanced up from the sports section of the *San Francisco Examiner*—Prescott had switched papers and was now covering baseball.

"What will that girl do next?" Adelaide was brandishing a copy of the *American Weekly,* a national magazine that the local paper carried as a Sunday supplement.

The headline read: "5 MILES DOWN UNDER THE SEA IN A BIG STEEL BOX."

The picture below was that of Alma, and the caption read, "Dr. Alma Reed, the Woman Explorer, who with the Distinguished Inventor, Dr. Hans Hartman, Will Make the Descent in the Steel Box."

"Dr. Reed is it now!" Horrified as he was at the thought of his daughter's latest escapade, Eugene felt grudging admiration for her impudent panache. One way or another, she was acquiring not only a practical education but the prestigious appearance of an academic one.

"The story refers to her as 'the well-known woman explorer,' " Adelaide read on. "It also says that the most modern diving apparatus will allow the wearer to descend five hundred feet. Just listen to this: 'The great steel cylinder will sink down into the sunless depth of the ocean where the two scientists will observe what no other eyes have seen before of life in the sea's abyss—gigantic octopuses which breed and live far below the surface, weird fish flashing with their own lights will reach out toward them and stare in at them, death will ride beside them every foot of the journey, but if they succeed, the sea and its hidden treasures will have been conquered.' "

"If they succeed, I certainly don't like the sound of that. . . ."

CHAPTER 10

The Further Adventures of Dr. Reed

Alma's diving career had its beginnings on the fabled island of the Lotus Eaters, a real-life place to the east of Tunis. A local sponge diver had told tales of a sunken city where brightly hued fish swam through windows of fabulous palaces. De Prorok was determined to investigate, Alma determined to accompany him.

It would, she feared, be the last story in her North African series. The well was running dry. *Times* readers, Ochs had recently cabled, were eager for fresh adventures, new destinations. Paid on a piecemeal basis, she was beginning to feel the pinch financially.

The island itself lived up to its classic reputation. Lotus Land, now known as Djerba, was beautiful. Three miles off the mainland, the island was an oasis torn from its moorings and sent floating out to sea.

But the people had changed a lot since the days of the Odyssey. Ulysses wouldn't have recognized the present-day inhabitants. Sober citizens now, they'd give him sailing lessons rather than psychedelic petals. Alma found the residents of Djerba to be serious, industrious people. Most of them, judging from their skill on the water, must have been born on ships under full sail.

Once on Djerba, they had found many divers who talked of "walls and windows" under the sea. Their dean was a seamy old buccaneer, whose face had a plowed look that reminded Alma of Carthage—after the Romans. On a preliminary sail, the man was too encouraging. When asked about the city, he pointed emphatically to the water and shouted, "Houni! Houni!" ("Here! Here!") Alma suspected that if every place he "hounied" had been part of the city, it would have been double the size of New York.

He was seconded by the caid of Adjim, another rogue, with a distinctly humoring manner. He was dubious of their sanity, his suspicions borne out one day when a visiting friend of de Prorok's asked about the possibility of getting a collection of scorpions together for transport to New York. Alma's rudimentary Arabic, acquired over the last few months, was quite sufficient to comprehend the man's remarks to his under caid: "Can you beat it? First these people want to hunt for a city under the sea—absolutely useless! Then they want to send scorpions to their relatives!"

It was easy for Alma to understand why these men might think them if not mad, then at least incredibly frivolous. A sponge diver's life was arduous in the extreme. She watched fascinated as they were rowed out to sea by Arabs manipulating their boats much, she imagined, as the slaves of Rome or Carthage must have done. The native oarsmen used gigantic sweeps, possibly between fifteen and twenty feet long, rowing with all the might and muscle of their bodies. Standing barefoot in the well of the boat, they gripped their prehensile, uncivilized toes that clung like fingers. Bending over the shaft of the oar, rising slowly, rising, gripping tightly, and grunting in unison, they flung themselves forward, then backward with all their strength.

On shore, Alma soon found the Greek sponge divers easy to recognize. The effect of working long stretches under such terrific pressure was readily apparent. Most of the men walked with difficulty, dragging their feet, a sign of the paralysis that claimed many of them. The incidence of death in their occupation, she was told, was ten percent a year.

The depth at which the men could lawfully work was established at thirty-eight meters maximum, but their overseers had a way of manipulating the recording instruments to show a different pressure. Divers frequently worked at fifty meters and occasionally even sixty, and, Alma was told, if an overseer thought a man hadn't worked long enough, he ignored the signal to return to the surface. Sometimes a diver would retaliate by inflating his suit, causing it to bob up like a cork—only to be driven down again at the foreman's whim. The diver's show of spirit could cost him dearly, for, by forcing himself quickly to the surface, he might cause his own paralysis. Alma heard horror tales of divers who'd disappeared and others who'd been buried at sea, sewn up in coarse sacking, their deaths never reported. A story still persisted of an old diver who was left below because he was too frail to continue working.

After much dickering with the French and Arab authorities and Greek ship owners, de Prorok acquired a small fleet, three Arab *feluccas,* and two small Greek coastal ships. They set off on their first venture with high hopes, but were rebuffed by choppy seas. The currents between Djerba and the mainland are strongest in May. Unfortunately, it was May when they discovered that significant detail.

Conditions were more promising on their second sally. At 4:30 in the afternoon of May 24, 1925, Michael Cocinos, one of the Greek sponge divers, went overboard. Alma watched the thin stream of bubbles that broke the surface, then scanned at a greater distance to see if anything threatened to break. She recalled the story of a man who'd been lost recently when his air tube and lifeline became tangled in what could have been the doorways or windows of the lost city.

Ten minutes later the sailor standing in the bow with the lifeline felt a tug, the signal that Cocinos was coming up. Alma rushed to the railing. She could make out his great helmet approaching through the clear green water. Tension mounted as they pulled the diver on board. The team could scarcely wait to get the man out of his gear, to hear the tale of his discoveries.

All they learned was that the currents were still strong and that Cocinos had been carried off his feet by currents, sometimes falling into deep hollows.

Another man, burdened with their hopes and fears, then went over gently, down, down. The record showed five, ten, fifteen, twenty meters, farther, faster. It was too much. The group held its collective breath, hoping that the rope would stop sliding into the sea, but it continued. Bubbles began to spread on the surface, indicating that the diver was being carried by the current. Orders were quickly given to haul him back aboard. The man emerged, white and exhausted. Nothing had been located. The current was just too strong to work.

The glances exchanged by Alma and de Prorok were mirror images—no Atlantis, no story. Wasted time, wasted effort.

Cocinos broke the silence. "There is a submarine city of which we do know," he ventured in Greek-accented English.

It developed that these ruins, located near the village Guallala, had been discovered at an uncertain time in the past by Berber sponge divers, but no one had ever bothered to explore them. Following Cocinos's directions, they immediately made for the spot. Before long, divers reported a well-constructed wall of white stone blocks. Their enthusiasm reminded Alma of Don Eduardo's fervor. Despite a hearing loss, he'd never regretted his diving experiences.

Neither threats of deafness nor warnings of paralysis could dissuade her. Determined to investigate for herself, Alma was screwed into a stuffy diving suit. The sensation corresponded with her sense of being buried alive. The more she looked at the sea, the darker it grew. Perhaps the risk was too great, perhaps she should renege, but even as the thought entered her mind, they were adjusting the lifeline and the full weight of the lead came down on her shoulders. Alma empathized with a mouse in a trap, a feeling she would retain. Two men lifted her weighted legs over the side—a sea burial! The crowd at the ship's side reminded her of mourners. Short of breath, Alma was certain the air pipe was out of order; she wondered about the durability of the lifeline. The heat was awful.

She was dropped over the side with a splash. Now the world was green and strange. There was a loud clatter in her ears. Alma fumbled frantically and at last found the valve located on the helmet that let the air out. Down she went faster and faster, watching the bubbles bobbing to the surface. Once on the seafloor, she discovered that, burdened as she was, it was impossible to walk and so set off at a crawl, clutching her lifeline for reassurance. Outside her window, the world was dark ink, a blend of green and blue that seemed somehow grotesque. Laboriously, she propelled herself along the white block wall. The suit was so heavy, it wasn't long before she was exhausted. Surely the neck pieces were heavier than necessary and the shoes far more cumbersome than the occasion demanded. Finally evidence of the potential began to dissipate her fear. She had to know what was beyond the wall; she would go around, but she was so very tired of crawling about with all that weight.

Then, unaccountably, everything went dark. The sudden blackness was terrifying; Alma started to scream, then stopped, half laughing at the awful irony of it. Who was there to hear her? Slowly, feeling like a mammoth bug, she forced herself to turn and crawl back in the direction from which she'd come. Some of the darkness faded. She kept on going and was again surrounded by the familiar blue-green. Managing to look up through the top window of her helmet, Alma realized that she had inadvertently crawled under the ship.

She was very tired now, ready to return to the surface. Grasping the lifeline, she pulled hard, three strong tugs. There was no response. Alma felt a trickle of water run down her neck and, thinking that her suit was leaking, knew a moment of panic. Then she realized that the water was her own perspiration. Alma said a little prayer to the water god and tugged again. No answer. Then she realized why. She'd been tugging at the cords that held the weights to her neck. An eternity passed before Alma located the real lifeline.

Something went "crack." It was her helmet hitting the hull of the ship on the ascent. Her suit was bulging like a balloon as she reached the surface, slamming against the hull as she rose. It was impossible to move her leaden feet. At last she was ignominiously dragged aboard.

As her helmet was whisked off, Alma breathed deeply, offered a silent thanksgiving to Neptune for heeding her prayer, then looked around. "How long have I been down?"

"Only about five minutes," the captain informed her. "We thought you'd stay longer."

If Alma had been impressed by the courage of the sponge divers before, she was overwhelmed now. She would never see a sponge without thinking of the risks involved: a choked air pipe, a vicious dogfish, a tangled lifeline, and, even more, the great silence, the intimidating isolation of the sea itself.

Remembering the weight of the diving gear and her own exhaustion, she was amazed when the next diver returned to the surface with a heavy object. It was an amphora that had been embedded in six inches of sea growth and covered with barnacles and mollusks. The diver explained that it was only with extreme difficulty that he'd been able to detach the relic.

Within minutes, Cocinos was again over the side, armed with a pickax and carrying a rope. When the rope had finally grown taut, they eagerly began to pull. An object slowly rose. It had little shape or form, but when it broke the surface, they saw with unutterable delight that it was the remains of three amphorae. Time and the weight and flow of the sea had cemented them together. Cheers went up in English, Greek, and Arabic—the hard work and numerous disappointments of previous days instantly forgotten. The sea was at last yielding up some of its secrets. They had worked hard and been rewarded by two or three bits of useless earth, but it had been worked by people who had made history and now they turned surmise into certainty.

Weather and tides turned against their party, but only for a few days. Soon they were back. This time the first diver had only been down eight minutes when the line began to jerk. A form showed through the green, and then that form took shape. Far below, Alma could make out an encrusted amphora—and what an amphora! The others paled by comparison. Carefully, as if it were delicate glass, the amphora was lifted from the water and gently placed on a mat in the center of the ship. It stood about four feet high, with its two handles still intact and its narrow base undamaged, a testimonial to the extreme care of the diver who'd recovered it. Mollusks, fungi, and sponges clung to the sides, but its general form and dimensions were similar to the amphorae that Pere Delattre had discovered in the earliest Phoenician tombs at Carthage.

In their excitement, they hadn't noticed that the day had turned windy, and waves were now breaking over the small ship; however, nothing could stop their No. 2 diver from going over. As the winds increased to even greater velocity, it was decided to raise him sooner than they'd anticipated. After repeated failure to respond to the rope signals, the captain started the motor and strove against the current, which, lashed by wind, was stronger than usual. The crew pulled at the lifeline to no avail. The diver was seventy feet down, caught perhaps in some submerged ruin. Then suddenly the line jerked, and the sailor holding it swore with sudden relief. The diver was loose at last.

Moments later, Alma saw the motionless form rise to the surface, floating face down. Her heart skipped a beat when his face became visible, dead white with a thin stream of blood trickling from his nostrils. The man lay motionless for several minutes, showing no signs of life. His suit was removed, his body wrapped in blankets. Then, as a strong stimulant was administered, the color slowly returned to his face.

The diver's story was horrendous. Alma listened as he explained how the current had carried him under some overhanging rocks. Imprisoned in total darkness, he sensed that the current had changed and was growing stronger by the minute, lessening the chances of escape. Desperately, he attempted to make steps out of the sand, to get leverage so that he might push himself out, but as often as he braced himself, the sand gave way, and he was washed back again into the recess. It was the changing position of the ship that helped him. Finally, and just as he swung clear, the diver had lost consciousness.

No more diving that day, and the next was to be their last. De Prorok had invited Monsieur Louis Pagan, governor of the Isle of Djerba; the Greek consul, and their old friend the wily caid to accompany them. The sea, accommodating the celebration, provided generously, yielding up pieces of bronze, a number of amphorae—one totally undamaged—as well as a large part of their luncheon menu. A small gramophone played Hawaiian music as they dined on the canvas-covered deck. It was a happy day that Alma would remember always. Ever the optimist, she struggled successfully to banish thoughts of her uncertain future.

Inevitably, Alma's role in the de Prorok expedition had come to an end. Once again, the count's funds were dwindling. What was left must be apportioned carefully. If the excavation at Carthage were to continue, he would have to defer his underwater search for Atlantis. Perhaps next year.

Then, just as he was making plans to return to the mainland, a new treasure hunter arrived on the scene. The U.S.S. *Vestal* was making waves in the small harbor of Djerba. Alma, sensing a story, set out to interview its commander, who was the internationally known scientist Dr. Hans Hartman.

Later, carrying her typewriter out to the small balcony of her hotel room, she surveyed the scene before her: the village an almost silvery white, its inhabitants dressed mostly in blue, the effect strangely cubist. Graceful *feluccas* skimmed across a sea that sparkled in the late afternoon sun. Recalling Fremont Older and the bedlam of the *Call* city room, she smiled at the contrast. Such tranquillity as this could never have even been imagined there. Yet even in paradise, a story was a story and deadlines remained implacable if one was to live. She anchored her notes with a large seashell and began to type.

The film industry has entered an underwater epoch and the enterprising producer may soon be seeking a "location" on the floor of the ocean. A vogue of deep sea studios may follow the discovery of an ancient submarine ruin and the perfection of subaqueous photography. The idea promises enough "super attractions" to keep Hollywood guessing.

The use of the improved subaqueous motion picture camera of Hans Hartman in recording the sunken cities of the Mediterranean will make possible the filming of "sets" that not even the most optimistic of scenario writers could have dared to suggest a few weeks ago. "Movie" audiences of not too distant seasons will view films showing monuments concealed in the mysterious depths of the ocean since the dawn of history. They will see reproduced on the screen those "vast heaps of stone—the vague and shadowy castles and temples clothed with ivy" so accurately described by Jules Verne when he predicted submarine archeology half a century ago.

Alma was excited. That afternoon, Hartman had taken her on a tour of the ship that President Wilson had fitted out to his specifications just prior to the Great War. The objects of the 1916 expedition were to locate sunken U-boats and to study on site the topography of the deep in comparison with the theoretical findings of the United States Coast and Geodetic Survey. Science, Hartman had told her, had recognized that the only accurate means of charting the mountains, hills, plains, and valleys of the sea was with the aid of a camera. The project had marked the government's initial attempt to record with accuracy the heretofore invisible contours of the ocean floor.

The *Vestal* became a veritable floating visual arts laboratory equipped with a huge deep-sea camera, which included a steel structure fifteen feet high and weighing more than one thousand pounds. The various parts of the mechanism included a submarine light projector, an additional electrically driven camera for still and motion pictures, a gyroscopic stabilizer to eliminate vibrations, and a propelling device for rotating the entire structure around its axis so as to obtain photographs in every quadrant.

Measuring instruments above and below showed the depths at which the devices were functioning. Others indicated the exact position or angle of the light projector and camera, and the speed at which pictures were taken. Sensitive microphones informed the operator above the water whether every part responded promptly and correctly to the control and also transmitted the faintest sounds coming from the exterior of the structure. "Feelers" reacted to the slightest touch by fish or other creatures of the sea. Instantly the light and cameras swung in that direction to photograph the cause.

Hartman was optimistic about a new invention of his, which he proudly showed to Alma. It was a method by which a passenger could descend into the sea riding comfortably with the camera in the steel cylinder while reporting everything to the scientists on the surface by telephone. The cylinder hung like a pendulum between the barges connected by a crossbar. From this vantage point, with the aid of a powerful searchlight in a watertight drum, the operator could direct excavations or salvage and control the camera.

"Would you like to take a ride with me in the cylinder?" Hartman asked.

Alma gulped, then replied almost instantly. "Yes—yes, I would indeed."

That evening Hartman came by the hotel to check the story for "scientific accuracy." Impressed with what she had written, he made her an offer. This time there wasn't the slightest hesitation. He needed an assistant. She needed a job.

The following day she waved good-bye to Count Byron Kuhn de Prorok as he and his roadster were about to be ferried back to the mainland. A colorful chapter of Alma's life was over. She felt few regrets, well aware that this particular party was over and none too soon. Clearly, she and de Prorok could no longer afford each other. Though a true adventurer like herself, the count was also something of a playboy. Archeology had currently captured his dilettante fancy, and he'd worked hard at it. Now he wanted academic recognition while keeping his antennae out for greater social access to the rich and famous, the International Set as they were known in those prejet times. Her aims were plain and simple. She had to feed herself.

Once again Alma Reed was a typewriter for hire. It was she who'd written the unsigned article that had stunned the folks back home.

Again her work was fund-raising, indirect but still fund-raising. After the war, Hartman had been allowed to retain his research ship, but with a diminished budget. For a time, as the protégé of Prince Albert of Monaco, he personally stocked the Museé Oceanographique with rare Mediterranean sea specimens. Now, that assignment completed, he, like de Prorok, had grand plans with little money to implement them. Alma, who would have been stranded in North Africa if not for his offer, chose to ignore the similarity. Surely a benevolent destiny had sent this exciting project her way just when she needed it most.

Confident that Hartman's work would result in a significant scientific breakthrough and that she herself would actually have a part to play in the grand adventure, Alma quickly found herself churning out press releases with great enthusiasm.

"In the course of the examination of Greek and Roman galleys in the Mediterranean, it is possible that Dr. Hartman's expedition will bring to light some of the most famous treasures in the world," she wrote.

> *The season's program calls for a survey of several triremes wrecked near Carthage in 455 A.D. as they neared the North African stronghold of the then Vandal King Geneseric after his sacking of Rome. They were a part of a four hundred vessel flotilla loaded with Roman loot following the pillage of the Imperial City for fourteen days and nights. The galleys contained silver and marble staves of the pagan gods which adorned the capital and the holy seven-branched candlesticks from the Temple of Solomon plundered from Jerusalum.*

Now, Alma speculated, who wouldn't thrill to that treasure hunt? Yet, if additional incentive was needed, she was ready to provide it.

> *Among the Grecian treasures was the golden roof wrested from Apollo's temple as well as shrines and altars of gold and precious stones from Christian churches and priceless ornaments from the Imperial Palace. Gold, silver and rare marbles were removed from the buildings and heaped upon the galley's decks. Nothing, in fact, that could be transported was spared.*

And that wasn't all, Alma reminded her readers. "The area had been the favorite haunt of the Barbary pirates. Hundreds of vessels listing under their golden cargoes have been attacked here and gone down with their treasures."

Then Alma had a brainstorm. Atlantis had proved a turning point in Don Eduardo Thompson's career. Perhaps it would do the trick for Hartman's as well. "Several of the archeologists who will accompany the expedition adhere to the lost Atlantis theory and hope to bring back photographic proof of the existence of the sunken continent, which tradition holds was the cradle of human civilization." But in an effort to be evenhanded and avoid putting off more conservative investors, she added, "Other archeologists of the party believe that actual observation of the submarine plain will tend to disprove the theory, and demonstrate once and for all that the 'lost Atlantis' is of mystical rather than historic origin."

Finally Alma concluded her flak:

> *Dr. Reed has written on the lost Atlantis theory in its relation to the baffling Maya race of Yucatán, which many scientists hold had its origin in an overflow of emigration from the submerged island continent. The Maya civilization produced an architecture second only to that of Greece and a time computing system that has been unsurpassed in the world's history.*

The time came for the proposed dive, but Alma's efforts to raise money had been less than successful. The necessary funds for a full-scale expedition were not forthcoming. Hartman was desperate. The next press release was picked up by all the wire services and seen throughout the world. It read:

GIRL TO PROBE
DEPTH OF SEA

> *The first to explore the depth of the ocean, 500 feet below the surface will be a woman. She is Alma Reed, former New York and San Franciscan newspaper woman and executive secretary of the Hartman deep sea expedition to the Gulf of Naples, who will probe for a buried city in a specially constructed diving bell.*

Alma was going down alone.

. . .

It was a visit to a new world almost beyond belief. Gliding downward, an infinite variety of deep sea creatures passed in review before the porthole. Some looked like large mechanical toys in their regular, deliberate movements. Others trailed their phosphorescent bodies through the darkness, giving the effect of illuminated airplanes performing nose dives and stunt figures in the night sky. Still others went through picturesque transformations of form and color with slow, undulating grace. All appeared to be attracted by the light, and many hovered in its beam as though hypnotized.

Using Hartman's state-of-the-art equipment, she photographed scores of odd and outlandish specimens. Some had vast eyes; others were apparently eyeless. Many had great heads out of all proportion to their tiny, dwindling bodies. Others were completely or partially luminescent in many colors and in varying degrees of brilliance.

One creature that stood out with unforgettable vividness was a large dark ball resembling a floating globe, without fins or projections of any kind. Striking the cylinder, it instantly changed into a long, tubular shape like an eel or python and measuring at least twelve feet in length. The change was so violent and swift that she was unable to follow the movement, but it seemed as if the long, stretched form had been shot from the globe's interior as a bright, phosphorescent bolt only to disappear into the darkness.

Another remarkable creature, whose color and luminescence were so faint and delicate that its very existence was uncertain, became entirely invisible without any apparent movement, only to reappear suddenly in the same form and at the identical spot. This weird disappearing act was repeated several times before the porthole.

Another specimen suggested the double-headed dragons of ancient legend. The uncanny creature, measuring about a yard in length and a foot in average diameter, seemed to be composed of two similar units, or to be a twin of double composition, joined at the side and making all motions in unison. The exact point of the junction could not be perfectly distinguished, but the two tubular bodies were closely separated for about five inches of the creature's length. There seemed to be two heads, each at least two feet high and ridiculously large for the size of the bodies. They were flat and extended far above and below the body proper. What appeared to be the mouths were constantly wide open and were highly luminescent.

Then, much as if it had been deliberately staged for Alma, there was a truly lurid drama. The first character to appear on the improvised stage in the spotlight's glare resembled a living, floating balloon. It constantly changed its dimensions, often attaining four times its original size. When largest, it measured about three feet in diameter; it was transparent and of a faintly rose color. When smallest, it was less than one foot and more luminous. One side of the body was a conical opening that increased and diminished according to the change in diameter. Around the body ran a circular line that was of very marked phosphorescence.

The second character of the deep-sea performance was a rarely beautiful creature, consisting of a dark purple globe from which smaller globes of a light red color protruded in all directions. The smaller globes were like lighted balls connected individually with the center body by thin, tubular feelers. At times the creature formed a radiant star. Later, all the little bulbs would drop downward, suggesting a delicately tinted electric fixture with a number of tiny lamps. Occasionally the little bulbs would concentrate closely around the center of the larger light ball, finally merging into a single, brilliantly lighted unit.

For a few moments this beautiful creature went through its romantic maneuvers as if tantalizing the sinister expanding, contracting balloonlike specimen. Alma was reminded of a slave girl dancing to please some bloated caliph. But in one graceful, climatic movement, it swept too close and in a flash was swallowed up or rather down into the ominous conical-shaped opening. The beautiful creature shrank violently within the transparent globe, which promptly contracted to its smallest diameter. The once lively, vibrant being disappeared into the hazy depths within the suddenly darkened body of its destroyer, where it continued to shine as a luminous ball.

Tragedy was followed by comedy on the submarine stage. Next came an oval-shaped buffoon with clownish antics. The creature measured about a yard in length, which it nearly doubled by throwing out a long fin or daggerlike projection with a straightforward motion.

As a charming finale, a flat, vertical, and slowly floating disk appeared trailing long streamers. These varicolored ribbons would close together at the center of the body in an umbrella shape from which they opened and curved upward like the petals of a flower.

It was an experience that Alma would never forget. Her sense of wonder at what she'd experienced helped immeasurably in writing about it—which was fortunate because Hartman was of absolutely no help whatsoever. When she sought his aid in identifying the exotic sea creatures who'd entertained her so royally, the bemused scientist merely shrugged.

"Really, my dear, I've no idea what you saw, I've never been down that far myself. *You* set the record. One day I'll have to to go check it out." In the meantime, his thoughts centered on money not fish. Funds he'd envisioned simply hadn't materialized. Alma's much publicized dive had been a last-ditch effort. For her the result was a personal triumph, for him a financial flop.

Alma had returned to the surface a media star, but her twinkle was a brief one. Headlines were breaking everywhere. Trouble with the Riffs in Morroco. Trouble with Serbs in the Balkans. Before her instant celebrity faded—a matter of days—Alma put her reporter's observational skills and dreamer's imagination to good use by selling a flamboyant description of her adventure to a news service.

Fortunately, the editor, overwhelmed by the sheer drama of the event, was content with colorful description. The sum paid Alma was substantial. The question was: How long would it last?

CHAPTER · 11

Alma Goes to Hell

After waiting almost twenty years, Alma finally found herself in a university lecture hall. It was the experience of which she'd always dreamed. She was in Naples attending the University of Southern Italy.

Lately Alma had become mildly dyspeptic. Was there anything to be gained from making plans? The harder she tried, the more effort and energy she expended, the faster they came "unmade."

Working with de Prorok, Alma had been guided almost unconsciously into the new field of public relations. Charming, attractive, and—when necessary—a convincing prevaricator, she was well suited to it. Then Dr. Hartman had entered her life at a point of near desperation. He, too, required financial backing, but, happily, there was no need to feign enthusiasm for his work. The exploration of the sea was enough to fascinate anyone. Hartman's track record was impressive and his goals plausible, but despite the media interviews Alma scheduled, the shipboard receptions she held, and the endless stories she wrote, the money didn't come.

When all else failed, Alma's dive was to have been the supreme attention getter. She'd always possessed a natural sense of adventure and this, combined with the fatalism that had developed since Felipe's death, rendered her virtually fearless. Frightening as the solo experience—a plunge five hundred feet beneath the sea—had been, she'd wanted to try again. Her dive had been duly recorded—a feat of daring, a record breaker—and that was it. If only she'd discovered a city or at least a salvageable ship, but she hadn't and her much publicized feat was a public relations disaster. Aside from the "girl diver takes the plunge" stuff milked to the limit, there was nothing else to report. Hartman vetoed the idea of a repeat. There wasn't enough money. He would have to get a job, perhaps hire himself out as a fish catcher to another celebrity like Prince Albert. Something would have to be done quickly, or his research ship would be lost to creditors. Clearly there was no place for Alma in his frantic schemes.

Then she learned that de Prorok was planning another expedition—this one deep into the Hoggar Mountains. A Franco-American committee had been formed to finance the expedition. No camels this time! Three powerful Renaults, six-wheelers, had been specially equipped. At a gala soirée, Madame Rouvier, wife of the late Premier of France and a friend of de Prorok's mother, had christened the cars. Chauffeurs would be included in the fleet. The count's man was named Martini. He was, de Prorok said, "as spirited as his namesake and as good a precursor to a meal."

But Alma wasn't invited. The *Times* was sending a Mr. Denny. His academic credentials were impressive. Despite her experience, despite her excellent articles, she was outgunned.

Then, while Alma considered her melancholy options, something reminded her of one of Mrs. Kelsey's protégés, Julia Brittain. As they'd worked together cataloging the bones of the Carthaginian children, Julia had talked of studying the classics in Italy. The more Alma thought about it, the more she wondered if possibly she just might qualify for a scholarship. Surely some of the people she'd met in the last eighteen months might be persuaded to write references. It worked!

Alma adored the University of Southern Italy. She'd studied Latin in high school and found it returned quickly. Now she was also learning Italian and Greek, and her special energies were lavished on the classical period. Alma's favorite instructor was Professor Amedeo Maiuri, a man of rare insight and humor.

On one occasion Maiuri took the class to the National Museum, of which he was director, and conducted them along a gallery flanked by marble busts of the former rulers of the world. With great curiosity, Alma studied the likenesses of Julius Caesar, Tiberius, Nero, Claudius, Trajan, Marcus Aurelius, and the young Octavian, who would later reign as Augustus Caesar. They were implacably realistic, chiseled by the great sculptors of the era.

Initially, Alma's fellow students, most a good fifteen years younger than she, showed little interest. Great these men might have been, but they were very long dead. Then Alma watched as Maiuri, a clever caricaturist, quickly captured their attention. From his sketches, cold marble was spontaneously reanimated, static features transformed with the lifelike suggestion of a smile, a sneer, an expression of haughty contempt, haunting fear, frustration, or an air of brutal cruelty. In other renderings, Maiuri was somehow able to highlight the nobler qualities of his subjects, revealing in some deep sympathy with humanity's problems, in others a spirit of mercy and altruism, or an idealism based on wisdom.

He had another trick as well, one that charmed as well as enlightened the entire class. The mere placing of a modern hat on the bust under discussion made that personage suddenly intelligible. Alma found the transformations extraordinary. Some of the Caesars reminded her of the captains of industry she'd glimpsed briefly in elevators of Manhattan skyscrapers, while others suggested supreme court judges or top echelon military men. The hat, in short, seemed to tear away the centuries that separated those mighty Romans from present-day affairs and to illuminate their vices and virtues with a clarity that historical record, even in their own times, could not evoke.

Alma was immediately challenged by this introduction to Roman antiquity. An eager scholar, always struggling to discover the link between myth and reality, it wasn't long before her efforts were noted by Maiuri. He invited her to accompany an archeological expedition.

"Where to?" she asked eagerly.

"The Abode of Shades," he replied with a mysterious smile.

When Alma shook her head in bewilderment, he referred her to an old friend, the *Aeneaid*. "Try Book Six," was the best he would do to relieve her curiosity.

Alma reflected: Book Six . . . Book Six. . . . Suddenly the narrative flashed through her mind. Aeneas, escaping Queen Dido's love net and after braving many perils on land and sea, finally arrived at Cumae. He'd come on a double mission—to consult the sibyl about his future but also to seek her guidance to the shade of his father in the netherworld beyond the River Styx.

"You—we—we're going to hell?" she asked him incredulously.

"Yes," the professor smiled. The mysterious realm of Hades was to be their destination.

In Maiuri's youth, Troy had been a myth. Now thanks to efforts of the great archeologist Heinrich Schliemann, it was a reality. The previous forty years had seen the transformation of archeology from mythology to science. Suddenly it seemed that anything was possible. He was determined to establish the geography of the *Aeneid,* a long overdue undertaking. After its centuries of isolation in the realm of poetic fancy, the classicist hoped to fix Hades on the map, validating it just as the once mythical Troy had been validated. Using the *Aeneid* as a guide, he planned to explore the Phlegrean Plains of southern Italy, a strange volcanic region associated in the minds of the ancients with mystery and terror.

He would follow the Trojan hero's wanderings from his arrival on the Euboean strand of Cumae "until he steered his galleys northward to the mouth of the Tiber." Alma was enthralled, already anticipating the article she would write for the *Times* Sunday Magazine (and the check). The headline would be a guaranteed attention getter: "VIRGIL'S HADES GIVES UP ITS SECRETS."

Maiuri's deductions proved largely correct. The *Aeneid,* a classic saga of the divine origin of the Roman Empire, provided an accurate guide for their travels over the Campi Flegrei. The land lay within sight of Vesuvius and just beyond the narrow ridge separating the Gulf of Naples from the Bay of Pozzuoli. Running westward to the Tyrrhenian Sea, it claimed a rocky strip of coast from Iseno's high, desolate headland to the lower tip of Gaeta's crescent harbor. A broken range of yellow hills marked its northern boundary.

Their investigation first centered on the Cumaean acropolis, and it was there that the ruins of the Temple of Apollo yielded fresh proof of the accuracy of Virgil's description. The caprice of nature and violence of man had left few vestiges of its former grandeur. Yet the archeologists were able to identify a great heap of broken stones as the stately temple hailed by Aeneas with hope and gratitude as he neared the Cumaean shore. Very soon Alma was carried along by the archeologist's enthusiasm, mentally striving to reconstruct the fallen grandeur.

The find bore little resemblance to the original perfection of the white marble temple with it golden roof credited to Daedalus. The unrivaled engineer, legend holds, in escaping King Minos's labyrinth, made wings of wax and feathers. He and his son, Icarus, took flight from Crete, but the daring youth flew too near the sun, melted his wings, and plummeted to the sea. Daedalus, however, landed safely at Cumae, where he erected a temple honoring Apollo. On its massive portals, he carved the legend of the cruel tragedy of the Cretan queen whose uncontrollable lust for a bull produced the monstrous Minotaur. Twice he tried to record the death of Icarus, but, overcome by grief, his hands fell helpless.

The temple was thought to mark the first Greek settlement on the Italian mainland and a seat of the cult of Apollo. Dotted with volcanic craters, the area was also held sacred to Pluto and his queen, Persephone. Art flourished in service to religion, helping to preserve the enduring flame of Hellenistic culture, which illuminated the western world for generations to come.

Alma spotted tombs cut into the huge pavement stones and found crude floor mosaics indicating the pagan temple's subsequent conversion to a Christian church. The golden gem-studded roof, regarded as one of the wonders of antiquity, was said to have been part of the rich loot dismantled and hoarded in the citadel by Goths and later hidden by them in an immense subterranean chamber after a siege made their position hopeless. The fire set by the imperial general Narses destroyed much of the ancient fortification. Alma looked with wonder at the vast pile of debris now overgrown by foliage which guarded the secrets of the Goths, but was more curious about other secrets—greater mysteries that might be locked in the depths of Apollo's shrine. It was here that the ancient oracle was thought to exist.

The task they had undertaken was more complicated than had been anticipated by the fact that the changes in Campi Flegrei that time had wrought in the past two millennia were even greater than they'd allowed for. Forces, natural and human, had raised unpredictably formidable barriers to their research. Despoilers had been particularly ruthless, and nature wanton. Earthquakes and lava flows had erased a number of significant landmarks. Mountains suddenly emerging from the depth of the earth had emptied lakes and diverted rivers. Bordered by submerged palaces, the golden shores of Baia gave dramatic evidence of the tidal waves that had swept wide areas into the seas. The enterprise of Roman emperors had also helped to alter the landscape. The twin lakes of Avernus and Lucrinus, once thought to be fed by the overflow from the Styx, had undergone marked changes. Originally, the "pestilent Avernus" had no natural outlet and was without birds or other life. None could survive the deadly vapors that drifted from the lake's surface. When Augustus connected it with Lake Lucrinus to form a naval harbor for the Roman fleet, it is said the poisonous fumes disappeared. Certainly Alma found nothing "hellish" in the sparkling lake frequented by Neopolitan picnickers.

Surrounding Avernus were the Tartarean forests, likened by Virgil to the gloom of the grave, and inhabited by the savage Cimmerians who dwelt in caves, rarely seeing the light of day. Another Augustinian reclamation project had cleared the impenetrable growth and drove out these ghoulish people, making way for vineyards and fragrant orange groves.

Had the confusion caused by such changes rendered the archeologist's job impossible? Alma wondered. Where, for instance, was the River Styx? She speculated that Lake Lucrinus, formerly separated from Avernus by the Tartarean woods, fit Virgil's description regarding position. As in his time, a wide causeway ran between it and the sea. Legend attributed the mysterious construction to Hercules, said to have built it as a means of crossing the marches. Unfortunately the greater part of Lucrinus now lay under Monte Nuevovo. During a volcanic eruption in A.D. 1538, the mountain sprang from a low crater in a single night, some five hundred feet high and and a half mile at the base. The eruption buried many Greek and Roman ruins and who knew how many secrets.

Perhaps the disturbances also destroyed the destination of the grim steersman of the Styx, for the scientists could find no clue to it, nor could they identify the stagant asylum of stillborn babies to whom "the pain of the wicked and the joy of the blessed alike are unknown." Alma was much sorrier to forgo the sight of the Mourning Meads, where suicides and love victims languished. Here it was that Aeneas was confronted by the ghost of Dido, who had ended her life in despair over him. Heedless to explanations and cold to his entreaties for forgiveness, she had turned from him to the arms of her dead husband.

Alma would have had a lot to discuss with Dido. What an interview! Dido and her first love were both dead, but would she continue to spurn Aeneas when—*his* life span ended—he joined them at last in Hades? Now, there was a love triangle. Alma thought a lot about love in all its ramifications. Busy as she kept herself, her thoughts turned invariably to Felipe. She'd met a lot of interesting, attractive men, but no one was able to displace him from her heart. Small wonder that her imagination often centered about reunions beyond the grave.

Less elusive, however, than the Mourning Meads was the domain where offenders against the gods were doomed to endless punishment. Most certainly, it matched Solfatara, that flat crater pitted with *fumaroles* steaming with boiling mud and sulfurous gases. One had but to stand beside these ugly gashes and listen to the seething fires beneath to understand why Virgil consigned the guilty to the Campi Flegrei.

The grizzled old guide who presided over the place, standing at the entrance to the Avernus passage, certainly had no doubt that this was the "Gate to Hades." The dark, wet tunnel, low, narrow, and forbidding, led from the southern shore of the lake to a destination known only to Pluto himself. The atmosphere was so gruesome that Alma found it easy to accept Virgil's account of the horrors the Trojans encountered along the route. The damp blackness ahead might well be infested by grief and disease, by old age, want, and fear. It reminded her a little of Loltun, but this time there was no Felipe to guide her.

With a torch, the old caretaker ignited the escaping gases and mumbled incantations for their amusement and their *lire*. At the close of his performance, he announced that he was the one person in all the world who was certain of heaven. When Alma dutifully asked why, his reply was ready: "Because I have lived in hell for forty years. . . . Plenty, plenty . . . for the worst of sinners."

Hades, for all its dark fascination, was not Alma's primary interest, though it did generate a sale to the *Times*. Attempting to match Virgil's ancient descriptions with present topography was an entertaining if frustrating bit of detective work; she found its precedent in the efforts of the French scholar Victor Berad, who some sixty years before had traced the wanderings of Ulysses.

Another aspect of the *Aeneid* intrigued her far more than geography.

Surely, Alma reasoned, the enigma of the Cumaean sibyl who'd conducted Aeneas on his journey to the underworld was of more significance than all the surrounding real estate—including that occupied by hell.

Since the dawn of history, the sibyl had dominated the Vesuvian region of volcanic fires. The wisest on earth had been helpless before her riddle. In the present day, the feeling of her extraordinary powers emerged clearly from the mass of ancient testimony, even though that testimony was vague and conflicting. It seemed to Alma that the sibyl and the oracular institution opened up two distinct lines of investigation. Could the sibyl's great wisdom and poetic inspiration ever be explained? Perhaps the woman or women who ruled the destinies of kingdoms possessed qualities that would forever elude the excavator's spade. But if archeology was never able to identify the most potent and baffling voice of the ancient world, it could at least shed light on the religious beliefs that were born of, took root in, and flourished from her genius.

Aristotle, Cicero, Livy, and others had sought the key to the sibyl's secrets in some analysis and much speculation. Alma urged her party to seek it in upturned soil. Perhaps in the depth of the rock-hewn chamber beneath the Cumaean acropolis, they might reconstruct the environment of the oracular shrine. Despite the ravages of centuries, the archeologists found the exterior of the sibyl's cave much as Aeneas might have seen it. Skillfully hewn out of rock, it gave, as was evidently intended, the impression of a large, natural opening.

As she explored the deep, recessed vault, Alma saw faint outlines of mystical symbols carved near the entrance. It was here, she realized with a shiver, that people, simple and great, had come from all parts of the ancient world to hear pronouncements revealed to them through the bronze lips of the goddess or to have her decrees inscribed for them on laurel leaves.

The *Aeneid* remained the expedition's lead string in the subterranean labyrinth. The poet's description of the sibyl was accepted as a composite of the legends and traditions surrounding the seer. As she attempted to read between the lines, Alma thought she detected a pathetic undercurrent suggesting enslavement by the rigorous and possibly cruel demands of the sibylline cult running throughout the chronicle of the seer's meeting with Aeneas. It aroused her sympathy as well as her wonder.

The tale revealed how the Trojan hero, passing through the Grove of

Diana, reached the Cumaean acropolis with its golden-roofed Temple of Apollo. Aeneas, summoned by the aged prophetess to her cave, asked her to reveal his future with her own voice. (If the medium used laurel leaves and the wind dispersed them, the prediction was void. Aeneas preferred not to risk this danger.) As the sibyl complied, Virgil described what Alma recognized as the contortions of a trance medium immediately before the "spirit control" took possession of her. Long hair falling about her in disheveled skeins, body shaking convulsively as she gasped for breath, the seer's facial features, a ghostly white, appeared to change.

Suddenly the sibyl's whole being seemed to expand as if she were seized with some violent rage. In this state, she pronounced the oracles that made Aeneas the prophet of Rome's doom. The hero heard that his descendants would rule Italy only to rue their coming when the Tiber ran red with the blood of savage wars. The seer didn't immediately regain her composure, and the Trojan chilled with fear as she flung herself wildly about the cave in an effort to shake off the torturing grip of the spell.

Alma found an ally who shared her fascination for the sibyl when Dr. Vittorio Macchiori, professor of the history of religions at the Royal University of Naples, joined the expedition. He pointed out that the sibyl's frenzied condition was peculiar to the initial states of the worship of both Apollo and Dionysus.

"In order to understand the sibyl," Macchiori explained, "it's necessary to imagine a time when the relationship to a supreme being meant something quite different from what it does today. In the worship of Apollo or Dionysus, the devotee became one with the deity, a merging filled with ecstatic madness. The result, for a few moments at least, was transformation. The frenzy that Virgil must have witnessed and then incorporated into his epic was doubtless a typical scene of frequent occurrence."

Scarcely pausing for breath, Macchiori continued in his professorial manner, "We're certain at any rate that the Cumaean oracle was the goal of a constant stream of travelers. While the average pilgrim probably received the answer to his query on laurel leaves, it's likely that many devotees—especially the rich and powerful ones—were favored with messages from the sibyl's own mouth. Virgil apparently regarded the sibyl as an unconscious prophetess who spoke because she was impelled to by an inward force. We may infer from her refusal to catch or rearrange the fluttering leaves or to recompose the oracles that she was not responsible for what issued from her lips, but made her predictions through an instinct that may even have tormented and dominated her."

Alma was surprised by his conclusions. "You really believe then that the sibyl was real—*I* felt she was—but Dr. Maiuri uncovered some 'mystery' paraphernalia. It made me wonder if the whole thing was a sham."

"You mean the speaking tubes?"

"Well, yes." They were standing beside the sibyl's cave, where a spacious, shelflike gallery had been hollowed out of the trachyte cliff. It had obviously served as a reception hall for the pilgrims. Around the walls were scores of little niches, the size of the terra-cotta lamps carried by Greek and Roman wayfarers. Ages had passed since the lamps were lighted, but the niches were still blackened by smoke from the tiny flames.

Macchiori was silent for a time, perhaps pondering the Apollonian cult whose beginnings remained lost in the dim unrecorded past. "I, myself, helped to excavate a series of underground passages that reach from the ruins of Apollo's temple to the inner sanctuary," he said at last. "We've discovered circular shafts communicating with the temple from the heart of the cave. Each mouth measured about two feet in diameter and was originally topped by a life-size statue of a goddess. Through the bronze head of each ran a little tube, terminating at her half-parted lips. So far we've located fourteen, but Virgil claimed there were one hundred."

Alma nodded. "It does make you wonder a bit about the sibyl's technique."

"Yes," Macchiori agreed, "that and other things. There's a small stairway in the reception room. Have you seen it?" He switched on his flashlight, lighting the way. "The stairs are treacherous, badly blocked, and impossible to navigate now, but I'm certain that once it was a very simple matter for a priestess to mingle with pilgrims who were no doubt sharing their needs and desires with one another. She could then slip away by means of the private stairs to the heart of the cave, where confidences she'd heard were divulged to the sibyl."

It was easy for Alma to imagine the rest of the scenario. Priestesses could then return to distribute numbers corresponding to the statues in the temple. The pilgrim would then stand beside the particular divinity to which he or she had been assigned and listen to the sibyl's pronouncements, perhaps on the very problem innocently confided to a disguised priestess. Alma sighed, shaking her head. "The indication of trickery just makes it all the more puzzling. It's such a curious contrast to the fanatical sincerity described by Virgil."

"A paradox," Macchiori agreed, "and I don't think we need rely solely on Virgil. Everyone who was anyone—not only the wealthiest, but the wisest and most powerful people of the day—consulted the sibyl. *They* didn't rely on leaves or speaking tubes; they had individual consultations. What was it your President Lincoln said: 'You can fool some of the people all of the time and all of the people some of the time, but . . .'?"

"Yes," Alma agreed, smiling. The investigative reporter within was at war with another part of her that sought credibility for the sibyl. There was balm to a troubled heart in the possibility that the seer might have been something more than a metaphoric link between reality and immortality. "It *does* seem as though something valid must have been going on or the influential people wouldn't have kept coming here for all that time—more than a thousand years."

"Indeed," Macchiori nodded, "but it also appears that some sort of complex priest craft was going on, too, employing trickery in which the truly gifted sibyl may have been the most deluded of all, the ultimate victim."

Alma, recalling her mother's card-reading sessions, hated the idea. Some people, she believed, perhaps all people in varying degrees, possessed the gift of intuition. How cruel to make a mockery of it. "What do you suppose the sibyls were like?" she wondered.

"Great age was attributed to them, at least by Virgil. He alluded to what must have been the current belief in his passageway scene—remember? As they returned from the abode of shades, the sibyl revealed to Aeneas an incident from her youth."

Alma remembered the part well. In his gratitude for the seer's guidance, the Trojan vowed to erect a shrine in her honor "even though she be mortal." The sibyl had replied that she might have been a goddess had she accepted the suit of Apollo. The god, she'd explained, had become enamored and offered to grant her dearest wish. Grasping a handful of sand, she had asked that the years of her life might equal the grains she held.

At thirty-six, Alma thought it a marvelous idea, but sighed inwardly at the way reality intruded into myth. It seemed there was no free lunch, not anywhere. Save for the injured vanity of the male, the plan would have worked beautifully. Apollo had complied, but unfortunately, when the sibyl refused to return his love, the god turned the gift into a curse by decreeing that she would live on while her beauty faded and her body withered with the attrition of the years. The tragedy had accelerated over seven centuries when Aeneas came to Cumae and would see half as many more before her years equaled the grains of sand. Her fate, she told Aeneas, was to shrink to a final dissolution, while her voice remained and was respected by future generations.

Alma speculated that the story just might have evolved in the high councils of the cult as a means of deepening the mystery surrounding the prophetess. The theory of a supernaturally prolonged life of one sibyl would explain the line of succession of gifted women to the exalted station. Might it not have been a veil concealing the record of their lives, a shroud flung over their human emotions in the darkness of the cave? The ironclad organization of the priesthood seemed apparent. Against a prying world, the secret of the personalities behind the inscrutable sibylline mask had been preserved for more than a thousand years.

"Ovid suggested reincarnation as an explanation for the continuance of the oracle," Macchiori reminded her.

Alma nodded, considering. The philosophy of reincarnation had grown increasingly appealing since Felipe's death. She speculated often about somehow being reunited with him. How easy to lose herself in dreams, how much wiser—she reminded herself—to keep busy with the work at hand. "Are there any legends of a sibyl's death?" she asked.

"Only two," Macchiori told her. "One of them involved a sibyl from Eritrea on the shores of the Red Sea. Apollo had granted her immortality on the condition that she abandon Eritrea and never behold the soil of her native land. Unfortunately, one day the sibyl received a letter from Eritrea sealed with clay and, beholding in the seal the Eritrean earth, she died on the spot. Her bones were interred in an urn in Apollo's temple."

"That Apollo!" Alma fumed. "Such a troublemaker."

"But such a power source," Macchiori reminded her.

"What about that power?" Alma asked, realizing that she'd never seriously considered the question. "Why was the Cumaean seer thought to be so powerful? Why was Cumae the world center of the cult?"

"The proximity to Rome may have had something to do with it, but also I think the Campi Flegrei—these flaming fields—was particularly adapted to a mystery religion. Then, as now, sulfurous fumes emanated from the soil; and, of course, there's the volcano, Solfatara, with those towering white columns of smoke."

Looking about her, Alma had to agree. It would be difficult to imagine a more dramatic setting. "Could it have been something in the fumes that brought on the sibyl's frenzy, perhaps the very oracles themselves?" she wondered.

Macchiori laughed. "It would certainly have been an extraordinary frenzy; the oracles were written in Greek hexameter, and two Greek interpreters assisted in their reading. Whatever their power source, the books of fate exerted tremendous influence on Roman history, becoming a kind of secret vigilante power, a court of last appeal in times of grave crisis. Those from the ill-fated sibyl of Eritrea were regarded as the most inspired—maybe that's why her bones were kept in the temple. Lacatonius, a priest of the Christian church, wrote in the third century, 'All sibyl songs are public and in use, except those of the Cumaean, whose books are kept secret by the Romans; nor do they hold it lawful for them to be inspected by any except the fifteen men'—presumably priests. That collection forms the basis of the sibylline poetry that's come down to us."

It was difficult for Alma, activist that she was, to imagine the procession of women who, for centuries, spent most of their lives in the dark cave. One had particularly stirred her fancy. She recalled the ethereal young face portrayed on Domenichino's canvas in the Villa Borghese of Rome. The sibyl wore the African turban of the diviner, and her slender fingers clasped the scroll of fate, but Alma imagined that her blue eyes followed some mortal lover with wistful longing.

Before Alma could complete her question, Macchiori responded. "Ah, I can tell you are thinking of Amalthea, no? She is a great favorite in southern Italy." A mischievous glint lit his faded eyes. "I believe that it's her gentle shade, rather than the stern and venerable guide of Aeneas, that walks with us over Campi Flegrei. Tradition has it that her prophecies were widely celebrated. The most renowned figures of the brilliant epoch in which she lived consulted her, but no less regarded was her rare loveliness. Even Agrippina, the mother of Nero and a most noted beauty of her time, was said to have marveled at it.

"But," the professor continued in the flowery manner that reminded Alma of an actor—she would attempt to recapture it in her *Times* article— "there was a trace of human dross in the nearly pure gold of this lovely sibyl's spirit, and the cruel god who always demanded his price had not succeeded in removing her heart when he made her being an instrument for his voice. She had not yet attained desirelessness, the goal of all the mystic paths since the birth of religious aspirations."

Alma smiled; she could guess what was coming next. "A lover, right?"

"Indeed, yes. She and the poet, Lucan, loved each other, but at first refused to recognize it. Amalthea had been drawn to him initially by a strong Platonic affection, and, for the poet, she was a kind of muse. The two often met in the forest, where Lucan composed poetry for her. Then Lucan incurred the wrath of Nero by besting him in a poetry contest, and the mad emperor forbade him to recite in public. The injustice of it drove Lucan into an assassination conspiracy that backfired. Nero ordered him to cut his veins and bleed to death."

Alma shuddered.

"Oh, my dear, such things weren't at all uncommon in those days. The tragic irony of it all was that Amalthea—unaware of what had happened—finally realized the true nature of her feelings for Lucan and resolved to leave Apollo's shrine and forsake her sibylline vows. Just as Nero's order was being carried out, the Campi Flegrei was rent by a violent earthquake. Amalthea, fearing for her lover's safety, asked Apollo for a sign. The word 'death' appeared on the prophetic laurel leaves. Alarmed, she rushed to the forest trysting place where Lucan came each day to compose songs to her.

"To take farewell of her, he'd bound his wounds and gone to the familiar spot near her cave. Before he could summon the somber words to describe his fate, her eyes told him the secret. 'Now I can die content,' he said sadly, 'for I see you love me.'

"Amalthea couldn't account for his words, nor for the sadness. 'I have already given you the devotion of my heart,"￼ she replied, trembling with emotion. 'Now I would give you my life. I break my vows. I renounce the deity who enslaved my youth. I am free, and I am yours.'

"It was too late. The flow of Lucan's blood could not be staunched. He removed the wrappings from his veins and the sybil realized the meaning of the prophesy. Pressing the dying poet to her breast, she forswore Apollo. The earth continued its convulsions, opening where they stood. The lovers, clinging together, sank into the yawning chasm. From the depths, Lucan's words echoed faintly: 'With your love I dream your soul into mine forever.' And Amalthea's reply: 'In your kiss I have found immortality.'

"And this," Macchiori concluded, "was the last time in legend or in history that the voice of the Cumaean sibyl issued from the darkness."

CHAPTER · 12

What the Oracle Said

It was inevitable that Alma's fascination with prophesy would take her to the most famous oracle of them all, the shrine at Delphi.

Her year's study in Naples had ended. While waiting to hear the results of her next scholarship application, Alma decided to make use of the money she'd received from her newspaper and magazine articles to holiday in Greece. It was there that she encountered Eva Palmer, a girlhood friend.

The wealthy Palmer family had had business dealings with Eugene during one of his more prosperous periods. Though a few years older, Eva had taken an interest in Alma, and the two maintained friendly ties until Eva's departure for Bryn Mawr. More than twenty years had passed, but Alma, who'd once had a schoolgirl crush on Eva, would have recognized her anywhere.

Eva was—and remained—absolutely stunning. Married now to the celebrated poet Angelo Sikelianos, she'd become totally Hellenized. When the two women met quite by chance, Alma thought she'd encountered a goddess. Eva's mass of flaming copper hair fell in two heavy braids far below her waist. Her short, pale gold tunic was of pure Macedonian silk, and circling her bare arms was a mantle or *stola* of the same glowing material. Both tunic and mantle had wide borders defined in deeper shades of gold in a design inspired by an ancient Greek vase.

"I made them myself, wove the fabric on my own loom," Eva explained to the admiring Alma. "You might say it was my first adventure into the Greek arts. When Angelo and I moved here, I was rather appalled at the way the peasant women dressed. In the museums, I fell in love with the magnificent works of Phidias, his graceful, rich drapery and beautiful, simple designs, but the present-day women wore plain, coarse clothing and any embroidery—instead of using the original Greek designs—was an imitation of something oriental."

"Well . . ."—Alma hesitated and then plunged in—"can you really expect peasants who're having a hard time even existing to appreciate ancient Greek art forms?"

"My little Alma, still the Bolshevik!" Eva's laugh was low, throaty, and vibrant, just as Alma remembered it. "Of course, I was unreasonable. I realize that now, but I was also, you might say, inspired. I knew that with patient effort and proper example, the women could be taught to imitate some of the ancient methods—that they could be valuable in improving their own local crafts. In order to attract their interest, I set up an experimental weaving center in my own home. I learned to spin and weave and studied the costumes of the ancient Greeks by reading and analyzing the rippling folds of the garments as shown in antique sculpture and painting. Finally, I concluded that the modern Greeks could imitate the wonderful old fabrics by using different combinations of warp and woof in their weaving. For some time I experimented, and everything I learned I taught to the peasant women, until today materials are being woven in Greece that I believe are identical to those of antiquity."

As Eva talked on, enthusiasm lighting her face, Alma noticed that her long fingers toyed absently with a large pendant that was her only ornament. "It's the moonstone, isn't it? Your mother's moonstone—I always loved it."

"Well, don't ever borrow it."

Alma sat back startled. "What are you talking about?"

Eva took off the crystal clear gem. "There's a strange story about it," she explained, handing the pendant to Alma. "For years it was said the family moonstone would bring tragedy to anyone who wore it other than its rightful owner. A few years ago Isadora Duncan was visiting and asked to borrow it. She wanted to wear it for luck to some special recital in Paris. On the very day of the performance, her two young children were drowned in the Seine. Soon afterward, Isadora returned the pendant to me—she brought it to Athens herself rather than risk bringing sorrow to some innocent person to whom she might entrust its delivery."

Alma shuddered, thinking of her own tragedy. "Never fear; I shall *never* ask," she assured her friend, hastily returning the pendant she'd been admiring.

Weaving was just one of Eva's Greek passions, Alma soon discovered. Her interest in ancient music was piqued by the ethnic melodies of peasants. Because their folk music was entirely different from either Western music or that of Oriental countries, Eva became convinced that it bore a direct relationship to the highly developed melodies of the ancient Greeks. Technical information, however, was limited; the music had to be learned by ear. The songs of peasants, shepherds, and bandits weren't written, but merely sung and passed on by memory from generation to generation. Furthermore, they couldn't be written in European notation, nor could they be played on a piano or other instrument with fixed notes.

"To Western ears, the songs sounded pretty monotonous," Eva admitted. "We're just not accustomed to the fine gradations of tone employed. There are forty intervals to the octave as against our twelve. I got a partial solution by studying the music of the Greek Orthodox Church, which is recorded in Byzantine notation. There I found the same strange intervals of half-tones, quarter-tones, and eight-tones on which peasant music is based. Unfortunately, there are very few people in the world who understand the Byzantine notation."

"Why?" Alma asked, her reporter's curiosity coming to the fore. Was there a story here?

"It's really rather sad," Eva lamented. "In the Byzantine notation, the musical literature is as great in bulk as the whole repertory of European music. But, because there has been no instrument on which this music could be played, and because its nomenclature is so difficult to master— fifteen years have been considered the *shortest* time in which it could be thoroughly learned—it has been practically unknown, but," she gulped, pausing for breath, "but, you'll never guess what—"

"What—what?" Alma answered, beginning to feel the tug of her friend's enthusiasm.

"I've located one of the few people in the whole world who has mastered it, a marvelous man, Professor Constantine Psachos, the greatest living authority on Byzantine music. And now he's invented a wonderful pipe organ with a huge keyboard on which the Greek music can be played. I had it built for him in Oettingen, Germany, and its been shipped here. The Orthodox music is quite distinctive. There are eight modes, eight manners of singing, each one having its own scale with intervals entirely different from one another, with its own sharps and flats and having different ways of unfolding the melody and different endings. We're absolutely certain that the little-known, eight-mode style of the church is a direct descendant of the eight modes of pagan Greek music, and, by studying it, we'll be able to approximate the music of Greece's golden age. You can imagine how excited I am! Now Professor Psachos is writing a special score for *Prometheus.*"

"Prometheus?"

"Yes, that's my new project. I'm putting on *Prometheus Bound* at Delphi."

Gulping at her friend's ambition, Alma wondered if the "I" part wasn't something of an exaggeration. Very soon she discovered that it was actually the Delphic Society that was putting on Aeschylus' masterpiece. But then it developed that the Delphic Society *was* Eva Sikelianos; at least she was its soul and its pocketbook.

Eva resumed their friendship with the same enthusiasm that she brought to everything. If Alma suspected that she, herself, was something of a reclamation project along with weaving and music, she did not complain. At thirty-seven, she found herself in something of a quandary as to what to do next—not to mention how to pay for it.

Alma's rather florid writing style was well suited to the flamboyant Sunday supplements popular in newspapers of the 1920's, but her ever-growing fascination with archeology also enabled her to uncover more esoteric subjects, which she turned into crisp, well-crafted articles for prestigious magazines such as *Interior Studio* and *Art and Archaeology.*

She was a natural communicator, a true journalist, whose fresh, original approach and natural enthusiasm allowed her to capture the essence of an often complex subject and make it informative and entertaining to her readers. Yet, talent notwithstanding, Alma had grown increasingly discouraged. Free-lance writing, she'd concluded, was a solitary act of courage performed without witnesses. She missed the lively camaraderie of her newspaper days, but not nearly so much as she missed the security of a weekly paycheck.

It was a dicey business. Periodicals went out of business. Carefully cultivated editors left or retired. The *Times,* her old standby, used less and less of her work. Alma was now competing with well-known scholars whose academic credentials apparently outweighed the nature of their prose in Ochs's opinion. Writing was an all-absorbing pursuit. Alma existed to write every bit as much as she wrote to exist, yet the frustrations involved grew increasingly onerous.

At the University of Southern Italy, her particular area of study had been the role played by the Orphic cult in the shaping of Christian ritual. Her private passion was prophecy. The desire to visit the world-famous oracle at Delphi had brought her to Greece. Perhaps she hoped the sacred site might inspire a sense of personal direction.

Now here was Eva possibly assuming the role of a latter-day priestess illuminating a new path for her that seemed tailor-made. First off, Eva and her handsome husband, Angelo, wouldn't hear of Alma staying anywhere but in their villa at Old Phaleron, a suburb of Athens. Alma had scarcely settled in before discovering that the place was a mecca for the intellectual and artistic elite of the day. Anybody who was anybody found his or her way to the Sikelianoses' doorstep. It was the golden age of Pericles reborn, and Alma, with her immediate sympathetic friendliness and mercurial wit, was in her element.

As a journalist, she had of necessity honed her interviewing skills to perfection. Alma could get *anybody* to talk and was a rapt listener, but, as a free spirit who'd lived, read, and traveled extensively, she was also a brilliant and challenging conversationalist. Quick, lithe, and graceful as she moved about the salon, Alma, in the prime of her beauty, was a distinct social asset to any hostess.

If Eva was delighted, Angelo was even more so. Acclaimed the greatest Greek poet of the day, he longed to see his sphere of influence extended. Very soon he recognized in his wife's old chum the perfect medium. Alma, with her linguistic skill, already possessed a good working knowledge of Greek from her studies at Naples. Now Sikelianos saw to it that she was able to continue her education at the University of Athens.

Before long she was a very busy woman. As if the heady social life that centered about the Sikelianoses wasn't enough to keep her occupied, there were her university studies and soon a survey of Angelo's poetry preparatory to translating it. Recognizing Alma's amazing genius for language, he was anxious to have an English volume of his poetry published. But this was by no means all.

Besides their city villa, the Sikelianoses had a home near Delphi. It was to be the launching pad for Eva's most ambitious project to date, the dream of which she'd only hinted to Alma. A Greek cultural renaissance was only the beginning; Eva intended to establish a world peace center at Delphi. The first test would be the production of a modern festival at the sacred site. It went without saying that both Alma and her typewriter were to be drafted for the cause.

If Alma had reservations, they quickly dissolved at the sight of Delphi, where awe turned to inspiration. Luminous and precipitous, the grandeur of the mountainous landscape, among the most solemn and imposing to be found anywhere in the world, spoke to her of the divine. If peace were ever possible for the race of territorial carnivores known as man, surely this would be its womb. During ancient times, warring factions laid down their arms and gathered every four years at Delphi in peace and harmony to celebrate the festival of Apollo and to compete in his sacred games. Perhaps there was some kind of precedent here. The tradition of a truce might offer hope for a new beginning.

The games were only a part of Delphi's illustrious past. Alma was far more interested in the oracle, for here, just as at Cumae, a priestess had been subsumed into a god—Apollo at work again. Prophecy was the result of their sacred union, but the collective memory of Greece went back further still. There had been a time, the legend said, a time just before Apollo when Gaia, the earth mother, had been worshiped at Delphi, and it was she who had revealed to humanity the natural order of things. Then Apollo appeared and slew Gaia's dragon, Python; after that, it was he who reigned as lord of the site and was responsible for the prophetic responses.

Alma noted with a certain satisfaction that crumbling layers of slate, while conducting cool spring water, also resulted in dangerous landslides that descended upon Delphi again and again in modern as well as ancient times. Obviously, the youthful god of light had not totally vanquished Mother Nature.

Still, Apollo patently dominated the area, and his prophetess, known as Pythia, gave voice to the oracle. There were no gases or vapors, Alma learned; the soil and rock at Delphi, unlike Cumae, was limestone, not volcanic. The Pythia also differed from the Cumaean sibyl in that she was not a trance medium. Though her words were believed to have been inspired by Apollo, she had spoken clearly and calmly in her own voice, uttering not actual predictions, but rather directions or sanctions.

Xenophon had recorded the two kinds of questions usually asked as well as typical responses. In doubt whether to accompany his friend on an expedition into Asia, Xenophon went on Socrates' advice to Delphi and asked in the labored prose of the genre: "To what god should I sacrifice and pray in order to accomplish with best result the journey that I intend, to fare well, and to return in safety?" The Pythia replied: "To Zeus, the King."

Socrates was disgusted with him for putting the cart before the horse. "You asked the wrong question," he chided his young friend. "You should have asked whether it was better to go on the expedition or stay home."

Clay tablets showed that both questions were couched in established formulas. Consultants queried either, "Is it better and preferable that I/we do X?" or, "To what god should I sacrifice in order to have success?" The response, channeled by the Pythia, came in the first case by picking up one of two rods, in the second from shaking a dish holding lots, so that one of them jumped out. The latter worked as well if Apollo was asked to declare which of various proposals had divine approval—which, for instance, of several rival chieftans should command a joint military action, or which among a number of mythical heroes should be honored as the tribe's progenitor.

There was no questioning the authority of the oracle. It was the god who had pronounced it through the agency of his servant; his wisdom had settled the matter. As an oracle by rod or lot cost less than one actually voiced by the Pythia, and because the majority of questions asked in a moment of indecision or dilemma permitted response by lot, this form of delivery was most popular. But Delphi would never have exerted the universal influence that prevailed for centuries if no spoken oracles had been given. Just as muses inspired creativity, so did Apollo fill his priestess with divine knowledge. From him, she received the insight that permitted her to draw on the full range of human experience.

Sometimes the oracle was clear-cut, as in the prediction that Athens would be destroyed by the Persian invasion, but for the most part it was oblique. The message sent King Croesus was classic: "If you cross the Halys, you will reduce a mighty power." Regarding the message as a promise of victory, he set off on a campaign that would cost him his own "mighty power." After that debacle, it was concluded that the oracle "neither states nor conceals but indicates," and prudent querists sought the aid of interpreters known as exegetes.

Noting the frequent use of the Delphic oracle by oligarchic Sparta, Alma found herself speculating as to the kind of advice Felipe might have received had he approached the Pythia. Apollo appeared to her as something of a conservative. What else could his traditional adages—"Know yourself" and "Nothing in excess"—mean but a warning that humans should be conscious of their limitations? Certainly, Apollo was not about change. He was a god of static forms, not dynamic forces. Small wonder he favored oligarchic systems of government over potentially volatile democracies where nearly everyone had the right to vote.

Alma laughed outright when her research took her to the submission of the Cnidians' plan to cut a channel across their peninsula. Apollo advised resoundingly against it: "If Zeus had wanted to make Cnidus an island, he would have done so." Obviously, Apollo, the son of Zeus, was a god of the status quo.

Despite her personal reservations about Apollo's politics, Alma could readily understand Eva's enthusiasm and share much of it. The Delphic ideal was practical and essentially peaceful. Alma saw Apollo's greatest gift as a realistic understanding of life patterns within the frame of which the future could be indicated. Advising, not foretelling, was the real thrust of his efficacy. The god's knowledge, as manifested by the Pythia, demonstrated a profound understanding of the fundamental causes of turmoil. He seemed to take particular notice of famine and discord, which were often caused by overpopulation, and reacted by recommending the establishment of new colonies on foreign shores. His directives proved so reliable that, without them, one hardly dared establish a daughter city. Besides being authorized in the adventure by Delphi, the leader of an expedition also learned the most favorable sites for a new venture.

Alma was impressed that the underlying motivation was not the development of a new power base, but rather the preservation of settled conditions at home by providing the surplus population with an opportunity to lead a healthy political life somewhere else—but yes, of course, Apollo's ordinances went with them.

Information about the Pythia was more accessible than that surrounding the Cumaean sibyl. The Pythia was, Alma learned, an elderly, worldly, though unmarried, woman chosen from among the highest-ranking families in the area. Very likely, she took part in the priests' deliberations over questions that had been submitted by querists. Yet, at least theoretically, when stirred by her higher calling and conscious of becoming the god's instrument, she mounted her tripod, it was Apollo's wisdom that she pronounced.

Realizing that it was the oracle around which everything else revolved, Alma marveled at the power that these women wielded. When, after the battle of Cannae, the Romans believed that the terrible disaster could only be repaired through the intervention of gods previously neglected, a delegation was dispatched to Delphi charged with learning from the oracle exactly which deities and rites would enable them to overcome the power of Hannibal. The Pythia's instructions worked, or at least everyone thought they did, and, Alma reasoned, wasn't that the very same thing?

It was easy for her to see clear parallels with the Maya. Again and again the priests of Yucatán had sought the future in the stars atop lofty pyramids or in the depth of sacred wells. Painful as it was to contemplate, the sense of destiny pervading Felipe's life continued to haunt Alma, driving her to reach for elements of truth in myth and legend. Wasn't the whole concept of prophecy—of destiny—merely a metaphor for humanity's desire to find a kind of order in the random chaos of life?

While Alma pondered metaphysics and the politics of prophecy, Eva was enthralled by the spectacle of Delphi itself. The sacred sanctuary had not only been the seat of the oracle, but also a center where both athletes and artists consecrated their triumphs to Apollo. It was the latter offering that Eva hoped to revive.

One day, walking beside her hostess up the steep hillside trail, it seemed to Alma that the entire splendor and tragedy of Greece were spread before her. Marble treasuries of once mighty kingdoms crowded closely around the sacred way, which climbed obliquely upward. City-states as distant as

Marseilles had sent tribute. Surely those attending the ancient festival, seeing the enormous number of costly gifts or the many splendid buildings, must have been keenly aware that this was the spiritual and artistic center of the world, in fact the very *omphalos,* or navel of the earth. Here was the common hearth of the Hellenes from whose flames the fires for local sanctuaries extinguished during the Persian War were rekindled.

It was this splendor, this spirit, that Eva hoped to recapture. Pointing to the ruins of the classic theater in the shadow of Mount Parnassus, she described her plans. Ancient dances, suggested by designs on antique vases and by bas-reliefs dating as early as 600 B.C., would be performed. Professor Psachos was busy composing music in the classical mode, and she herself was designing costumes that would be handwoven from silk born of her own mulberry trees.

Alma was quickly swept along on the wave of her friend's enthusiasm. On the way to becoming a professional houseguest, she could scarcely avoid it. Fortunately, the scope of the project and its grand concept could not help but engage her. The Delphic Festival, held May 9 and 10, 1927, was a glorious event. Eva's costumes in soft shades of blue, mauve, yellow, green, and purple, suggested the various moods of the Aegean Sea as they rippled and flowed like waves over the supple young bodies of the chorus of "oceanaides," fifty beautiful young women from the most prominent families in Athens.

The festival received international recognition. A *London Times* reviewer gushed:

> *Art and nature combined to produce a perfection, and the light effects as the sun set behind Parnassus were heavenly. While eagles soared over the theater, the musical setting enchanted the ears. It was scored for harps, woodwind, and brass. The Prometheus music had a free harmonic spirit in keeping with the majestic beauty of the surroundings.*
>
> *M. and Madame Sikelianos were accorded a tremendous ovation at the end of the play, and the lining of the route from the theater back to the village by torchbearers accentuated the termination of an artistic festival unprecedented in modern Greece. Archeologists agree that the production in its details was archeologically in keeping. Although the present performance was*

*probably a financial loss, hopes are generally expressed that it will
be possible to repeat this Delphic Festival annually.*

The reviewer's surmise was correct. Everyone agreed that *Prometheus
Bound* was a creative success. Too bad it wasn't a financial one. "Well,
money, what's money"—Eva shrugged. "This was the beginning. We'll do
it again and recoup everything. In the meantime . . ."

She was off and running with more plans for the Delphic Society and
soon had Alma corresponding with Jane Addams, the pioneer social
worker; and Henry Morganthau, later secretary of the treasury; and the
presidents of Harvard and Princeton. Angelo also kept Alma busy with
translations, and a volume of his poetry was soon ready for publication. The
Greek government was delighted at the prospect of the international ac-
claim that they were certain would be accorded to the work of the man
considered a national treasure.

At a special ceremony, the Order of Welfare was conferred on Alma.
Walking home that night through the pine grove that fringed the Sikelianos
villa, Eva made an announcement. Alma was reminded of the Pythia as her
friend turned dramatically to face them. "I have made a decision," she said.
The moonlight shone on her great mass of auburn hair, and the line of her
silken tunic was as purely classic as any ancient sculpture.

"It is time we returned to America. You will take care of things here,
Angelo. Alma and I will visit our friends and families in San Francisco. We
will then stop in New York for a few months."

"A few months!" her husband repeated in dismay.

"Yes, the time has come for the Delphic Society to expand. We will
establish our first colony in New York."

Alma's family. Standing (l. to r.): Walter, Alma, and Murial. Seated: Florence, Adelaide, Prescott, Isabel, and Euegene. (Courtesy: The Sullivan family collection)

Alma dressed for a family gathering. (Courtesy: The Sullivan family collection)

San Quentin front gate, circa 1928.

E. H. Thompson standing by dredge, 1907, Chichén Itzá.
(Courtesy: Peabody Museum, Harvard University)

Thompson's hacienda at Chichén Itzá, Yucatán, Mexico.
(Courtesy: Peabody Museum, Harvard University)

Alma in native dress on her first visit to the Yucatán in 1923. (Courtesy: The Pablo Bush Romero collection)

Felipe Carrillo Puerto as a young man. (From the author's collection)

Ricardo Palmerín, one of the composers of "La Peregrina." (From the author's collection)

FESTIVAL EN YUCATAN

Un aspecto del festival verificado en Yucatán, con motivo de la inauguración de la carretera a Chichén Itzá

Cuadro de señoritas que ejecutaron la "Danza Sagrada", en Chichén Itzá", uno de los números más atrayentes del festival

Ejecución de la "Danza Sagrada"

El señor Gobernador de Yucatán, pronunciando su discurso en el idioma de la raza, durante los festivales que presidieron a la inauguración de la nueva carretera

The opening of the road to Chichén Itzá. (From the author's collection)

Workers on a henequen plantation in the early 1920's.
(Courtesy: The Universidad Autónoma de Yucatán Facultad de Ciencias Antropologicas Collection)

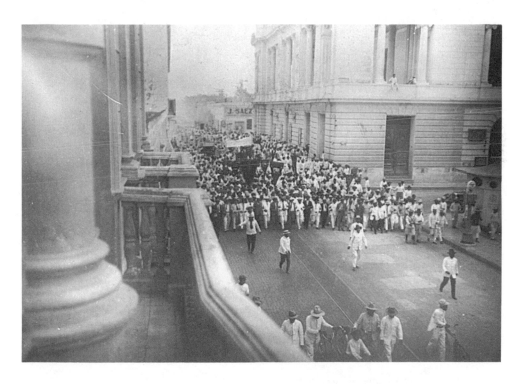

A gathering of Felipe's socialist party in Merida in the early 1920's.
(Courtesy: The Universidad Autónoma de Yucatán Facultad de Ciencias Antropologicas Collection)

Members of the "Feminista League" formed by Felipe Carrillo Puerto.
(Courtesy: The Universidad Autónoma de Yucatán Facultad de Ciencias Antropologicias Collection)

Felipe's honor guard in Merída.
(Courtesy: The Universidad Autónoma de Yucatán Facultad de Ciencias Antropologicas Collection)

The Carrillo Puerto brothers
(clockwise from the top):
Wilfrido, Benjamin, Edesio,
and Felipe.
(From the author's collection)

Mural by Diego Rivera depicting the
martyred Felipe Carrillo Puerto.
(From the author's collection)

Byron de Prorok on the dunes south of Carthage. (From the author's collection)

A diver from de Prorok's expedition to locate Atlantis off the Tunisian coast with salvaged amphorae. (From the author's collection)

Eva Sikelianos in costume for the production of "Prometheus Bound." (From the author's collection)

Alma with the poet, Angelo Sikelianos, in Greece, 1927.
(Courtesy: The Sullivan family collection)

Alma's dive as reported in "American Weekly." (From the author's collection)

Alma in 1928, shortly after her move to New York. (Courtesy: The Sullivan family collection)

Alma with José Clemente Orozco. (From the author's collection)

Alma back at Chichén Itzá. (Courtesy: The collection of Pablo Bush Romero)

Alma—picture used for her U.S. lecture tour in 1960.
(Courtesy: The collection of Pablo Bush Romero)

Pablo Bush Romero holding a skull he recovered diving in the sacred cenote at Chichén Itzá.
(Courtesy: The collection of Pablo Bush Romero)

Pablo Bush Romero beside Alma's grave.
(Courtesy: The collection of Pablo Bush Romero)

Alma's funeral, 1967. (Courtesy: The collection of Pablo Bush Romero)

PART IV

CHAPTER · 13

Prometheus Unbound

In early 1928 Alma's girlhood dream of living in Greenwich Village actually came true. The apartment was perfect; it even had a "past."

"Maksim Gorky used to live here," Syud Huessain told Alma as he handed her the lease. Huessain, a Moslem disciple of Gandhi, was editor of the *New Orient* and a frequent lecturer on Indian independence. He'd become a friend of Alma's and an active supporter of the Delphic Society. If Eva had reservations about the revolutionary associations, they were forgotten when Alma showed her the apartment. "My dear, you were right; the vibrations are divine!"

Perhaps they were, for soon the women were referring to their new quarters as the "Ashram." The Indian name was selected in honor of Mahatma Gandhi, whom both women greatly admired. They regarded the apartment as appropriately named for a number of reasons. Like the dwelling and teaching center of the Hindu leader—the celebrated ashram, or shelter, at Wardha—their Manhattan home was dedicated to communal

uses; and, again like Gandhi's ashram, theirs was the headquarters of a
cultural movement with a philosophic base. Moreover, because of its Indian
associations, distinguished spokespeople for the independence movement
were accustomed to gravitating there.

Soon the Ashram's activities were worthy of its colorful past. Creative
spirits from many lands gathered around the fireplace. The guest list was
a roster of members of many of the arts and professions: poets, dancers,
philosophers, archeologists, scientists, and theater people. Largely
through Alma's efforts, these were joined by men and women devoted to
public causes as directors of or associated with humanitarian organizations,
for the goal of both women continued to be the reestablishment of ancient
Delphi, the *omphalos,* or navel of the earth, as a center of universality and
the source of a peaceful new world.

The decor of the living room reflected their passion. Around three sides
of the long room were divans covered with hand-loomed woolen textiles
and comfortably backed with brightly colored square *sakouli* of primitive
patterns converted into cushions. The handwoven rugs and vivid silk hangings, the hammered brass, the low, carved, cedarwood chairs and tables,
the brilliantly glazed ceramics, and the embroidered linens had been made
by skilled native craftspeople and brought from Greece.

It seemed to Alma in retrospect that she'd scarcely settled into the new
quarters at 12 Fifth Avenue, and begun laying the public relations foundation for the 1930 performance of *Prometheus,* when the course of her life
was changed suddenly and forever.

Though Alma could scarcely have realized it when the lease was signed,
the apartment, with its commanding view of Washington Square and its
triumphal arch, was a portent of events to come. Soon the arch would
symbolize for her the dreams of thousands of struggling artists irresistibly
drawn to the area. Hardly a day passed that someone didn't call with the
hope that the Ashram might sponsor an artist with a reception or that Alma
might write an article, arrange an introduction . . . it went on and on.

Then one day she received a call from Anita Brenner, a young writer who
shared her fascination with Mexico. "We have a mutual acquaintance,"
Anita announced. "He's a celebrated artist, but sad, lonely, and neglected."
Anita didn't add "impoverished"; she didn't need to. Both women recognized a too-familiar pattern.

"Someone I know?" Alma asked tentatively. There were so many
causes, so little time—almost none for herself.

"Surely you remember José Clemente Orozco?"

Of course she did! The name triggered a parade of memories, many of them painful. Had only six years elapsed since that first trip to Mexico City? It was a moment before Alma could bring herself to speak. "Oh, I remember him so well, those wicked political cartoons and the magnificent frescoes at the National Preparatory School."

"That's the man, but he's fallen on bad times. He's here in New York. No one knows him, and he's flat broke."

Alma was shocked and incredulous. She regarded Orozco as a genius whose epic murals had not only revived the long-lost technique of true fresco but substantially enriched the classic medium.

"I really don't know what, if anything, can be done for him," Anita admitted. "He isn't easy to be around. As a rule, he's either unhappy or furious. He has the habit of pain."

Alma understood the latter well.

Her first impression of Orozco against the simple, austere background of his little studio was puzzling. Not quite forty-five, the artist looked several years younger. Slender and of medium height, his youthful build, tiny cropped mustache, and fine-textured wavy black hair were vaguely debonair. Alma noted that Orozco's suit was carefully pressed, the garnet red tie clipped into place. The artist's meticulous neatness extended to the well-scrubbed cleanliness of his sparsely furnished quarters. On his small worktable, tubes of pigment had been laid out in orderly arrangement. Well-washed brushes, placed according to size, protruded from glass jars. Recalling the radical carictures in which the artist portrayed himself as an unkempt, wild-eyed anarchist, Alma was surprised by the air of gentle efficiency about the man before her who might easily have modeled for a portrait of an earnest, responsible, "solid" citizen.

Had Alma not known about the distressing condition of the artist's finances, she would never have guessed that grave worries burdened him. As Alma renewed the acquaintance, she marveled at the illusion of high morale that his rigid discipline and intense pride had created. Even more amazing was his capacity for the sustained physical labor demanded by his enormous mural projects. Realizing that the fresco medium requires strong manual pressure with a trowel, a variety of incidental chores, and intense concentration over long working periods, she was poignantly aware that his left coat sleeve was folded back to disguise the absence of a hand.

Alma sensed how bleak the previous winter in New York must have been for the artist as he spoke of his family. Orozco's voice became animated as he handed her a group snapshot of his wife, Margarita, and their three children. Smiling from her mother's lap was a dark-eyed, curly-headed baby girl, Eugenia Lucrecia. Standing manfully on either side were two small boys, Alfredo and Clemente, Jr. The picture had been taken in the doorway of their cheerful, white-walled home on Avenida Madrid in Coyoacan, a charming suburb of Mexico City.

The six months since his arrival in December 1927 had been *muy duro*—"very hard." With amusing gestures, he demonstrated how nearly every morning that winter he'd had to dig himself out of the snow-blocked entrance to his subterranean dwelling, a basement apartment on Riverside Drive.

"But why did you come?" Alma wanted to know.

Orozco outlined his hopes and plans, attempting to bring her up to date on developments in the Mexican art world—developments that had ground to a standstill. Frequently when swept along by the emotional current of an idea, a Spanish phrase would fill a void in his English vocabulary. "There is nothing for me in Mexico professionally. You see," he emphasized, his early reticence melting, "I am a *public* painter. For public painting, one needs walls—big walls. Here you have such fine walls—such pretty walls." He glanced with longing through the window of his tiny studio where a skyscraper could be seen thrusting its mighty bulk behind a row of small dwellings across the street, then laughed in good humored frustration at the inadequacy of his English to describe Manhattan's towering forms.

For Alma it was wonderful to hear Spanish spoken again.

As they talked, she noticed a dozen or so canvases facing the wall and asked to see them.

"You will not find them cheerful," he replied, placing them one by one on the none-too-substantial easel next to the one window.

It was hard not to smile at the understatement. Each canvas was undeniably cheerless, each a synthesis of Mexico's revolutionary struggle that had brought death to an estimated two million human beings and untold agony to a whole nation before running its bloody course. The starkness of the subject matter itself and the focus of overwhelming emotional power in its presentation was painful, yet she could feel the sense of mysticism that was so distinctly Mexican still dominating the macabre.

Alma scarcely knew what to say. It was a time when most New York painters confined themselves to apples and bananas on tidy kitchen tables, to luscious *dames au toilette* or glimpses of lively Riviera beaches with an occasional red barn as a bold patriotic assertion.

As though reading her mind, the artist shrugged. *"Si,* I realize they do not reflect the mood here. They are not *suave y armonioso."*

Alma couldn't help but laugh. "Sweet and harmonious," they were not! Orozco's canvases portrayed death with life as only an incident. The subject matter, born of his own poignant contact with the revolution's toll on Mexican manhood, approached death's mystery with the authority of a timeless, universal statement. Each picture spoke intimately to the human heart. The artist's message—"I know your pain; I comprehend your loss"—would have been equally intelligible to a Chinese, a Berber from the Atlas, or a Parisian boulevardier.

As Alma studied the paintings, she felt as if she were attending a funeral as the only mourner. Orozco had stripped death to its symbolic essentials—the white winding sheet, the flickering flame of the candle, a weeping woman, her black shawl drawn tightly about her head as she sat beside a silent corpse in blind anguish. As a spectator, Alma shared the subject's vigil, read what was in her heart, followed her thoughts in their dazed and helpless surrender to the common fate, knowing that one who walked with her yesterday would not walk with her tomorrow or ever again.

Alma didn't attempt to rationalize her sudden resolve to help José Clemente Orozco pursue his career in the United States. There seemed sufficient reason for the action in the fact that a great artist was friendless and in need during a period of creative crisis.

Everything was against it. At the time Alma was wholly absorbed in her own life and work. Her only association with art had been as a student. She was fully aware of the difficulty of launching the uncompromising Orozco upon New York's already monopolized art community. Yet it was clear to her that an artist of Orozco's caliber deserved, demanded, recognition. Alma was determined to provide the exposure that would, she was certain, insure that recognition.

There could be no long-range campaign. In a few months she would return to Greece with Eva to meet her next commitment as the translator of the Sikelianos poems. In the meantime, Alma intended to introduce Orozco's work to every conceivable exhibitor and buyer; surely somewhere in her circle there must be some perceptive gallery owner with the vision and enterprise to sponsor him.

Time was vital to the artist. His financial situation demanded immediate attention if he were to continue for even one more month his heavy struggle in the New York art arena. The support of his family, filial duties to his mother, his own livelihood—these were serious and pressing problems. At the creative level, it was urgent that the artist have the peace of mind and freedom from embarrassment necessary to cope effectively with the challenge of his new and different environment.

What he needed was a commission. Alma thought immediately of Eva—a portrait of Eva.

The next day, Orozco called at the Ashram, a portfolio of his wash drawings tucked under his arm, work that would one day be celebrated as the "Mexico in Revolution" series. Over preserved orange blossoms and rose-flavored Turkish coffee, the three discussed the pacific doctrines of Jesus and Buddha, Lao-tzu, Zoroaster, Walt Whitman, Emerson, and Gandhi—everything it seemed, except Orozco's painting, his career. A flood of ideas emerged as to how these doctrines might be applied to the emerging conflicts of the time in ways that might be consistent with the highest ideal of civilized behavior and yet realistic in their approach to the primal impulses of individuals and groups. The stock of the League of Nations was at a low point in 1928, yet Orozco was adamant that some world agency must take its place. Humanity's sole hope for survival, he believed, lay in a strong and permanently functioning body that was empowered to settle differences between nations by negotiation. The day must come, he assured the two women, when spokespeople for all the peoples of the earth—bound together by a new moral code—would gather around a conference table on terms of equality and respect for the solution of their common problems.

The artist could hardly have imagined that he was actually painting in words the precise image of the "Brotherhood" panel that he was to paint in fresco two years later on the walls of the New School of Social Research in New York. Nor could he know then that the spokespeople for all races and creeds, to be seated at this envisioned table of universality, would be drawn from distinguished models whom he was soon to meet in the Ashram's living room.

Eva listened eagerly and then explained to Orozco that the concrete, operative realization of his concept of brotherhood was the lifelong dream of Angelo, her poet-philosopher husband. She explained how for twenty years she had worked with him in an effort to restore world harmony in the spirit of the ancient Amphictyonic League, which for several centuries had functioned at Delphi as a precursor, she believed, of the League of Nations.

Where other efforts to unite humanity directed by militarists and politicians had failed, her Delphic Society hoped to succeed by bringing together the intellectuals, the great minds, the true elite of the earth in order that they might pool their genius for the advancement of mankind. "The mountaintops see one another," she added, "while the valleys do not. Creation and achievement at the highest level in any land is always understood by creators at the same level in other lands."

Alma, sensing how elitist this must sound to the Mexican revolutionary, tactfully pointed out that Orozco's work transcended even this most lofty ideal. His drawings of war could be understood by every mother—however humble and unschooled—in the world.

He nodded, explaining, "In the tragedy of war, time and place are not important. In Mexico, the fighting men of the revolution wore huaraches and sombreros—when they had them. The ancient Greek warriors wore white-crested helmets and classic sandals, but in both epochs the suffering was the same, for woman's sorrow is universal. Everywhere the waste of youth is equally senseless." Orozco grew more and more intense, frequently lapsing into Spanish, and Alma found herself translating for Eva. "The cruelty, the brutality, the stupidity are the same in all countries and in all periods—except that now war is more sinister than ever because the toll of life increases as weapons of mass destruction are steadily perfected."

Idealistic Alma was rhapsodic, recalling the meeting years later in her biography *Orozco.* "Nothing less than an aesthetic miracle could have brought together such a painter and such a subject. For on that June day in 1928, Orozco saw Eva Sikelianos as an embodiment of the integral beauty that was Greece."

Actually, Orozco's point of view was a bit more cynical. Alma would have been surprised indeed, and Eva horrified, if they could have seen his reaction expressed in a letter to a fellow artist written that day,

Indians from Greece shall be introduced to civilization. Same as in Mexico, the same worn-out cliche. Greek folk art shall be

*fostered—their serapes are just like ours—dancing there shall be
to the tune of Greek bagpipes. All that will happen in Delphi, plus
Olympic Games, and for a finale, a play, "Prometheus."*

*Thus plans an aged lady, an American millionairess, wed to
the Greek poet, Sikelianos. A beautiful woman, Miss Alma Reed,
is active in the goings-on. She admires me and bought one of the
tragic drawings.*

Alma, in the new intermediary role she had created for herself, often found
it difficult to reconcile the backgrounds of both her benefactor and her new
protégé. It was hard to remember that the themes of Orozco's revolutionary drawings, subjects tragically familiar to herself, were totally foreign to
Eva's experience. The most terrifying and brutal works were interwoven
with events in her own life. Scarcely a day had passed in the last four years
that she had not involuntarily reconstructed them in her own mind. She was
unable to obliterate the memory of the cemetery wall in Mérida where
Felipe had been assassinated. Even though she'd confronted the documen-
tary photographs in Yucatán, Alma had to literally force herself to look at
Orozco's drawing, "Against the Wall," with the blindfolded victims drop-
ping before the fusillade or kneeling in their last agonies to receive the coup
de grace.

The drawing that best embodied to her the artist's most poignant and
insistent message was "The Wounded." Her funds limited as usual, Alma
was still determined to have it. The work that she purchased that afternoon
was not only a treasured possession, but a means of both morally and
materially supporting the artist. The scene depicted was a railroad station
hastily converted into a field hospital. Its floor was strewn with the dead,
the dying, and the mutilated. Sitting upright in the foreground was a quadru-
ple amputee, a nude youth with his stumps of arms and legs swathed in
bandages. His eyes, too, were bandaged, but an accusing gaze seemed to
burn through the cloth to direct a curse upon an insane world that could
find no better use for his virile young manhood than to hack it to pieces.

Within a week Orozco was a regular feature at the Ashram. His skill with
a single hand at performing all kinds of physical tasks was a constant source
of amazement to everyone. He deftly set up his easel at the south end of
the living room, where a large window looked down on Washington Square.
That working setup was to remain just as the artist arranged it long after
Eva's portrait was completed. Soon the spot was known as "Orozco's

corner," and it was here over a period of months that he was to paint a least a dozen important oils for his first New York exhibition.

Alma would recall later in her biography,

> *Each day, after painting, Orozco would carefully remove the easel and other equipment to a room at the rear of the apartment which he had dubbed the* pulquería. *His subtle humor took varied forms. Later, he decorated odd pieces of home-made furniture and painted two canvases for the adornment of what he called the Ashram's "Mexican Sector." The smaller of the pictures showed a band of little cupids holding a scroll in which appeared the well known* pulquería *slogan:* echate la otra, *an invitation "To have another," with romantic instead of tippling implications conveyed by the feminine ending of* otra. *The larger oil,* The Temptress, *depicted a lush-full bosomed blond, seated in semi-nude splendor upon a serpent-encircled throne, while a thin-shanked and considerably less deadly appearing male crouched humbly before her.*
>
> *Orozco's finishing touch to the room's exotic decor was a long, narrow, ornately lettered sign reading* El Atoron *(literally, a holdup), a favorite name for the drinking shops patronized by the Mexican proletariat.* El Atoron *designates the popular alibi of the philandering Mexican patron who, having spent the night at a* pulquería *or some equally seductive haunt of forbidden pleasure, returns home in the small hours minus his week's wages. To appease his wife's wrath, the culprit dramatically relates how a terrible creature (it is not clear whether human, animal or just plain demon) gripped him by the leg as he was dutifully trudging homeward along the road and, having robbed him of his last peso, held him prisoner until dawn, when the monster vanished with the crowing of a cock. The amusing pictures, the still more amusing furniture, and the signboard were painted in the gaudy ultramarine and vermilion with dashes of bright yellow favored by the professional* pulquería *decorators.*

Possibly the decor was a subtle declaration of masculine independence on the artist's part. He was openly critical of the gifted Dutch poet Leonard Van Hoppen calling him shy and pusillanimous because he frequently altered his work in response to suggestions from the women who frequented the Ashram. Well aware that many were wealthy socialites cultivated by Eva or Alma for their potential financial benefit to Greek revival and/or Indian independence, he regarded them as dilettantes and stood ready to resist the slightest possibility of undue feminine interference.

Once when guests were gathered around the tea table, someone asked how Orozco had lost his left hand. The artist was casual, matter-of-fact, as he explained how he'd been experimenting with chemicals as a seventeen-year-old student when an explosion destroyed his left hand and badly shattered the other.

Casually, he assured the sympathetic group that his reaction to the accident had been one of relief. "I was studying to be an architect—the practical thing to do—but this is a very social occupation in Mexico. Architects enjoy great prestige and even carry a title; they are prominent in diplomatic circles, ornaments of society. My accident had suddenly made me unfit for all that. My first thought was, 'Now, at last, I can be a painter.' "

Alma, who was coming to know the artist very well, recognized his sincerity, but was also aware of Orozco's aesthetic preoccupation with hands; they appeared frequently as a motif in his work, surely indicating a subconscious awareness of his physical lack as well as his tactile sense. She knew, too, that the accident had also impaired the artist's vision and hearing.

Working for the first time in three years under conditions of economic security and realistically based hope, Orozco painted daily for the rest of the summer and into the winter of 1928. In rapid succession, he turned out several major canvases and a number of color sketches for future development.

Eva had paid several hundred dollars for her portrait and had purchased Alma's favorite of the new oil paintings, "The White House," as a gift for her.

Ashram evenings were devoted to literature and philosophy. Often Alma recited her translations of Sikelianos's epic poems. The artist felt inspired by both the medium and the message. He thought a poetic reference to a new generation of gods particularly splendid. But she, concerned that he might feel somehow left out, overwhelmed by so much Hellenic fervor, was careful to accent the similarities she saw linking Greece and Mexico.

There was, she pointed out, the same primitivism, the same good taste in shaping and coloring objects of daily use, the same ferocity in defense of liberty. Alma brought out snapshots taken on her journeys, pointing out that photographs of Greek farmers standing with their burros in front of their huts might well have been taken for photographs of Mexicans.

The artist was touched; despite his talent and confidence, the ambience of the Ashram could be daunting. One day Greeks would come, among them Dr. Kalimacos, patriarch of the Greek Orthodox Church of New York. Orozco couldn't help but be impressed by the sight of Alma conversing with him in what appeared to be perfect Greek. Another day there would be Hindus, bronze-faced and turbaned, devoted followers of Mahatma Gandhi. Sarojini Naidu would make her majestic entrance, followed by a train of young women secretaries, all clad in saris of silk and gold. Mme. Naidu, a close associate of Gandhi's, had been educated at Oxford and filled Orozco with envy at her command of English. There was another guest as well, also a brilliant spokesperson, who, it was said, was directly descended from Muhammad. Alma, along with the other ladies, was "quite bowled over," the artist confided to a friend, but he was forced to add that the potential rival gave a series of magnificent lectures thoroughly documented and most instructive upon comparative religion.

One night they were all invited by Van Noppen to his home on Staten Island. The poet deferred to Alma, who recited Sikelianos's Delphic poems, among them "Prologue to Life," "Calypso," "Resurrection," and frag- ments of his tragedies, *The Sybil, Daedalos,* and *Asclepios.* Dr. Kalimacos rose and solemnly declared: "To the Greeks, all true artists the world over, of whatever period, are Greeks." Orozco and Van Noppen bowed their heads while the Greek patriarch crowned them with laurel wreaths and bestowed new names upon them. Orozco was baptized with the name Panselenos, a brilliant Greek muralist of Byzantine times.

The ferry ride back to Manhattan was enchanted, the night clear, the full moon reflecting as though on polished ebony. The artist dreamed many dreams, saw many images, not the least of them the worldly and beautiful woman beside him.

The Hellenic community that had now embraced him evinced much contempt for Rome. Greece alone was the creator of beauty. Rome was monstrous, hard, heavy, the home of slaves and despots. That didn't inhibit Eva from having as one of her closest friends a Roman princess who frequently invited her along with Alma and Orozco to her elegant residence. In the princess's grand salon there were neither chairs nor divans, but rather polished floors strewn with soft, sensuous bearskins and silken cushions. Orozco would never forget the image of Alma in that setting, her white perfumed body shrouded in silk.

The artist's presence brought about a change in the Ashram's evening programs. Previously devoted chiefly to poetry, philosophy, and music, now it was decided to set aside time for art discussions. For the first, centered around Orozco, the walls of three rooms in the apartment were appropriated for his work, with other paintings hanging in the reception room.

Limited to sixty guests, this event, held in late September of 1928, was Orozco's first one-man show in the United States. No longer did he feel like a prophet crying in the wilderness; at last he was experiencing the satisfaction of finding himself honored in his own time and in a foreign country by a discriminating audience drawn from many lands.

The critical success of the event made it possible for Alma to set up a two-week exhibition of the wash drawings in the "Mexico in Revolution" series at the Marie Sterner Gallery at 9 East 57th Street. It was she who paid for the framing of the drawings as well as for the printing and mailing of the exhibition catalogs and the gallery guarantees.

When Orozco demurred, Alma bravely assured him that she regarded his works as beyond price, and therefore he would always possess the means of repaying her.

Alma had thought herself fortunate to have talked the well-connected Marie Sterner into agreeing to the show. On October 10, 1928, as she and Orozco welcomed guests beneath the newly hung drawings, Alma began to have misgivings. The rococo Nile green and gilt decor was an incongruous setting for Orozco's virile creations. She could not rid herself of the illusion that the paintings were glowering down with indignant scorn at the guests, as they sipped their cocktails and gossiped in a studied manner about art and literary celebrities. Orozco smiled blandly, his face a polite mask, as cultural issues were discussed and disposed of between nibbled petits fours. In marked contrast, his black-and-white dramas suggested, in their enormous implications, giant cacti of the windswept Mexican desert vainly trying to accommodate their bulk to a a hot house filled with delicate, short-lived blooms.

The lorgnetted matrons and their paunchy escorts who'd responded to the invitation—largely, Alma realized, out of deference to Marie Sterner, a grande dame of the art world—showed far more interest in Sterner's Biederman furniture than Orozco's portrayal of revolutionary violence. Too late she recognized that the gallery, like many other chic East Side establishments, channeled its publicity mainly through society columns. Younger art collectors and intellectuals were noticably absent.

Years later, Alma recalled,

> *The 1928 New York art season coincided with the full momentum of an era that suggested Roman Imperial decadence. Their common excesses, born of unbridled power and irresponsible wealth, were reflected in the vogue of extremes—the trivial and the bizarre. In both epochs the considered judgment of the mind, the spontaneous impulse of the heart, were at low ebb of influence. On the American scene, particularly in New York during the golden-hued Indian summer of 1928, joy was unconfined. Diversions were startlingly unrefined even at the level of innocuous pastime.*
>
> *Weekend drinking orgies were the rule at crowded house parties on Long Island estates. The corpulent stock broker played games with childish abandon. His favorite outdoor sport was pushing his fully clothed female companion into the swimming pool. It never occurred to him to associate the big splash with impending disaster. Besides, in the blinding glare of the false dawn before the Depression's gathering storm, omens of gloom were not easily detected. Anyway, why look for trouble? And, in Heaven's name, why mess up the walls with tragedy? In the feverish buying market, when almost anybody would take a chance at almost anything, "unpleasant" subject matter was a rejected commodity.*

What Alma and Orozco had hoped for was a critical success. What they encountered was oblivion. After eagerly scanning the *Times,* they found halfway down the page an unsigned column headed "Local Notes." There Alma spotted a two-line item: "An exhibition of the work of Orozco, the

Mexican artist, opened last week at the Marie Sterner Gallery and will last through October 22nd."

It was obvious to Alma that no member of the *Times* art staff had attended the exhibition, and it was terribly embarrassing for her to point out the brief notice to her friend, who was eagerly awaiting his first New York criticism. Orozco's reaction was a characteristic shrug and a patient smile. "Well, Angelita," (his nickname for a woman who was "always flying around") "they credit me with something. They say here that I am an artist and a Mexican. It could be worse, you know. They might have omitted both *calificaciones!*"

They'd begun the endeavor with high hopes and a spirit of adventure, yet neither was unduly discouraged by the disappointing results. Enthusiasm now tempered with grim determination, their mutual confidence was undimmed. Orozco had found a champion, but Alma's reward was far greater. She'd at last discovered the purpose in life for which she had been searching.

Eva was returning to Greece. Their American sojourn had failed to net anticipated endowments for the Delphic movement. Now, with some promise of European financial support, she was focusing her efforts on the organization of a second festival. Alma was to remain temporarily in charge of the organization's interests in the United States until those responsibilities could be disposed of. She'd promised to sail for Greece in May.

Concerned that Orozco's career might not gain sufficient momentum by then, Alma doubled her efforts on his behalf. Ranking Orozco's work with that of the great masters, she regarded its promotion as a near sacred trust. Important as her friend's present work might be, she perceived its recognition and sale merely as a means to an end. Each picture was an essential step in the larger aim—the execution of heroic murals. Alma was determined to devote every resource of time, energy, and, yes, money to finding a forum for the registry of his vision. To the exclusion of her own writing ambitions, she found herself concentrating exclusively on ways and means. Her goal was one of those "pretty walls" he'd described with such longing on her first visit to his studio.

With a typical flair for auspicious beginnings, Orozco selected January 1, 1929, to begin work on a portrait of his working muse. He had decided to paint her in profile, a pose that reminded Alma of the first photograph to accompany her column in the *Bulletin* nearly eight years before. She inwardly whistled at how much had happened in that brief period!

As he penciled in the preliminary sketch, Orozco expressed satisfaction at finally being able to settle down to a "very *simpático* task." The portrait had been planned almost from the beginning but had been delayed several times because of the artist's continued preparations for increasingly frequent private and public exhibitions and Alma's out-of-town trips on behalf of the Delphic movement. That evening she noted in her diary, "The little painting gives promise. I already see myself."

Alma posed for brief periods the first week of January, and on the following Sunday the artist applied the finishing touches and affixed his signature to the sixteen-by-twenty-inch canvas.

Visitors to the Ashram who saw the finished portrait considered it a penetrating and sympathetic likeness. But Orozco was disappointed. He appeared downcast whenever he looked at the painting and asked Alma not to display it further until he could give it more leisurely study. Finally he admitted that he much preferred a likeness by Kahlil Gibran to his own work.

It was quite an admission. Though devoted to his family, Orozco had the typical Latin temperament. He and Alma were constantly together. She was very beautiful; they were both lonely and vulnerable, drawn to one another by philosophy and inspiration as well as chemistry.

Kahlil Gibran, the Lebanese poet and philosopher, whose mystical writings had at the time captured the imagination of the entire world, was also drawn to Alma and was a frequent guest at the Ashram. On one of these occasions, Gibran, who was also a critically acclaimed artist, had done a sensitive crayon portrait of her.

This was the first praise that Orozco had ever given to any of the poet's pre-Raphaelite inspired drawings, many of which illustrated his books. From the very beginning of their acquaintance, a controlled but active antagonism had existed between the two men. It took its outward form in artistic dispute. While Orozco maintained an ominous silence on the subject of Gibran's drawings, Kahlil was outspoken regarding what he called "the violent art of Mexico." He often asked Alma how she could endure living in the Ashram when Orozco's scenes of horror and tragic death covered the walls.

Despite their rivalry, there was an honesty and magnanimous spirit about the two men. Alma counted herself fortunate to have them both in her life. That same week she launched the Ashram's international social schedule with a party honoring the poet's forty-sixth birthday. The event was celebrated on January 6, rather than its proper date, January 8, so as not to interfere with the Syrian colony's observance of Gibran's silver jubilee.

The poet was then at the height of his fame. An exile from his native Lebanon because of his vigorous protest against governmental injustice and oppression, he spent his youth in Paris, where he studied under Rodin. Alma's program included a reading from his masterpiece, *The Prophet,* which was enjoying worldwide popularity. It had been translated into twenty-two languages.

Gibran, who, unknown to anyone present, had just been diagnosed as having a fatal illness, himself read parables from some of his earlier works. One was a particular favorite of Orozco, who requested it that night. The parable that had pleased the Mexican artist the most—one that he often chuckled over and frequently retold himself—was the tale of the fox included in *The Madmen.*

Before Gibran read it, he explained that he did so in deference to the Mexican artist, "who tells it even better than the author." The parable related how a fox, looking at his shadow at sunrise, said: "I will have camel for lunch today." All morning he went looking for camels. At noon he saw his shadow again and said, "A mouse will do." For years afterward Orozco would greet Alma with the phrase, "I'll have a camel for lunch today," meaning that all was well with him.

But all was not well with the poet. As the guests continued to press him for more parables and aphorisms, he read on in a voice that betrayed deep emotions, until at last he was no longer able to control his feelings. Excusing himself, he fled the room.

Alma followed and found him shuddering with deep sobs. "What a tragedy," he said, struggling to regain his composure. "I have lost my original creative power. I know the truth, and I face it. I can no longer write as I once did."

"Surely *The Prophet* and the new work, *Lazarus,* are as great as your earlier writings; it's only that they are different," Alma assured him, but Gibran continued to weep.

Orozco, entering, overheard the conversation. *"Hombre,"* he said, grasping the poet in a warm *abrazo* so common among men friends in Mexico, "don't regret that your latest work is different from your early work. I find it good—in fact, wonderful—that you change. It would indeed be a calamity if you did not. Who knows—your new work may be even better than your old. Give it time. You may not be the best judge of its worth. Meanwhile, be happy that you are young enough to grow—that you are not an ossified academician. To stagnate even at a good point is living death for an artist."

As they talked, Kahlil regained his poise. Together they walked back into the living room, composure restored.

For nearly a year—whenever Alma was not occupied with the demands of the Delphic Society—she and Orozco had talked of opening a gallery to feature his work. Alma, whose job would be its management, was keenly aware of the obstacles: her other obligations and their lack of money.

Then very suddenly both were dramatically eliminated, or so it seemed.

First came a cable from Eva. The second Delphic Festival would be held May 1930 with the financial aid of a joint Greek and French committee. Alma was to remain in New York, continuing her efforts at the movement's American center. A collateral duty would be to organize and to promote as many tours to the event as possible.

That same month Alma received a phone call from Adelaide. Eugene, despondent over continued business reversals, had disappeared. Adelaide was certain that he'd taken his own life. Alma somehow knew it was true and was stricken by memories. She recalled her father's enthusiasm that previous summer during her brief visit. Another business deal. This was it! They would all be wealthy beyond their wildest dreams. She was devastated by the loss of this man who'd first introduced her to the world of art and literature that had become her life. If only she'd told him how much she appreciated what he'd done for her, if only they'd talked more that last time, if only she'd stayed longer or gone home again at holiday time. Her remorse was unbearable.

Then another phone call. This one brought news that the entire top floor of a building at 9 East 57th Street was available. With it came the realization: Nothing could change the past; she could only move forward. Surely that was exactly what Eugene would have wanted.

Thoughts of her father brought back myriad memories of their days together, among them her time spent assisting him at the real estate office. Over the years—particularly when financially pressed—Alma had checked on the lot she'd bought on speculation nearly twenty years before. For years it had remained virtually valueless, but on her last trip home Alma had noticed that neat little bungalows were beginning to encroach on the solitude of dunes and ice plants. San Francisco was moving southward, just as she'd once thought it would.

In 1929, it seemed that prices of everything had reached an all-time high and yet people were buying. Surely the land was worth something. To Alma's great delight, the sale of of the lot did fetch a small sum. And as for the rest of the money . . .

As always with Alma the end justified the means. Furthering the career of one of the greatest artists of the time was certainly in keeping with the Delphic ideals—or so she rationalized. The prospective gallery was spacious enough to accommodate large scale exhibitions *and* Delphic activities. Surely the one could subsidize the other. Later Alma would say that an inheritance financed the gallery, and in a sense it was true.

One morning Orozco appeared with a partnership agreement. The Ashram housekeeper witnessed their signatures as Orozco joked about the party of the first part and the party of the second part. At his insistence, theirs would be an equal partnership. "I can rest better and work better if you are protected and our affairs clarified and in order."

Alma made the stipulation that the arrangement be for one year only and that either could terminate at the end of that time. Actually, both believed that the gallery would no longer be necessary after a year. Their mutual goal was the acquisition of fresco commissions. They were confident that a rush of architects clamoring for Orozco murals would eliminate the need for a showcase.

Art magazines described the gallery as a "handsome and stimulating addition to 57th Street." Orozco had mixed a sample for the wall paint—a warm French gray—for the decorator's guidance, and his sketches for the functional, streamlined furniture, finished in flat black lacquer, were faithfully executed by a skillful craftsman. For the convenient showing of his graphic work, the artist had designed an oversized table with concealed shelves at one end for the lithograph cases and, at the other, upright divisions for framed drawings. The matching chairs were of striking lines and ample proportions; the low window benches were covered with dark blue velour cushions. The whole art deco scheme was completed with a large, circular, hand-hooked woolen rug designed by Thomas Hart Benton.

Orozco returned to Mexico that summer to visit his family. Alma saw him off at the railroad station, painfully aware that he was returning to another woman. Despite the attraction that had flared between them, despite their shared visions and her worldview of which his was a mirror image, Orozco remained deeply committed to his family. He would never be another Felipe, sacrificing all for a grand passion. Nor did Alma want him to be. The artist's fiery nature and creative genius had brought much needed direction to her life while offering solace to an aching heart. The early heady months with Orozco and the deep, mutually sustaining friendship that evolved, coming as they had in her fortieth year, had brought a kind of renaissance, yet she knew that nothing would ever replace the love she would always feel for Felipe. Nothing or no one could ever take his place. A relationship with built-in limitations seemed somehow right to her, providing focus, companionship, and a degree of romantic excitement without demanding total commitment. Nevertheless, despite her realism and resolve, saying good-bye was harder than Alma had anticipated. Fortunately, there was plenty to keep her busy and no doubt that he would be returning in fall.

From its opening in June 1929, the gallery became a rendezvous for students and fanciers of avant-garde trends, but soon directors of the country's leading museums found their way there as well. The gallery was flourishing. Sales of works by Orozco and other Mexican and American artists in the "Delphic group" were daily occurrences. There were numerous inquiries from collectors, requests for circulating exhibitions, and sometimes Alma even had to assure would-be purchasers that the gallery furnishings and decorations weren't for sale. Buying had become a mania in this summer before dark. A feverish eagerness for swift profits and a fear of sudden losses had seized Manhattan like an epidemic. Alma saw the language of the stock market invade all levels of social life, heard the word *margin* dominate the vocabulary of nearly everyone.

When Orozco returned, Alma, basking in the warm pleasure of their renewed closeness coupled with a sudden heady success, eagerly persuaded him to attend a luncheon given by a Park Avenue socialite. Though the hostess had expressed deep admiration for the artist and a desire to meet him, the stock market preempted all other topics. A few guests even left the dining room between courses to telephone their brokers. Presumably they'd gathered to meet Orozco, yet no effort was made to discuss art or Mexico or any other subject with which he was familiar.

Throughout late September and the first weeks of October, the sale of pictures had become increasingly involved with market transactions. Deposits were paid on paintings by Orozco, Benton, Merida, Maroto, and others with the understanding that the purchases would be concluded when this or that security advanced forty or fifty points. Thus, the first major break in the market in late October was cataclysmic. Important sales were canceled, deposits refunded. Then the paralysis set in.

"One morning in 1929 something very serious happened in New York," Orozco would later recall in his autobiography.

> *The people ran about more than ordinarily. They talked heatedly in little groups. The sirens of the fire engines and of the Red Cross ambulances howled fiercely on all sides. Newspaper "extras" were carried in great bundles by trucks, then passed from hand to hand. Wall Street and its vicinity became a great infernal sea. Many speculators had already thrown themselves to the street from the windows of their offices and their remains were gathered up by the police. The office boy no longer wagered if his boss would commit suicide or not, but at what time he would do it—before or after lunch.*

Exaggerations, of course, but Orozco was, well, Orozco.

> *Thousands and thousands of people lost their money and whatever else they possessed in a few moments. The market values went down to zero. A fantastic debt took the place of a fortune. The Crash! Over production for lack of exportation. The world markets were crammed full of merchandise that nobody bought. The factories closed and great business firms disappeared. Panic! Lack of credit!*
>
> *Millions of people suddenly left without work while the numerous employment agencies on Sixth, Seventh and Third*

avenues were stormed in vain by the jobless. Those in power had
promised prosperity without limit and assured the public that there
would be a "chicken in every pot." But now there was not even a
fire in millions of homes. The city was obliged to distribute
rations of soup and coffee. In sections of New York there were
formidable lines of strong men, hatless and scarcely protected by
their old clothes, suffering long hours outdoors in freezing
temperatures, standing on a layer of hardened snow. Red-faced
men, hard, angry, desperate, with dark looks and closed fists. By
night people begged in the streets in the cover of the shadows for a
nickel for coffee. And it was true, how true, that they needed it. It
was The Crash—the Disaster."

Panic seized everyone professionally connected with painting, the first field
of enterprise to be classed as "nonessential." The anxiety of the advertising solicitor who served the gallery was typical of the defeatism that
enveloped 57th Street. As part of her plan to keep Orozco's name continuously before the public, Alma had become a heavy advertiser in newspapers and art journals. Soon after the second market break on November
13, the solicitor, who was an amateur painter and an Orozco fan, called as
usual to arrange for the weekly art page announcements. At least that's
what Alma assumed, until he announced that despite the loss of his commission, he felt duty bound to discourage her from expensive advertising
during the economic chaos. "You're doing a public service presenting
Orozco's work to the American people; I don't want you to be hurt," he
explained.

Alma continued to make the rounds of architects' offices armed with her
album of Mexican fresco photographs and to write glowing letters to the
heads of schools, colleges, and charitable foundations, refusing to believe
that the Crash had made a chance of securing a mural commission virtually
impossible. Construction had practically ceased and there was no money
available for the decoration of old buildings.

Then suddenly, unexpectedly, an opportunity opened up in an area
seemingly light-years away. Professor José Pijoan, the brilliant and highly
controversial head of the art history department at Pomona College in
California, was eager to secure a mural for the recently completed Frary
Hall refectory. Mutual friends enthusiastically recommended Orozco. Writ-

ing about this exciting development more than twenty years later, Alma would recall:

> *The sum mentioned as available for the mural was five thousand dollars, and we were given to understand that the money was already on hand or had been guaranteed. At the time, there was no reason to suspect that the optimistic Pijoan had based his calculations on wishful thinking rather than contributions in the bank or signed pledges of the local orange growers.*

(Pomona College, student population eight hundred, was located in the semiagricultural community of Claremont, some forty miles east of downtown Los Angeles.)

Both Alma and Orozco considered the amount very small considering the size of the wall to be painted (some one hundred square yards) especially because the amount would be greatly reduced by the heavy cost of materials, scaffolding, fees for the mason and assistant, as well as the artist's cross-country travel expenses. After much discussion, they agreed that their main objective was to secure a wall—almost any wall would do—to enable Orozco to function as a public painter. His morale, his survival as a creative artist and even as a self-sustaining citizen with family responsibilities seemed to depend upon obtaining an immediate mural commission.

The discovery on arrival that no money had actually been raised for the project was almost too much for Orozco. A young reporter on the college weekly *Student Life* recalled that the artist, grown suddenly pale on learning the distressing facts, quietly asked: "Do you still have the *wall?*" Assured that the wall at least existed, Orozco wrote Alma immediately, "Drop everything, come West at once, and bring plenty of paintings." He had decided to go ahead with the mural. If funds weren't available, they would finance the work themselves through the sale of his pictures—sacrifice sales.

For Alma, her friend's choice of subject mitigated some of the disappointment. Orozco's theme was *Prometheus Bound.* Well aware of the Mexican revolutionary's initial cynical reaction to her Hellenistic fervor, she recognized that his two years of living and working in an environment colored by both the practical and spiritual implications of Aeschylus' drama had had their effect. The art might be his, but the inspiration—the divine spark—had been hers.

With some degree of satisfaction, Alma recalled her efforts to stimulate interest in the upcoming Delphic festival. She had scheduled a series of programs at which distinguished Hellenists read and interpreted *Prometheus Bound*. These prefestival programs placed special emphasis on her translations of the writings of Angelo Sikelianos. The Greek poet was frequently quoted on the relationship of the Aeschylean drama—written four centuries before the Christian era—to contemporary problems.

Before introducing the speakers at any evening, Alma invariably described the original Delphic Festival production of May 1927, then outlined Sikelianos's plan to reestablish a world center on the site of the first United Nations, the ancient Amphictyonic League. Ashram forums dealt with the message conveyed by Aeschylus through the medium of myth. The supreme God who figured so prominently in the drama appeared as a prototype of a Greek tyrant—a deliberate device on the part of the author, Alma felt certain. The play, which had no parallel in ancient literature, appeared to her a foreshadowing of twentieth-century totalitarianism, and she had frequently drawn analogies to contemporary problems.

Orozco, Alma recalled, had quickly perceived similarities between the prophetic, defiant giver of fire and the intrepid, lonely rebel in the arts and sciences. The artist, hearing the play read for the first time, listened raptly, swept along by the grand scale of the drama's human action. Later he'd observed that the protagonists, whether divine or supernatural, were just average men and women who remained the slaves of every mortal weakness—desire, hate, jealousy, or fear. One evening he'd delighted the others by remarking that the Olympian deities in general, and Zeus in particular, reminded him of present-day "stuffed shirts" with all their bourgeois vices. On another occasion, he'd spoken admiringly of the "grandiose" concept of the suffering Prometheus chained to the Scythian crag while vultures gnawed at his liver, all the while defiant of the mighty tyrant. And now, Alma marveled, here he was about to depict the war between brute force and unbending knowledge, between the reigning monarch of the universe and the patron of suffering mankind on a colossal fresco.

The lengthy historical interpretation of *Prometheus Bound* appeared to her as a mirror of life itself. While social innovators found mythological justification for romanticism, liberalism, and socialism, authoritarians resoundingly approved the crushing punishment accorded to the rebel against supreme authority. Surely Orozco had chosen a highly controversial subject for his Pomona mural.

Antagonism was inevitable. Alma saw the climax of public agitation reached one Sunday, during a special service in Claremont's principal church, when several of the local clergy denounced the mural on three distinct grounds. These "critics" felt that Prometheus was an unsuitable subject for a college wall because the myth symbolized rebellion. The second objection was based on the painter's nationality. Mexicans, it was charged, were known to be a people without respect for established institutions. Many of them were, in fact, outlaws—as the revolutions of 1910 to 1921 had demonstrated. The third objection held that the interpretation of a theme as daring as Prometheus should not be entrusted to a foreign artist because of his unfamiliarity with American customs and beliefs. The men of the cloth declared that the symbolic Prometheus was likely to prove disturbing, even provocative of dangerous reactions, leading youth and law-abiding citizens to heaven only knew what flouting of the law, to what disrespect for recognized authority—religious or political.

The trustees, patrons of the college, were equally divided. It required some fast talking from Orozco's proponent, the fervent, rapturous Pijoan, to persuade them to permit what he had retreated into calling "the experiment."

Alma had closed the Delphic Studios and joined the artist in Pomona with a shipment of canvases, drawings, and prints. Sales kept them going—just barely—while Orozco completed his fresco. Later in *Orozco,* she would glowing recap a dedication dinner for the mural, vividly describing the enthusiasm of Pomona College president Edmunds as he praised the "moral effect of the artist's stay at Pomona" and "the fine example set by Orozco through his faithful observance to working schedules, his meticulous regard for craftsmanship, rare modesty, integrity, his simplicity and kindliness of manner, his devotion to purpose, and his high standards of personal conduct." A check was then presented, albeit for "less than half the originally stipulated five thousand dollars" but with "expressed regret that the amount was not many times larger."

Once again Alma was rewriting history to suit herself. Actually there had been no official dedication, no acknowledgment, and no payment whatsoever. Upon completion of the mural, the artist simply bade good-bye to the students and more liberal faculty members who'd become his friends and left with Alma for San Francisco.

. . .

The Sullivans took Orozco to their collective bosom, and he stayed for a time with Alma and Adelaide at the family home on Buchanan Street. It was a difficult period for Adelaide. Eugene's body had been found in San Francisco Bay, but the insurance company was stalling. There were endless forms, embarrassing questions, delays. It would be a year before the policy was finally paid. Alma was assailed by memories. Confronted by a familiar painting, "Mother of the Sorrows," a portrait of Mary, her heart pierced by seven arrows, she found it typical of not only Adelaide but the many vicissitudes to which the family had been subject. It was a pattern she'd sought to escape in childhood only to encounter again and again in historic themes as well as personal life. Sacrifice and suffering, suffering and sacrifice.

Alma's concern that the appearance of the controversial artist would be a strain on her mother was a mistake. The two were drawn to one another from the start. Orozco, who adored his own mother, found a ready substitute in Adelaide, who was charmed by his Latin courtliness. Alma's siblings planned modest outings for the artist—theater parties, tours, dinners, but it was soon obvious that the painter was happiest in the company of Adelaide, conversing animatedly about his home and family, about the Mexican capital, and about his native Guadalajara, which he said had so much in common with her lovely San Francisco. If the mother had questions about the exact nature of her daughter's involvement with this attractive, volatile man, she didn't raise them. The years had mellowed everyone.

Frequently Orozco tested Adelaide's skill at tarot card reading, confiding to Alma that she had hit upon the truth with "remarkable accuracy." Alma remembered one occasion when Orozco's mood turned unusually serious. Adelaide ran through the pack in the customary fashion. At the end of the reading, she announced that his wish would not materialize. "Ah, that is bad—very bad," the artist exclaimed. "Why, what was your wish?" Adelaide asked. "I wished for peace and happiness for all humanity," he replied.

Orozco never forgot this particular "reading" and, as war clouds gathered in the late 1930's, he referred to it often.

They spent the summer in San Francisco, and Orozco worked hard producing several canvases for the fall gallery opening in New York, yet still found time to paint an oil portrait of Alma's niece, Patricia. "Patsy," a young schoolgirl in her middy blouse, thought the sittings an awful chore and hated the result. "I look so grim," she protested. "Darling, he has captured your soul," Alma airily explained. Patsy was not mollified.

Back in New York, Orozco's next public work, a mural for the New School for Social Research, was a speculative effort underwritten unknowingly by the Delphic Society. Subsequent sales would soon enable her to reimburse the fund, Alma reassured herself. In the meantime, this was a date with destiny that could not be ignored. In writing to Dr. Alvin Johnson, the school's director, she outlined her position:

> *It is only right and proper that this cheerfully assumed (though at the time very difficult) responsibility of making it possible for Sr. Orozco to meet his personal and family needs during the progress of the work at the New School, remains my own, since the whole idea of the frescoes for the New School originated in my own mind because the work itself represents profoundly my own point of view and idealism, and because, with the Mexican panel, my name will be associated with Mexican history.*

Alma had a sense of fate about the frescoes, the theme of which combined her own past and present with historical events. In contrast to "Prometheus" the New School murals depicted specific twentieth-century revolutionary struggles that held great meaning for Ashram members and most specifically for herself.

On January 19, 1931, she went with Orozco for the final inspection of his work before the official preview and reception. "You're going to feel very much at home here, Almita," the artist said as he lead her inside. "You will be among your friends; it is just another Ashram." He referred to the "Table of Brotherhood," where several of the seated figures were portraits of her dearest friends, courageous forerunners of an enlightened order, among them the poet Leonard Van Hoppen and the French philosopher Dr. Paul Richard, responsible for the abolition of the notorious Devil's Island.

But for her, the room was dominated by another mural—one that Orozco had kept her from seeing until now. This one immortalized Felipe. Orozco led her to the west wall, where they stood silently before his stirring tribute to the Yucatecan leader. "Well, Almita, here it is," he said. "I hope it pleases you. At any rate it is the first monument in your country to Felipe's memory. Some day there will be others—and on a grander scale."

Alma struggled for words. No memorial, however grand, could have moved her more. The New World panel in the "Struggle in the West" showed the martyred governor of Yucatán in the characteristic pose of a little framed photograph that always stood on her desk. In the background was the pyramid of Chichén Itzá, which she and Felipe had climbed together so long ago. Below, an armed guerrilla and a group of women and children recalled the Leagues of Resistance and the feministas who had fought for improved education, hygiene, and child care.

In "Struggle in the Orient" on the opposite wall, Mahatma Gandhi also made his first United States appearance in a public monument. The other world leader was Lenin—a presence that did not set well with the backers of the school, who had made the building possible. "How could I ignore Lenin in any factual evaluation of the world 'as is'?" Orozco had reasoned. He'd hoped that within the context of a twentieth-century overview, the inclusion of such an influential thinker would appear logical.

Not everyone agreed. The Lenin portrait and the appearance of a black man at the "Table of Brotherhood" caused the withdrawal of subscriptions to the New School Building Fund by some of the richest patrons. This was not to be the end. Twenty-two years later in 1952, the McCarthy influence forced school authorities to cover not only Lenin's portrait, but Felipe's as well.

The same *New York Times* article that made the announcement disclosed that the appraised value of the murals was seventy thousand dollars. The artist never received a penny for his work.

One of the few who initially recognized Orozco's genius was Frank Lloyd Wright, who, immediately upon visiting the New School, telephoned Alma, requesting that she set up a meeting with the artist. The famous architect approached Orozco with a surprising offer. "José Orozco, you are an authentic master. At last, I find in you a painter with whom I wish to collaborate on great projects. I'm willing to form an exclusive working partnership with you for the rest of our days. Never before in history have an architect and a painter of our ability and our vision had the good fortune to create and execute together. Let us take advantage of the unique circumstances for the enrichment of contemporary art and life."

Wright's plan was extraordinary. He would not only guarantee the artist an affluent living, but would send for his wife and children and arrange accommodations for them at Taliesen, his home and teaching center in Spring Greens, Wisconsin, where the children would enjoy the finest educational facilities available anywhere. Wright went on to describe living conditions in his model community that seemed to fulfill simultaneously every dream of the creative artist as well as the solicitous parent.

Alma was stunned. The proposed association could not help but affect, possibly even terminate, her relationship with Orozco. All needs both personal and professional would be met by others. Yet what could she say? At a time when the economic situation had reached record instability and her friend's most recent artistic creation was under attack, Wright's offer seemed heaven-sent.

She looked at Orozco, anticipating the luminous expression that appeared as refracted light on his thick bifocals at moments of supreme pleasure. To her surprise, his face was impassive. Thanking the architect for the honor paid him, Orozco asked for "a few moments to discuss the matter privately with Mrs. Reed."

The minute the door closed on Wright, Orozco turned to Alma. "That man would devour me!" he fairly exploded. "He has exceptional ability, but he is also an egotist. He believes that architecture is greater than art. That is a false idea. He thinks, too, that architecture is the father of the arts. He is wrong again." Alma was appalled at the tirade, mostly in Spanish, which went on and on as Orozco outlined the differences between art and architecture to the advantage of the former. "I cannot accept his offer and you must tell him so because your English words are better than mine. I want him to understand that I appreciate his good opinion of my work, but if I were to live at Taliesen it would be the end of my independence."

When she reluctantly pointed out the advantages of the offer, Orozco shook his head, "No, Almita, that is not for me. He would be the master, I his slave. I do not care how much money or how much fame would come of it. I could never live nor create under dictated conditions. I must be a free man."

"I can't tell him that," she protested. "I can't insult him."

Orozco thought a moment, then suggested, "Ask him how far the town where we would live is from—well—some large city and ask him how cold it gets in winter. You could then say that I am a man for the big cities, and I cannot stand extreme cold. This much is the truth, and it is enough for him to know."

Years later, when Frank Lloyd Wright was eighty-two, Alma smiled when she chanced to hear him interviewed on the radio. "Early in my life, being very sure of my star, I had to choose between honest arrogance and hypocritical humility," he explained. "I chose honest arrogance, and I'm still at it." She recalled the memorable meeting between Orozco and the world's leading exponent of organic architecture. Obviously the latter had met his match. Recounting the event in her biography, *Orozco,* she wrote,

> *In words and personal bearing Orozco was the most modest of men, but he never lost sight of his true worth as an artist. He realized that his own gifts were at least equal to those of the older man, who represented the greatest single influence on contemporary architecture. Orozco suspected too that Wright's "honest arrogance" would eventually try to dominate their artistic partnership and impose the personal ideas of the Master of Taliesen upon mural theme and composition, despite the architect's admiration of the artist's knowledge and power.*

Orozco's confidence in his own ability was inspiring, but it didn't pay the bills. Now even Eva was feeling the pinch. The Delphic fund had shrunk; there was little to divert. Alma gave up the spacious apartment and moved to a much smaller place on 57th Street near the gallery. The murals that Orozco painted for her kitchen made the art pages of *Time.*

Fortunately, Orozco's faith was miraculously born out. Soon after the meeting with Wright, Stephen C. Clark, collector and trustee of the Museum of Modern Art, bought two drawings and commissioned several large-scale canvases. The money enabled Orozco to bring his family to New York.

Alma and Orozco's wife, Margarita, achieved a working truce. Well aware of the other's value to the man they both loved and admired, each was willing to make concessions and achieve compromises in order to effect the fulfillment of a shared vision. If Orozco was to manifest his full artistic genius, they would just have to put up with one another. The children, though the more obvious obstacle to a permanent union between Alma and Orozco, were somehow easier for her to deal with.

She became a kind of "Auntie Mame" figure to the three active youngsters, introducing them to the wonders of Manhattan. Clemente, Jr., seven at the time, has mixed memories of the flamboyant *norteamericana.* On the one hand, she was an exciting companion, a fairy godmother from another world—the person who gave him his first birthday party; on the other, she was a mysterious siren who clearly exerted a strong influence on his father.

Alma was also busy exerting an influence on his behalf. Her goal was the new Baker Library at Dartmouth College. Alma had been following this tack for some time. On February 20, 1931, she wrote a reminder to Professor Artemas Packard, chairman of the art faculty:

> *Last summer you suggested the possibility of a mural. . . . I am wondering how such a possibility may be furthered into reality. Orozco is now free for a few months. . . . He has just completed the murals in the New School of Social Research (and) is eager to go on with what he did in Pomona College and which he calls the New World epic painting—taking traditional themes—such as the "Prometheus" and giving them a meaning for today.*

It was another year before the project, underwritten by a special Rockefeller fund (Nelson Rockefeller had been graduated from Dartmouth in 1930 and was becoming interested in his mother's hobby, the Museum of Modern Art), came together. Once again Orozco's theme was the heroic self-sacrifice of the rebel or artist for the benefit of humanity. And once again, Alma was at least partially responsible for that theme—the greatest figure in indigenous American mythology, the Indian Prometheus, Quetzalcoatl. For her, Quetzalcoatl and his Mayan embodiment, Kukulkan, would always symbolize Felipe and the ideals for which he died.

Alma and Orozco worked together on the concept of the murals, which was then submitted to the college—no Pomonalike debacle this time, Alma saw to that. It was a source of tremendous personal satisfaction to her to see the pictorial evolvement of Quetzalcoatl. After scenes illustrating the violence and brutality of ancient Mexican society, the first panel of the Quetzalcoatl series shows the god ascending like the sun of a new day. The vital, civilizing force of Quetzalcoatl overcomes the malevolent, unproductive qualities of the other gods and instills new and positive energy into humanity. Like Felipe, Quetzalcoatl brings the ideals of humanism, work, unity, loyalty, honesty, wisdom, and dynamism to a lethargic society. The effect of his heroic influence is shown in a series of creative achievements and advances in agriculture, art, and science. The final panel portrays the fatal opposition of the magicians to Quetzalcoatl's determination to change the course of his, and by extension, human existence, by following his existential mandates.

Few social critics could complain about Quetzalcoatl. It was Orozco's other subject matter that drew inevitable controversy; "Stillborn Education" was an example. Here was a savage denouncement of what the artist saw as the sterility and meaninglessness of modern education embodied in a grotesque scene in which a skeleton gives birth to a dead fetus surrounded by cadavers in academic garb.

The last of the Baker Library panels, "Modern Migration of the Spirit," provides a final thunderous crescendo. Here a mutilated Christ returns to destroy his cross, a modern Last Judgment illustrating the abject failure of modern American society. By his act of self-sacrifice, Christ calls for liberation of twentieth-century humanity from the terrible waste of nationalistic chauvinism strikingly symbolized by a junk heap of weapons and the useless remnants of outworn creeds and religions. In the wrathful and powerful portrayal, Orozco drew parallels between Christ and Quetzalcoatl. Both represented higher forces that attempt humanity's salvation through the purification of self-sacrifice; here, in contrast to the positive achievements of humanity made possible by Quetzalcoatl, Orozco's concern lies with humanity's commitment to violent destruction. Though cynical and pessimistic in the extreme, there remains a slim degree of hope for humanity's future in the Christ image, a force capable of destroying the old order as Prometheus did in order to prepare for the "modern migration of the spirit."

The response from press and public was vitriolic. Opponents deplored the Mexican "craze," the "deformed" modernism. Yet the *Boston Globe,* Orozco's most militant adversary from 1932 to 1934, would announce early in 1935, "People from all over the United States have been more interested in the great mural painting by a Mexican artist—José Clemente Orozco— than in any other thing at the college." By 1940, the now-famous murals played an important role in Dartmouth's burgeoning art program, with some four hundred students a year enrolled in art and archeology courses. Today the murals have come to be accepted, as was the case with "Prometheus" at Pomona College, as the single most important artistic and cultural resource at the school.

Unfortunately, those glory years were far in the future. Alma, desperate to shore up Orozco's career, published an art book featuring his work, which she sent to art critics all over the world. The book, published in 1932, cost ten thousand dollars. Alma financed the venture by selling precious treasures that she'd collected over the years in her travels—as well as a few of Eva's left in her keeping.

When Orozco was invited to exhibit at the Arts Club, where membership included some of Chicago's wealthiest art patrons, Alma went with him. The artist was greeted with admiration and enthusiasm, many lookers, but no buyers. It seemed a time for taking stock. Orozco hated Chicago and decided to take the train from there to Mexico, where his family was again living. "I see no hope of anything worthwhile here, Almita. Please go back to New York as soon as you can. Don't waste your time, as no good can be accomplished in this environment. They are interested only in *puercos* [pigs]—the Chicago kind, live or roasted, or the Mexican variety, *painted.*"

Waiting at the depot, they weighed the events of the last six years. Alma voiced her extreme frustration at not having translated Orozco's genius into a comparable financial success. But he was quick to remind her that their goal had been walls not wealth. This they had achieved—in New York, in California, and in the heart of conservative New England. Surely in these places his name would be forever identified with the beginnings of truly American continental art. Alma was certain that nothing would succeed at home like recognition abroad. Surely Orozco's new international status would open walls to him at last worthy of his art.

It was a sad parting.

Alma returned to New York to reopen the gallery for the Fall 1934 season. As usual, a Mexican exhibition was the inaugural event and, as always, a section was reserved for permanent showing of works by José Clemente Orozco.

The months and years that followed were busy ones, full of plans, receptions, promotions. There were friends, many of them, but no one filled the void left by his departure. In 1936, Orozco returned briefly as the Mexican delegate to the American Art Congress. It was as though he'd never been gone, their rapport unbroken.

A year later, visiting in Guadalajara, Alma saw her intuition born out. Orozco's genius was at last recognized. He had become that most fortunate of creatures, a hero in his own land. Twice they visited the Hospicio Cabañas to marvel at the grandiose dimensions of the ancient chapel that the governor had invited him to paint.

Alma went on to Mexico City, her first visit in more than ten years. She had not wanted to return during the influence of Alvaro Obregon, but now he was dead. As planned, Calles had succeeded Obregon as president. Then in 1928, again as planned, Obregon was reelected. While celebrating his victory, the president-elect was shot and killed by a Catholic fanatic. "A monument has been erected at the restaurant where it happened; would you care to see it?" someone asked.

"No thanks," Alma's replied emphatically. She preferred to visit instead with old friends who remembered happier times. At one affair Luis Rosada de la Vega sang "La Peregrina" for her. Too soon it was time to return to New York.

In 1940 Orozco rejoined her for a few months. He'd come to paint a mural at the Museum of Modern Art. Alma planned reunions with old admirers from the Ashram days and a reception in his honor at her apartment. Orozco appeared healthy—a fact he attributed to a diet limited to uncooked vegetables. Alma refused to become a convert.

On the morning his mural was unveiled, he asked her to accompany him to see the completed work. It was a dramatic moment for them both, representing as it did the conquest of the last stronghold of Manhattan's art establishment—a belated but total victory in their campaign begun twelve years before. At last they were witnessing the capitulation of the mighty Museum of Modern Art.

Orozco's mural was the featured exhibit in the contemporary section of the vast panorama of creation entitled, "Twenty Centuries of Mexican Art." Though Alma knew the theme and was acutely aware of Orozco's motivation, she nonetheless recoiled slightly. The focus of each of the six panels was a weapon of mass destruction. "Why did you paint a dive bomber?" she asked.

"His answer," Alma wrote later,

> *was a significant prophecy, not only in view of world developments and ever-increasing violence, but of the menace that continues to hang over the human race as a result of the potential of unleashed atomic power. His voice and his expression became more serious as he said, "You ask me, Almita, why I have painted a dive bomber. I answer by asking you, "Will there be anything else in our world as important as this instrument of annihilation for the next half century?"*

CHAPTER · 14

A Legend in Her Time

The gallery was foundering. Over the years Alma had used every possible means to keep the Delphic Studios afloat. She'd begged, borrowed, and even stolen. Once when finances were really tight, she recalled Orozco's portrait of her young niece, Patsy. "The painting is needed for an important exhibition," she explained in a hasty note. "Send it immediately. You'll have it back as soon as possible." The next time that Patsy was to see her portrait was in an art book, a focal point of someone else's collection.

Rules, Alma had always believed, were written for someone else; they didn't apply to her. If she needed something, she thought of a story to sell or *tell* to get it. Because the cause generally involved the advancement of some worthy artist, the end—at least in her mind—justified the means of achieving it. She had always done whatever was necessary to attain her goals. For herself, Alma desired very little. When an occasional windfall came her way, she invariably spent it on a painting or a piece of sculpture, sometimes for the pleasure of owning a treasure, always as a means of

aiding and encouraging the artist. Her life-style centered around art, literature, and philosophy. A popular guest, she was also a frequent party giver.
If, of necessity, the food was a trifle spare and the drinks slightly watered,
few noticed, for the conversation sparkled and one simply never knew who
might turn up at Alma's. Actually, it could as easily be Albert Einstein as
Nelson Rockefeller.

Alma had put on weight over the years, but carried it well. Her smile
was just as dazzling, her skin still so flawless, her eyes such a vivid blue
that people accepted, even admired, the eccentricity of her clothing. She
favored long, flowing skirts, flamboyant shawls, large hats. Financially
unable to follow the styles, she created her own. Tall and statuesque, she
was a spectacular figure even for New York.

The attack on Pearl Harbor in 1941 created a new set of problems. A
public confronted by life-and-death issues had little time for art. The timing
for the dire and prophetic messages of Orozco couldn't have been worse.
Even the most liberal collectors were alienated. Eventually the effort of
making ends meet was just too much. At fifty-two, Alma finally paused to
take stock of her life and sensed the end of an era. She had been too long
in one place.

When a suggestion came from an art collector in Mobile, Alabama, Alma
discarded it as outrageous. Then she thought again, and retrieved the
letter. A job was available on the *Mobile Press Register* as art editor. Writing
had been her first great passion, yet years had passed since she'd done
anything but press releases—might it not be exciting to cover news events
again? Somehow the assumed somnolence of the southern city appealed
to her. Wasn't a change exactly what she'd been seeking?

Alabama offered more opportunity than anticipated. In addition to her
work at the newspaper, Alma produced and "starred" in a weekly radio
show, which eventually drew such sponsors as the Industrial Bank of
Mobile and the Davis News Company, at that time the largest distributor
of books, magazines, and newspapers in the South. The show's format was
a discussion of various cultural events, but Alma frequently managed to
introduce Mexico into the subject matter. Eventually she was the guiding
light behind the formation of the Society for the Friends of Mexico. Wearing the pendant that Felipe had given her some twenty years before, the
bell retrieved from the *cenote* at Chichén Itzá, she cut a wide swath and
loved it.

Still, as the war continued and a series of wire stories described the fighting in North Africa, Italy, and Greece, Alma's thoughts often turned to her own adventures in those far-off places. Cultural events seemed tame indeed. Her most exciting newspaper assignment came in April 1945. An International Peace Conference was to be held in San Francisco, and she was determined to cover it. When the *Mobile Press Register* balked at the expense, Alma, with her usual enterprise, found others to help defray the cost. On April 25, when she presented her credentials at the preliminary session, Alma was representing a chain of southern newspapers, a southern monthly magazine, and a foreign language feature syndicate based in New York.

Though Europe was at last at peace, war raged on in the Pacific. San Francisco officials, fearing sabotage, had placed antiaircraft guns atop their skyscrapers, heightening the breathless excitement of the event. Theatrical glamour enveloped the delegates from the moment they left their limousines at the canopied sidewalk to ascend the carpeted steps of the Opera House. Flanking lines of reporters, photographers, and city officials cheered their advance as any crowd of first-night fans might have greeted stage or screen favorites.

From a choice spot near the stately bronze doors, Alma watched the global pageantry unrolling like a digest of all the newsreels of the past five years. Even the missing top-flight headliners were all the more conspicuous by their absence. She was deeply aware, for instance, of Winston Churchill's impressive contours, as Britain's dapper Anthony Eden, sartorially and tonsorially impeccable, stepped briefly into the foyer. Alma saw the steel-like glint of Stalin's enigmatic smile as the stockily built Molotov crossed the threshold. The alert bodyguards and the huge, shaven-headed generals, balancing overstuffed epaulets and dripping bejeweled medals, who preceded and followed him, emphasized Russia's recent dominance in Eastern Europe.

"The delegations of the Lesser Nations—the Little 45," Alma noted in her story,

> *supplied many vivid personages. The handsome prince of Saudi Arabia, wearing the traditional white burnoose and flowing gold and black headdress of the desert sheik, evoked gasps of feminine approval. And the applause was loud and long as the several dark-skinned delegations, notably those of Ethiopia, Haiti and Liberia, joined the colorful diplomatic review.*

Once inside the klieg-lighted Opera House—its galleries, loges, and main floor filled to capacity with wearers of the little red, blue, and gray enamel buttons issued by the International Secretariat—another absent figure was to dominate that heterogeneous assembly. The spiritual presence of Franklin Delano Roosevelt, only months dead, was hailed as the most vital integrating force of the inaugural conference session. Poignant memories assailed Alma of the careworn face, tired, kindly eyes, and charismatic voice. "There seemed," she told her readers,

> *a perfectly natural acceptance of the theory of the 6th Century Spanish mystic, Saavedra de Fajardo: "That which was can never cease to have been." By common and solemn assent, this was F.D.R.'s day. The United Nations representatives refused to let the mere accident of death rob him of his full glory.*
>
> *The profound feeling was expressed in words that were broadcast from the White House to formally open history's most significant proceedings: "In the name of a great humanitarian," said the then unfamiliar radio voice of the nation's new chief executive, "I earnestly appeal to each of you to rise above personal interests and adhere to those lofty principles that benefit all mankind."*

Alma thought President Truman's plain Missouri twang lent substance to the collective wishful thinking. The human race seemed nearer the goal of permanent peace then than at any other crossroads in the long trek from cave to cyclotron.

Her presence at what she believed to be a pivotal moment in history, her coverage of such an event, was undoubtedly the high point of Alma's career at the *Press Register.* Soon the war in Asia ended. The men were coming home seeking their old jobs, and women were urged to relinquish them. It was the patriotic thing to do. Besides, as everyone knew, women didn't really *have* to work.

Alma returned to New York and attempted to reestablish the Delphic Studios, featuring the work of many talented Mexican artists, Orozco, Rivera, and Siqueiros among them. It was a struggle from the start. Eva, warm, generous, idealistic, and, yes, somewhat gullible, was dead now— Alma's last-ditch source of income lost forever. At last it appeared that creditors could no long be cajoled.

At sixty, Alma felt the urge to move once again. The time had come; she knew it had. It was 1950, and La Peregrina was returning to Mexico. No, not to Mérida; the associations were still too deep, too painful. She would go instead to Mexico City; surely this was a place where a *norteamericana* on a limited income might live comfortably, *if* she was careful, *if* she was lucky. Alma had always been a gambler. She had just enough money to transport herself and her last remaining art treasures to the Mexican capital and to pay the first month's rent on a pretty apartment at 31 Alba, a pleasant district just off the Reforma.

The next step was a job. The ghost of her younger self walked beside Alma to the recently established *Mexico City News,* an English-language paper. It seemed that thirty-five years had passed in the blinking of an eye. A vision of that first onslaught on Fremont Older strengthened her resolve.

"I was here in the postrevolutionary days—nearly thirty years ago. All the old-timers know me; I'm La Peregrina," she explained to the young editor, Bill Shanahan, who'd only been in Mexico a few months. "What I'd like to do for you and for your paper is a column highlighting what's going on now in light of your past history. My viewpoint is fresh—having just returned—yet seasoned. It would, I believe, add a note of authority to a newspaper that's just getting started."

She then went on to embroider her ancient connection with the *New York Times* until the young editor, himself something of an adventurer, felt ashamed to make his best offer—twenty-five dollars per weekly column. Actually it was as much as the full-time reporters made in a week. Over the years, Alma had grown adept at masking desperation, disappointment, and relief. She accepted his offer graciously, as someone generously granting a personal favor.

Alma wrote knowledgeably about sociopolitical matters, about the art scene, Mexican festivals, and scenic attractions, but soon she was branching out. Archeology remained her greatest passion; it was inevitable that she would return to Yucatán for subject material. (The burgeoning tourist industry was only too willing to underwrite her junket—once she had, with characteristic tact, flair, and enthusiasm, outlined the ultimate advantages of the exposure she proposed.)

Confronted once more by ruins of the Mayan civilization, Alma was assailed by impressions formed from old memories. For nearly thirty years she had been acquiring experience culminating in expertise in both classic and modern art. Now here was the Mayan city of Uxmal once more spread before her. This architectural monument, ancient yet so "modern" in its design and execution, had been constructed between A.D. 987 and 1174, a time when European nations were still groping in the intellectual obscurity of the Dark Ages.

Settling down in a shady corner, Alma wrote in longhand what would be the lead for her *News* column:

> *The analogy between Time and the spiral which, in its return,*
> *brings some half-forgotten yesterday closer to an unborn*
> *Tomorrow than to the passing hour, occurred to us with more*
> *than the usual emphasis as we traveled over Mexico's great*
> *Southeastern archeological zones. The proximity of Past and*
> *Future seemed dramatically evident at the magnificent Maya city*
> *of Uxmal. . . ."*

Unwittingly, she had created a metaphor for the final sixteen years of her life.

Within a year Alma, in her reportorial capacity, was again breaking new ground. Seated in a small bush plane, she was flying over the Tabasco jungle on her way to search for a "missing link." Was it possible that Columbus had in some mysterious way actually touched a Hindu outpost on his voyage of discovery? Did the Great Navigator, seeking a direct trade route to the Indies, unknowingly claim for their most Christian Majesties of Castile and Aragon a continent where age-old religions of the East had flourished and decayed centuries before his little vessels dropped anchor in their New World port?

The likelihood of contact between Buddhist-Hindu India and early American peoples suggested itself to her as the tiny plane touched down near the colossal stones of La Venta. This isolated site of a forgotten civilization, with its marvelous black basalt monoliths, did at the very least emphasize the antiquity of the Middle American culture. The massive, carved stones, between two thousand and three thousand years old, corresponded to the period of dominant influence of both the Hindu and Buddhist cultures.

The most prominent of the carved figures was seated in the familiar posture of the Lord Guatama Buddha, as he is represented in innumerable images throughout the Asian world. The facial expression, the cast of features, and the attitude, together with the particular feeling or tone subtly projected by the artist, combined to present a completely new type of pre-Columbian art. It bore little resemblance to that of any hitherto identified people. In one of the three gigantic heads—weighing approximately ten tons—the eyes look inward like those of a person completely absorbed in meditation, a mood peculiar to Buddhist art.

The heads, as well as nearby bas-relief figures, showed a rounded cranial formation, a broad forehead, regular features with a small nose, and full but well-modeled lips. The effect strongly indicated Aryan racial origin. Alma found them curiously Anglo-Saxon and was reminded of Winston Churchill and Theodore Roosevelt.

A possible Far Eastern connection had also been found in Palenque, deep in the Chiapas jungle. Cortés's army had apparently marched within twenty miles of this magnificent site but missed it. Alma could understand why after taking the train from Coaztzacoalcos, at that time the only mode of access. She'd had ample opportunity on the twelve-hour ride to question her own determination to go there. The site was a long way from anywhere. But once reached, Alma found Palenque stunning—well worth any effort. Here was the most beautiful Mayan city of all, each building a work of art, intricately carved stone with the elegance of marble against a backdrop of emerald green jungle.

Quartered once more with archeologists, Alma felt like a girl again responding with youthful enthusiasm to the findings of Albert Ruz Lhuiller. Lhuiller, leading her up a steep hill to the Temple of the Foliated Cross, pointed out a carving decorated with a kind of monster mask at its center and a bird in the upper branches. "It's exact counterpart can be found at Angkor Vat in Cambodia," he told her and produced a photograph to prove it.

Alma was shown a number of other striking parallels between Palenque and Southeast Asia. Scientists had been speculating about such possibilities for years, but the newest and most significant find was the one that Alma had come so far to see. The premise universally agreed upon by archeologists had been that Mayan pyramids were just that. Pyramids—not tombs as in Egypt. But that was pre-Lhuiller.

Alma had studied his report carefully. It seemed that one day the archeologist was staring at the floor of the Temple of the Inscriptions. Its flagstones were beautifully made and fit together almost perfectly. Some were particularly large. One slab had a double row of holes bored into it, so that the heavy stone could be lifted. When Lhuiller investigated, he found that the floor appeared higher in places than the bottom of the walls. Realizing that another hidden room must lie below, he had the heavy flagstones lifted. Beneath was a passage and stairs blocked by sand and rocks. It took four years—four archeological field sessions—to reach the foot of the stairs. The concealed staircase led down into the interior of the pyramid. At the foot of the stairs, the archeologists found sacrificial offerings consisting of jade earplugs and beads, red shells, and a perfect tear-shaped pearl. Another wall was removed, and behind it were the skeletons of six young men. Eighty-two feet below the floor of the temple and six and a half feet below the base of the pyramid, the passage ended.

A closer scrutiny, however, revealed that its apparent terminus was a triangular stone slab. On June 15, 1952, Lhuiller and his patient, hardworking crew were rewarded when the slab was removed and they saw before them the tomb of a Mayan king—with all its priceless array of funerary gifts—quite intact.

Only days later Alma arrived, determined to see this historic find for herself. The scene that awaited her was the remains of a great ruler and his accompanying attendants on their final journey into the afterlife, buried with a splendor then thought to be unique in the Maya civilization. The tomb chamber itself was large with a vaulted ceiling and containing a bas-relief of nine great figures slightly larger than life, forming a procession around the walls. In the center lay a sarcophagus with a huge, elaborately carved stone lid. The skeleton inside was lavishly arrayed with jade jewelry, which included a headdress, a necklace of beads in many forms, and elaborate, delicately incised jade earplugs.

At the time of burial the great lord had been wearing a jade mosaic mask with inlaid eyes of shell and obsidian. In his hands he held large jade beads, and in his mouth was another jade bead. Even more jade objects were arranged about his feet. The coloration indicated that ground cinnabar had been sprinkled over the body, the jade ornaments, and the interior sides of the sarcarphagus. The color red, Alma knew, was associated with the rising sun and may have been symbolic of rebirth.

"What can you conclude from this," the archeologist asked, "other than a link with Egypt? Once we grant that the pyramid, though supporting a temple, was constructed as a grandiose funeral monument, how can Palenque's royal tomb not bring us closer to the Egyptian concept?" Calling attention to the grandeur of the Palenque tomb, he pointed out that, as in the case of Egypt, thousands of hands were required to build and adorn the colossal temple with its sarcophagus weighing some twenty tons and entirely covered with bas-reliefs of extraordinary artistic quality.

Contributing to the theory was the magnificence of the buried Mayan personage. Expressed in terms of expense and toil, the rich jade ornaments, jewelry, and other finery found with the skeleton suggested that there existed in Palenque a theocratic system similar to that of Egypt, where an all-powerful priest-king was considered during his life as well as after his death to be a god. Palenque's royal tomb was also a strong indication that the Mayan attitude toward death was very close to that of the pharaohs.

An Egyptian link? A Hindu link? Such controversy was food and drink to Alma. Back in the field, it was easy to imagine nothing had changed, that she was a young woman again on her first expedition. But, returning to Mexico City and the *News,* she was frequently keenly aware of the passage of time. Watching the reporters, particularly the "girls," dart from one assignment to another, trim, shapely and so very *young,* Alma felt light-years removed from them. Busy with the demands of their careers and love lives, the women did nothing to bridge the gap. To them, the flamboyant Alma in her flowing garments was as out of place in a newspaper as a Gutenberg press. She tried sharing her own experiences back on the *Call,* the murders, the trials, the hangings. "I covered the Fatty Arbuckle trial," she ventured. Her reward was a blank stare. Alma also found it strange to take orders from men half her age. Jim Budd, the editor, a ladies' man who would once have flirted with her, was polite. Where *had* the years gone?

But Alma was nothing if not a survivor. She had not succeeded this long in public relations without learning adaptability, perfecting the art of flattery, and developing intuition. She would never win a popularity contest at the *News,* but, over time, cultivated some warm friends there. Though Alma's often florid writing style contained more than a hint of the 1920's, the enthusiasm she brought to her subjects, coupled with a bloodhound flare for sniffing out rare, original subjects and following them through, compensated to a large degree. Colleagues respected the scholarship and enterprise, while deploring her infuriating insistence that *nothing* be cut from her stories. The last-minute typographical errors, however inevitable in the day-to-day deadline crunch of any metropolitan paper, were unforgivable to Alma and had to be publicly atoned for in boxes that frequently appeared beside her column the following week.

A routine developed by which she brought in her column and then returned the next evening to oversee its transition to type. Often the vigil lasted late into the night. Many times Alma was accompanied on these pilgrimages by old friends from the New York days who happened to be in town. Former *News* employees remember seeing Jackson Pollock and Truman Capote helping her to proofread.

As always, money was a problem. Any needy artist knew that he or she could get help from her, but the fast-talking Alma wasn't always too scrupulous about the source. Living on the edge herself and observing young people barely hanging on by their fingernails, she would use any means necessary to keep herself and her numerous protégés afloat. On one occasion, she borrowed prized paintings from Sloan Simpson, the beautiful model and former wife of William O'Dwyer, the American ambassador. They were to be displayed at an exhibit of Mexican art that Alma was arranging. Sloan, having heard of La Peregrina, was only too happy to assist the woman who was rapidly becoming a living legend. Eight paintings were borrowed, only seven returned. The missing painting was never recovered. There were those who believed that Alma had sold it to meet some pressing need—just as she'd sold her niece's portrait.

It wasn't that Alma didn't try the conventional route. There was some additional income from articles for *Mexican Life* as well as *Gourmet* and *Art Digest,* but the demands on her largess were so many.

For a time in the early 1950's, she lived well on the proceeds from *Orozco,* the biography she wrote as a memorial to her dearest friend, who had died of a heart attack in 1949. No one bothered to notify Alma; she learned of his death from an article in the *New York Times.* The book was a labor of love, a very personal tribute and a nostalgic memoir to the many years they'd shared. If all of it was not *quite* true, well, at least it was true in spirit. A slight revisioning here and there gave some individuals an opportunity to say and do the things they might later have *wished* they'd done in light of the artist's subsequent success. For the most part the book was well received, the advance a windfall, and the royalties better than expected. Alma refurbished her apartment, bought a few more paintings and artifacts, and lent money that she would never see again, but it wasn't long before the royalties dried up and she was struggling once more to supplement her salary with articles.

Then suddenly, unexpectedly, came a lucky break in the form of a swashbuckling entrepreneur.

Pablo Bush Romero, Mexico's leading Ford distributor, also dabbled successfully in real estate. Having stalked big game in Africa and India, he now turned his sights on a more elusive target. An avid diver, Bush was determined to plumb the secrets of the sea. His vehicle was CEDAM, an organization he had recently founded to promote underwater archeology, exploration, and history in Mexico. The name was an acronym for Club de Exploraciónes y Deportes Acuáticos de México.

When Bush and Alma met by chance at a cocktail party in 1956, it was a case of fantasy colliding with destiny. As Bush outlined his extensive plans, Alma remembered the dreams of Byron de Prorok and Hans Hartman and was swept with nostalgia. She was also aware of opportunity knocking.

Bush was a realist with the wherewithal to implement *his* dreams. Now listening to this sixty-something lady recount the most amazing adventures, he looked beyond the broad-brimmed picture hat and the ankle-length gown, recognizing a kindred spirit. CEDAM lacked a historian, a post that Alma could easily fill; it also needed an unofficial publicist. Multilingual and already employed as a feature writer by the country's leading English-language newspaper, she was ideally suited for both roles.

Alma's publicizing of CEDAM's initial treasure-hunting expedition put Cozumel on the map. Historically, the island had been sacred to Ixchel, the Mayan goddess of childbirth, fertility, creativity, the sea, and the moon. The moon goddess's effect was easily observable. At the new moon and at its fullest, the sea tides were at their highest, bountifully spilling fish and crabs onto the beach—a lavish feast waiting only to be harvested. Obviously, Ixchel was a deity to be venerated. Fishermen made sacrifices at her shrine before setting out to sea, and pilgrims from as far away as Belize, Guatemala, Chiapas, and Tabasco came to pay homage.

The goddess also possessed the power of prophesy. Sometimes she employed a medium who worked in the same manner as the oracle at

Delphi, only here the seer was a man inside a large hollow idol who received her messages and transmitted them to the waiting populace. Pilgrimages from the mainland were considered a holy obligation and were particularly popular with pregnant women or women who wished to become pregnant.

It was this Mayan equivalent of Mecca, Rome, or Jeruselum that had received the first thrust of Hernán Cortés's idol-smashing crusade in 1519. When the conquistador arrived with his eleven ships and six hundred men on their way to conquering all of Mexico, he'd found an island of some forty thousand inhabitants—ten times the population that existed when Alma arrived. Few remnants of Cozumel's grandeur survived his stay, and once the orgy of vandalism was over, the Spaniards lost interest and abandoned the island to less hypocritical predators. When the pirates arrived, there was nothing left to plunder, but Cozumel was so desolate that it provided a convenient hideout. When piracy drifted out of fashion, Cozumel was abandoned once again.

Now here was Alma in a small plane seated beside the bush pilot as he navigated between the twin blues of sea and sky. Below her the water was so clear that she could see sandbars and coral formations. When they landed, it was near a charming village, and Alma felt the reluctance that all travel writers experience. If she wrote about this forgotten island paradise with its incredibly blue sea and talcum-powder sand, its warm, friendly natives and ready accessibility to North America, it must invariably change. *But* Cozumel was the site of the CEDAM lab, and she had a job to do.

Sure enough they did—and fairly soon—sight a sunken ship. Objects large and small were salvaged; tankards, pewter plates, cutlery. A Spanish galleon, they assumed, until a large gold watch dated 1739 was discovered. Inside the massive case were a few scraps of the *London Daily Observer* containing an advertisement for a gout remedy with a glowing testimonial from the mistress of the bedchamber of the prince of Wales. Then packaged needles stamped Achen, Germany, were discovered and, after that, white enamel shoe buckles of various designs thought to be either Dutch or French. There were tiny hand-shaped amulets, clearly a product of Brazil, and thousands of crucifixes thought to be of Italian origin. Certainly an eclectic band of adventurers. Eventually the ill-starred ship was identified as the paradoxically named Spanish vessel *Nuestra Señora de los Milagros* ("Our Lady of the Miracles").

In 1960, Alma, representing CEDAM at the Third International Congress on Submarine Biology in Barcelona, reflected that it was from here that Columbus had reported to Ferdinand and Isabella the discoveries of his first voyage. She found it "fitting that the same city should serve as a forum for the consideration of an equally vast enterprise—nothing less than the exploration of another New World—the immense expanse of sea that occupies almost three-quarters of the planet's surface."

Soon Alma was writing about submarine entrances leading to the palaces and temples of Tulum on the mainland coast of Quintana Roo and the discovery of Chunyaxche, another "lost" city, located by following two lakes connected by ancient Mayan canals. Quintana Roo was a territory then, wild, uncultivated, the jungle everywhere—dense, exotic, nearly impenetrable, a place where jaguars came down to the beach to eat turtles. There were human predators as well, descendants of the Caste War, who still viewed outsiders with hostility. It was a grand adventure and, despite her advancing years, the heat, the primitive conditions, Alma was happy to be in the thick of it.

The ghost of Jean Lafitte was a constant specter shadowing the 1960 expedition. The pirate had secured his place in history when he marshaled a brigand band to save General Andrew Jackson at the Battle of New Orleans. Following the British defeat, Lafitte was pardoned for his pirate past but couldn't seem to stay away from it. During the 1820's, he sacked and burned Galveston.

One day Bush quietly told Alma of a rumor he'd heard. The body of the pirate was said to be buried in the Yucatecan village of Dzilam-Bravo. "We've *got* to go there," Alma insisted. "We absolutely must." Traveling to the tiny town, the CEDAM group had no difficulty finding the Estrada family, who claimed to be Lafitte's direct descendants. Don José M. Estrada proudly introduced his blond, blue-eyed family, who bore little resemblance to their Mayan neighbors.

Alma's pen was fairly flying across the paper as Don José recounted the family legend. Lafitte had come to Dzilam-Bravo with a beautiful mulatto woman, Lucia Allen, whom he'd kidnapped from Mobile. Apparently happily reconciled to her fate, Lucia settled down with him in the remote village, where the reformed pirate reportedly lived a long and honest life. One child, a daughter, was born to the couple.

Don José obligingly conducted the CEDAM party to the cemetery and pointed out a worm-eaten wood plaque at the head of one of the graves. Carved on its surface was a rose, a cross, and the words "Jean Lafitte." What a story! Alma was thrilled. Bush struck a deal. In exchange for the wooden marker from the pirate's grave, which he wanted for the CEDAM museum, he would provide a new marble gravestone. Don José agreed.

Following a month of diving for sunken ships and jungle exploration, the group returned with the new gravestone and retrieved the old wooden one. Alma's *News* exclusive was picked up by a wire service. Soon a storm of controversy broke. One historian claimed that the Dzilam-Bravo tomb was actually that of Lafitte's brother, Pierre. Jean Lafitte had, he said, died in a naval battle while fighting in the service of the Latin American patriot Simón Bolívar. A reporter from the *New Orleans Times-Picayune* asked, "What of all those people who believe that Lafitte is buried in the Bay de Barataria?"

Alma took advantage of a visit to New York to do some research at the Central Library, where she made an amazing find: the diary of Jean Lafitte, which had been published by the buccaneer's great-grandson, John Lafitte. He wrote that it was the pirate's wish that his diary not be published until one hundred and seven years after his death.

It appeared that the Lafitte brothers had hit upon a convenient escape route. When either ran into difficulties, he would simply "die," be "buried," and then "reincarnate" somewhere else. Still tracking, Alma found a descendant of the buccaneer who told her that "Jean Laflin," last alias of the "gentleman" pirate, had been head of an honorable family and who showed her his original *Memoir Journal* recounting Lafitte's pleasant days spent at Dzilam-Bravo, where he "rested at ease and formed intimate attachments difficult to sever." Apparently the fake death was a tactful release from a relationship and life-style that had become restrictive. Eventually Lafitte "retired," married a childhood sweetheart, and used some of his immense treasure to fund the writings of two obscure young men whose sentiments he admired, Karl Marx and Friedrich Engels.

Lafitte had opened an account in a Paris bank to finance the two while they completed the Communist Manifesto, an undertaking that would alter the course of history for more than a hundred years. "They are working on it now," Lafitte recorded in his journal,

drawing up laws in Germany, Belgium and Holland. I hope the new doctrine and manifesto will overthrow England. Spain is

*now weak. It was always my pleasure and intention to embrace
every cause for liberty, to tear up and snatch away kingdoms from
monarchs. The pen is stronger than armies. I have donated my
resources to those men in Germany and France to draft a
manifesto for the liberty of the working man.*

Lafitte had died in Alton, Illinois, on May 5, 1854, and was buried there in
the family cemetery.

Alma loved the story and hoped that it was true. One thing was certain;
Lafitte was her kind of man.

CHAPTER · 15

Forever Alma

In January 1961, Alma at seventy-one, returned to Chichén Itzá. The occasion was CEDAM's most ambitious expedition. The group planned to descend into the sacred *cenote* and were joined in the enterprise by the Mexican National Institute of Anthropology and the National Geographic Society.

Alma, arriving on the scene in the late afternoon after the archeologists and divers had completed their first day's work, was overcome by forty years of changes. On her first visit the mood was one of romantic desolation. The whole place seemed caught in some strange spell, the city a scene of ruined splendor trapped in a dense maze of tropical growth. The majestic Temple of the Warriors, with its now-gleaming expanse of white columns, had been completely hidden by the brush, with only here and there a fleeting suggestion of stone protruding above or through the vegetation to guide the archeologists. Now the foliage had been trimmed back, the debris removed, the buildings reconstructed; she was amazed by the transformation. The lost city of the mysterious Itzas had become a park.

The *cenote* alone seemed unchanged. Except for the dredging machinery, everything was precisely as Alma remembered it from her first visit. As she lowered herself gingerly onto the granite platform, the years seemed to roll back. Again the setting sun bathed the tiny temple in purple and gold; again an iguana crawled from beneath the rocks to watch her. The pool loomed before her like a great cavernous mouth opening with startling abruptness in the midst of the jungle. After all these years a sense of sinister mystery, even of horror, remained.

It was hard for Alma to believe that so much time had passed since her first visit. She was actually ten years older than Don Eduardo had been then. How very ancient he'd seemed! Poor Don Eduardo, the years had not been kind to him. The bitterly fought lawsuit instituted by the Mexican government following the appearance of her story had marked one of the least cooperative periods in Mexican and United States history. After many expensive legal battles, the two million-dollar case had finally reached the Mexican Supreme Court, where the controversy was finally settled in Thompson's favor. The court ruled that no adequate local or federal laws existed at the time to prevent the exporting of archeological treasures and because the Hacienda Chichén Itzá, on which the objects had been found, was Thompson's property, Mexico had no legal redress.

Vindicated at last, Thompson had attempted to rebuild the hacienda, hoping to turn it into a hotel. The idea was later realized by his successors, but at the time, his financial difficulties made it impossible. Disheartened, the explorer of the Well of Sacrifice left the only home of his adult life and his beloved ruins, returning to the United States, where he died in 1935. The knowledge was still traumatic for Alma. Although she'd had Don Eduardo's permission, even his encouragement, to publish the story, the fact remained that but for it his life would have been much different.

The decision that awarded the treasure to the Peabody Museum was a bitter blow to Mexico. Scholars and the general public alike argued heatedly that the sacred *cenote* treasure represented an important cultural heritage of the Mexican people. Finally, in December 1959, during the Fifty-Eighth Congress of American Anthropologists, at least partially as a result of a campaign instigated by Alma, ninety-four precious pre-Columbian objects—gold discs bearing hieroglyphic inscriptions—were "spontaneously" returned to Mexico by the Peabody Museum.

Don Eduardo had always believed that he'd only scratched the surface.

Now, a team of experts from both countries was attempting to prove him right. And this time there was no question but that the treasure would remain in its homeland, where not only natives, but people from all over the world would come to see, admire, and study it.

The latest modern equipment included a method of raising the bottom material by suction, and a large floating platform was constructed where the recovered matter was cleaned and sorted before being placed on the conveyer and hoisted to the *cenote*'s edge. Divers worked in pairs, with one on the *cenote*'s floor and the other on the platform holding a connecting rope used as a signal to stop the compressor and the tube's suction in an emergency. Guiding the mouth of the tube in the darkness was dangerous. The operator had to push the mud close to the mouth of the tube with his hands, being careful not to be grabbed by the powerful suction.

One of the first artifacts brought up was a rubber ball. Alma was thrilled, realizing that it had come from the ritual ball game, well established in Mayan life five hundred years before the Greeks founded the Olympic games during the first century B.C. When this find was followed by two idols made of rubber—something never seen before—Alma could stand it no longer. Watching from the parapet was too far from the action. "Take me down!" she insisted.

A cheer went up as Alma—in her large hat and flowing gown—was slowly lowered in a canvas sling to the platform just above the surface of the water. It was a whole new view. She marveled again at the near architectural perfection of the *cenote*'s circular rim, the dazzling whiteness of its perpendicular walls, and their evenly eroded horizontal markings as if carved by some master sculptor. Far above her were the tall, dark trees that surrounded the water pit. Seated on the platform, she had the very first opportunity to examine rubber figures, jade pendants, coral beads, golden earplugs, and obsidian knives that were handed to her by the surfacing divers. These were hours of both excitement and contentment, hours that she would remember always with pride and satisfaction. Life might not begin at seventy, but it certainly wasn't over!

In 1961, Alma received two awards. The first, the Royal Order of Benefactions, a high order of Greece, was presented to her by the Greek consul general in Mexico City on behalf of his country's sovereign, King Paul. The decoration, a medal in the form of a gold cross, plus a citation "in recognition of her sincere efforts in the further of Greek culture in this hemisphere," commemorated both her translations of the Sikelianos poems years before and her efforts in founding a Hellenic Cultural Center in Mexico City. Eva would have been pleased.

Later in the year, Alma was awarded the Aztec Eagle, the highest decoration the Mexican government can bestow upon a foreigner. She received the honor from Foreign Minister Manuel Tello. It commemorated nearly forty years of writing about the Mexican culture, with particular emphasis on art and archeology.

A few months later, Alma returned briefly to San Francisco, where she delivered an illustrated lecture on Mexican art and archeology at the M. H. de Young Museum in Golden Gate Park. Alma was touched by the many accolades to her newly published book, *Mexican Muralists,* but her thoughts drifted to the past.

The stylized facade of the museum, suggestive of an ancient temple on the Nile, evoked persistent ghosts—her eight-year-old self running ahead of her father and the younger children to view the Egyptian hall. Surely her love of archeology had begun here. Now, as then, Alma felt Eugene close by encouraging, approving her scholarship, her enthusiasm.

Of all the paintings, the work that had impressed her most and would remain indelibly imprinted on her memory was a huge canvas commemorating the driving of the last spike—a golden one—at the completion of the Union Pacific Transcontinental Railroad. The artistic merit of the painting was indifferent, but her father's patriotic enthusiasm, reaching its apex here as he singled out with local pride the various personages portrayed, worked a singular magic. The hero of this pivotal event in the building of the nation was James G. Hill. Attired in a long frock coat and in an attitude of official dignity, he stood in a central group of "empire builders" that included Senator Leland Stanford, founder of the university, and Senator George Hearst, father of the newspaper publisher. Behind them was a crowd of notables. In fact, there were so many portrait heads in the enormous composition that years later Orozco, when accompanying her on a nostalgic pilgrimage, referred to the canvas as "an outstanding achievement of the 'confetti' school of painting."

Many times that evening Alma's thoughts were drawn to Orozco and the enchanted hours they had spent together in the museum during that long-ago summer in San Francisco. It pleased her to imagine that perhaps somehow, somewhere he and Adelaide were together, for now Alma's mother, too, was gone.

There was little time for introspection. A nation-wide lecture tour took her from one end of the country to the other, and then it was back to Mexico, where she resumed her work at the *News*—guest columnists, diplomats, or historians filled in during her absences.

Occasionally there were visits from the family. Alma's beautiful niece, Jane Wallach, came with her daughter, Kim. The vivacious teenager caught everyone's eye. It was an unforgettable experience for the girl. Her aunt's apartment was a veritable museum, but cluttered, confusing. There was a litter of books, scattered jewelry, North African rugs, Hindu statues, trailing gowns of silk and velvet, Gypsy shawls, things from Greece, things from Italy, stone idols from heaven knew where and paintings from everywhere. It was clearly the home of a woman who had lived her own life for her own self. Most surprising, her aunt—whom the rest of the family thought eccentric, perhaps a little mad—was a heroine in Mexico. Sometimes orchestras changed their tunes spontaneously to "La Peregrina" as Auntie Alma entered the room. People bowed, often clapped, heads craned, someone invariably murmured: "It's she; that's Alma Reed."

Despite the adulation, Kim was a little embarrassed by her aunt's sometimes outlandish attire, bizarre costumes of another era. The stares often bothered her, but she said nothing, a little in awe of this remarkable woman.

Not so Prescott. When Prescott came to Mexico City, he was still Prescott. Nothing or no one awed him. In fact, Alma's baby brother had become a legend, too. "San Francisco without Prescott Sullivan is like San Francisco without cable cars, or at least San Francisco without saloons," a newspaper crony once remarked. A sports columnist straight from central casting, Prescott had a mouth designed to hold a cigar. His crumpled hat rode jauntily above two of the most impressive ears ever seen; it was said that he changed his shirt daily, his suit annually.

To Prescott, Alma was still his same bleeding-heart sis. A pain in the ass at times. "For Christ's sake, take off that hat, or we're not going anywhere," he'd invariably demand as the two set off to attend some reception in her honor.

Alma had grown used to the recognition. Frequently on press assignments with Jim Budd, her boss at the *News,* their train would reach some remote town, where a dignitary would suddenly appear with a bouquet of flowers, behind him a motley band playing "La Peregrina." Alma invariably nodded graciously and smiled her still beautiful smile, accepting it all as her due.

Unquestionably, Alma Reed had become a legend in her time; yet despite her many real accomplishments, the need to exaggerate, even prevaricate, remained. As if the reality of her early days in Mexico wasn't enough, she could not resist embroidering the truth. One of her fables had her acting as a spy on a secret mission for the *New York Times.* Her task, she said, had been to obtain a copy of President Obregon's budget, which would presumably reveal his intentions for Mexico's future. According to her apocryphal tale, the information obtained by sleuthing was responsible for the eventual recognition of Mexico's then-revolutionary government by the United States. It was certainly not the first time she'd arranged facts to suit her fancy.

Fortunately this propensity for personal exaggeration never intruded into her reportage. Despite her advancing age, Alma remained true to the ideals instilled in her years before by Fremont Older. She was fast, and she was accurate. Proud of her many exclusives on a variety of subjects, she still refused to be bound by rules. When had they ever applied to her? Often Alma's stories ran long, far exceeding the number of pages assigned.

No editor wants to redo a completed page in order to incorporate a jump from an overlong story from another page. The obvious solution lay with editing. "Cut the picture," he'd suggest.

"Never!" was Alma's inevitable response. Her pictures, she insisted, were treasures that enhanced the text, beautified the paper.

"Then cut a few paragraphs," the editor would shrug.

"Absolutely not! This story is a scoop."

If an editor refused to yield, Alma had no compunction about going over his head. Once she awakened a publisher of the *News* in the middle of the night. The word came down: "Give that lady what she wants."

The obstinacy of this older woman amused some, infuriated others. A resentful young reporter, surprisingly a woman, sniped back with a cruel review of Alma's newest book, *The Ancient Past of Mexico,* generally considered a landmark contribution to archeological scholarship. Alma was heartbroken by this attack from one of her own *News* colleagues, but, as always, the prospect of a change of scene never failed to raise her spirits.

That book came out early in 1966, and soon Alma was off on a national lecture and book-promotion tour. In San Francisco at the Century Club, one of the oldest and most prestigious women's clubs in the city, she spoke on the conquest of Mexico from the viewpoint of the conquered—a startling revelation in those days. In New York during the observance of Pan American Week, she was interviewed on national radio. Discussing her newest work, Alma confided: "This isn't a book I decided to write recently. You might say I've been working on it since my teens when I came to Mexico as a young reporter for the *New York Times*. I was a young archeologist whose prime interest was and is the ancient past of Mexico." Well, some of it was true.

Alma, as usual, spent that summer in Cozumel with CEDAM divers and then in September flew to Argentina, where she reported on CEDAM's progress at the biennial Congress of Americanists. Along with her travel, CEDAM reports, and weekly columns, she had begun another book. This one a biography of Felipe. "I have only to close my eyes to see him standing before me," she confided to Pearl Gonzalez, a young reporter, one of her few women friends at the *News*. "He has never left me."

Rosa Lie Johannsen, a needy houseguest who ended up staying a year with Alma in her Mexico City apartment, would recall how hard her benefactor worked—often fourteen hours a day at her typewriter. "There were always money problems; I would worry, but Alma remained confident. 'The money will come from somewhere,' she would say, and somehow it always did."

On November 19, 1966, Alma wrote her column as usual. It was a commemorative piece on the subject of the fifty-sixth anniversary of the *Revolución Social* to be celebrated the following day. Solemnly she recalled the death of the first martyrs in the revolt against the dictatorship of Porfirio Díaz and the two million others who were sacrificed for the cause in the following decade.

Recapping the evils of the Díaz dictatorship, she focused on the henequen plantations of Yucatán, where the Maya were kept under what has been described as the last vestige of chattel slavery in the New World. Glancing at the framed photograph next to her typewriter, Alma continued: "Kept in ignorance, these Maya workers did not even know their rights under Mexican law. It remained for Yucatán's martyred governor, Felipe Carrillo Puerto, to translate for them the Mexican constitution in their own Maya tongue, a 'crime' for which he was imprisoned by General Díaz."

Gathering up the pages of her article, Alma placed them in a briefcase.

She patted her hair in place before a mirror framed in antique silver—a gift from a long-ago admirer—then donned her broad-brimmed hat. Alma picked up a small overnight bag, which she had carefully packed, and walked down the stairs to the street below. She hailed a cab and went first to the *News,* where she asked the driver to wait while she dropped off the column. Returning in minutes, she directed him to a nearby hospital, where, on the following day, she was to have surgery to correct an intestinal obstruction.

That evening, from the hospital, Alma talked on the phone with Eulalia Guzman, archives director of the National Anthropology Museum. The two chatted briefly about a proposed trip to the ruins at Tajin. There was another call to Joe Nash, a young reporter at the *News* who had become a close friend and occasional escort. "I've nearly finished the biography, Joe—just one more month and it'll be done."

"Perhaps they'll make a movie of it."

"Perhaps. Budd Schulberg wants to do a script."

"Who do you want to play you?"

"Anybody but Elizabeth Taylor!" Alma laughed, then hesitated. "There was an actress who reminded me a bit of myself as a young woman, Dolores Hart. I met her once, a very nice girl—maybe too nice—she entered a convent." Alma hung up the phone still chuckling.

There was no need for a sedative. She had actually looked forward to the prospect of a short rest in the hospital. It was nice to have a little quiet time just for herself. After all, she *was* seventy-seven—not that anyone would ever know it!

The following morning she joked cheerfully with the nurse who prepared her for the operation. It was minor; she'd been told. Alma was certain the recuperation time would be brief, and soon she'd be ready to pursue all the exciting projects she had planned. There was a festive atmosphere about the hospital. It was Revolution Day.

As the anesthetic began to take effect, Alma smiled sleepily. "I'm being liberated, too," she murmured as her still beautiful blue eyes closed for the last time.

And so it ended. A legend in life, a legend even in death. Alma Sullivan Reed, La Peregrina of fact and fantasy, never awakened from the anesthetic that did indeed liberate her.

EPILOGUE

Alma's death was attributed to an arrhythmia that developed suddenly during the operation and couldn't be controlled. Concerned friends demanded an autopsy. The findings surprised everyone. Alma's intestinal problem was by no means "minor." She suffered from an occlusion caused by cancer of the colon, which had reached an advanced stage. The sudden, painless death was considered a blessing.

Her body was cremated, and three days later a memorial service was held. Many longtime friends spoke, including Emilio Portes Gil, former president of Mexico, and the Greek consul general, Leander Vourvoulias, who'd known Alma since Delphic Festival days.

As a conclusion to the services, Ricardo Palmerín accompanied by his daughter and Jacinto Vargas, professor of music at the National University of Mexico, performed "La Peregrina." They had played and sung the selection many times at parties as well as on the radio and television, but this was the first time with tears in their eyes, and it was the last time for Alma Reed.

Stanley Sullivan, who represented the family at the service, felt that his sister's heart had always been in Mexico, and that's where she would remain. For a time the ashes were stored at the Eusebio Gayosso Funeral Home in Mexico City, awaiting the return of the globe-trotting Pablo Bush Romero, whose *destino* it would be to return Alma Reed to Yucatán and the lost love who waited.

NOTES AND SOURCES

PROLOGUE

The account of Alma Reed's interment was taken from interviews with three of her friends who attended, Pablo Bush Romero, Dr. Prospero Martínez Carrillo, and James Budd, editor of the *Mexico City News,* who covered the event. Also accounts in the Merida papers, *Diario de Revista* and *La Revista de Yucatán.*

CHAPTER ONE

Kevin Starr's book, *Americans and the California Dream* and *Suddenly San Francisco* by Charles Lockwood, were immensely helpful in providing background on early San Francisco as were contemporary newspapers, the *San Francisco Morning Call* and *San Francisco Examiner.* Reed's nieces, Mrs. Jane Wallach and Mrs. Patsy Berman, provided much information about her girlhood. Mort and Elaine Levine's Fremont Older archives; Older's autobiography, *My Own Story;* and his biography, *Fremont Older,* written by Evelyn Wells, a contemporary of Reed's, provided a vivid picture of Reed's early newspaper career.

CHAPTER TWO

Sources here included Alma Reed's own account of the Simon Ruiz case, which appeared in the *San Francisco Morning Call,* as well as other contemporary accounts in the *San Francisco Bulletin* and *Sacramento Union.*

CHAPTER THREE

David Yallap's *The Day the Laughter Stopped* provided much valuable background on Roscoe Arbuckle. His trial and that of The Reverend John Spencer was reconstructed from both Reed's accounts in the *Bulletin* and those in the *San Francisco Chronicle* and *Examiner.* The section on postrevolutionary Mexico was drawn from Reed's contemporary reporting of her travels, later reminiscences published in the *Mexico City News,* as well as private anecdotes to friends. John Mason Hart's *Revolutionary Mexico* provided excellent background information.

CHAPTER FOUR

The works of John L. Stephens, *Incidents of Travel in Central America, Chiapas and Yucatán* and *Incidents of Travel in Yucatán,* as well as *Mysteries of the Mexican*

Pyramids by Peter Tompkins, were rich in the archeological history of Yucatán. Another important source, supplementing Reed's own extensive writings, was *Digging in Yucatán,* a contemporary account of the Carnegie expedition by her friend, Ann Axtell Morris. *Felipe Carrillo Puerto* by Jaime Oroso Díaz provided background on this man supplementing contemporary accounts in *Las Revista de Yucatán.*

CHAPTER FIVE

Once again, *Digging in Yucatán* provided background, as did Edward Thompson's story as told to C. W. Ceram in *Gods, Graves and Scholars,* but the most significant accounts were Reed's own, which were published contemporarily in the *New York Times* and later as retrospective pieces in the *Mexico City News.* More additional information on Felipe Carrillo Puerto was provided by Díaz's previously mentioned biography.

CHAPTER SIX

The archeological content of this chapter was taken from articles written by Reed that appeared in the *New York Times* and *Mexico City News.* The facts relating to Reed's relationship with Felipe Carrillo Puerto came from her personal reminisces and writings as well as Díaz's biography. The events surrounding the governor's assassination were reconstructed from the before-mentioned biography as well as from contemporary newspaper accounts. Richard Joseph's *From Caste War to Class War* was an invaluable source.

CHAPTER SEVEN

From Caste War to Class War again provided background information leading to the conclusions regarding Carrillo Puerto's death discussed in this chapter. Other valuable research material was contributed by *Revista de la Universidad de Yucatán, Revista de Yucatán,* John Mason Hart's *Revolutionary Mexico,* and, of course, Reed's own writings.

CHAPTER EIGHT

The information for this chapter was taken largely from Reed's contemporary accounts in the *New York Times* as well as her reminiscences that appeared years later in the *Mexico City News.* De Prorok's book, *Digging for Lost African Gods,* was also extremely helpful, as was *Carthage* by David Soren, Ben den aben Ben, and Hedi Slim Simon. Contemporary accounts in *The National Geographic, Art and Archeology, Mentor,* and *Saturday Evening Post* furnished additional background. Scullard's *From the Gracchi to Nero* brought a historical perspective to the narrative, as did *The Aeneid.*

CHAPTER NINE

Alma Reed wrote extensively about her travels through North Africa in *New York Times* articles. There was also general news coverage. De Prorok's book also contains some descriptive information.

CHAPTER TEN

Once again, Reed's writings in the *New York Times* as well as her subsequent reminiscences both verbal and in the *Mexico City News* formed the basis for this chapter. Other sources included de Prorok's book as well as contemporary news accounts of Hartman's and Reed's article "Five Miles Under the Sea in a Big Steel Box," in *American Weekly.*

CHAPTER ELEVEN

Reed's pursuit of the Aeneas legend and most particularly her fascination with the sybil of Cumae was covered extensively in her writings both at the time of the expedition and years later. She spoke often of this time in her life, changing the dates to suit her fancy. Other aspects of her life during this period came to light through her writings in *Interior Studio* and *Art and Archaeology.*

CHAPTER TWELVE

There are many family anecdotes regarding Reed's friendship with Angelo and Eva Sikelianos and her years spent living in Greece. Her association with the *New York Times* ended at this time, possibly because of her full-time studies in Athens and the commencement of her translations of the Sikelianos poems, although she did write extensively of her life and work in Greece at a later date in the *Mexico City News.* The Delphic Festival was covered extensively in *The Mentor, The Independent,* and *The Literary Digest.*

CHAPTER THIRTEEN

Reed wrote about her friendship with Orozco in her biography of that name. Other primary sources included Orozco's own autobiography and writings, as well as Laurence P. Hurlburt's *Mexican Muralists in the United States.* The chapter also draws from personal anecdote, recollections from the Sullivan family as well as Alma's close friends and colleagues.

CHAPTER FOURTEEN

Alma Reed cut a wide swath in Mobile and is remembered by many who worked with her at the *Register*. Articles written by her from 1950 to 1966 for the *Mexico City News* proved invaluable, as did the firsthand information regarding this period obtained from interviews with Pablo Bush Romero and Reed's editors on the *News*, Jim Budd and Bill Shanahan.

CHAPTER FIFTEEN

In addition to Reed's *News* articles, much anecdotal information about the last years of Reed's life was provided by the previously mentioned Bush, Budd, and Shanahan, as well as by members of the Sullivan family, Jane and Kim Wallach, and her *News* colleagues, Pearl Gonzales, Joe Nash, and Jackie Peterson.

BIBLIOGRAPHY

BOOKS

Aeschylus. *Prometheus Bound.* Translated by James Scully and John Herington. New York: Oxford University Press, 1975

Ceram, C.W. *Gods, Graves and Scholars.* New York: Alfred Knopf, 1951.

de Prorok, Byron Kuhn. *Digging for Lost African Gods.* New York: G.P. Putnam's Sons, 1926.

Díaz, Jaime Oroso. *Felipe Carrillo Puerto.* Mérida, Yucatán: Mandonado Editores, 1983.

Flaubert, Gustave. *Salammbo: A Romance of Ancient Carthage, Volumes 1 and 2.* New York: Walter Dunne, 1904.

Hart, John Mason. *Revolutionary Mexico.* Berkeley: University of California Press, 1987.

Hurlburt, Laurence P. *The Mexican Muralists in the United States.* Albuquerque: University of New Mexico Press, 1990.

Joseph, Richard. *From Caste War to Class War.* Mobile: University of Alabama Press, 1986.

Kandell, Jonathan. *La Capital: The Biography of Mexico City.* New York: Random House, 1988.

Lockwood, Charles. *Suddenly San Francisco.* San Francisco: A California Living Book, 1978.

May, Antoinette. *The Yucatán, A Guide to the Land of Maya Mysteries.* San Carlos, CA: Wide World Publishing, 1987.

Morris, Ann Axtell. *Digging in Yucatán.* New York: Junior Literary Guild, 1931.

Older, Fremont. *My Own Story.* New York: Macmillan Company, 1926.

OROZCO Iconografia Personal. Mexico City: Fondo de Cultura Económica, 1983.

Reed, Alma. *Orozco.* New York: Oxford University Press, 1958.

Reed, Alma. *The Mexican Muralists.* New York: Crown Publishers, 1961.

Reed, Alma. *Submarine Archaeology Congress Reveals Amazing Results of Oceanic Exploration.* Mexico City: Publicaciónes C.E.D.A.M., 1961.

Reed, Alma. *The Ancient Past of Mexico.* New York: Crown Publishers, 1966.

Scullard, H.H. *From the Gracchi to Nero.* London: Methuen, 1959.

Soren, David: Aicha, den aben Ben; and Simon, Hedi Slim. *Carthage.* New York: Simon & Schuster, 1990.

Starr, Kevin. *Americans and the California Dream.* New York: Oxford University Press, 1973.

Wells, Evenly. *Fremont Older.* New York: Appleton-Century Company, 1936.

Wilson, Earl J. *The Mexican Caribbean.* Smithtown, NY: Exposition Press, 1980.

Yallap, David. *The Day the Laughter Stopped.* New York: St. Martin's Press, 1976.
Young, Barbara. *This Man From Lebanon.* New York: Alfred Knopf, 1965.

ARTICLES

Austin, F. Britten. "Delenda est Carthago." *Saturday Evening Post,* March 19, 1927.

Courtellemont, Gervais. "Tunisia, Where Sea and Desert Meet." *The National Geographic Magazine,* April 1924.

de Prorok, Byron Kuhn. "The Ancient Basilicas of Carthage and Early Christian Ruins in North Africa." *Art and Archaeology,* January 1923.

de Prorok, Byron Kuhn. "The Excavations of Carthage, 1921–1922." *Art and Archaeology,* January 1923.

de Prorok, Byron Kuhn. "Unearthing Ancient Carthage." *Traveler,* January 1923.

de Prorok, Byron Kuhn. "Ancient Carthage in the Light of Modern Civilization." *The National Geographic Magazine,* April 1924.

de Prorok, Byron Kuhn. "Through the Layers of Ancient Carthage." *Mentor,* April 1924.

de Prorok, Byron Kuhn. "The Excavations of the Temple of Tanit at Carthage." *Art and Archeology,* January 1925.

de Prorok, Byron Kuhn. "We Haven't Found Much in Carthage." *Collier's The National Weekly,* July 5, 1925.

"Five Miles Under the Sea in a Big Steel Box." *American Weekly,* August 30, 1925.

Fuller, Raymond. "The Glory That Was Carthage." *The Mentor,* March 1927.

Gruening, Ernest. "A Maya Idyl." *Century,* April 1924.

Kelsey, Francis F. "Tanit." *Art and Archaeology,* February 1926.

Mead, Dorothy M. "The Delphic Festival." *The Mentor,* May 1927.

Morgan, Clayland T. "The Spell of Africa's Vanished Cities." *Art and Archaeology,* October 1928.

Rapp, William Jordan. "Greece Looks to Her Fathers." *The Independent,* April 30, 1927.

Reed, Alma. "Restored Farnese Tazza." *Interior Studio,* July 1926.

Reed, Alma. "Antique Italian Tomb Paintings." *Interior Studio,* August 1926.

Reed, Alma. "Lost Tombs of Canosa." *Art and Archaeology,* September 1927.

Rodriguez, Jorge C. Gonzales. "Felipe Carrillo Puerto." *Revista de la Universidad de Yucatán,* August 1973.

Sheldon, Lee. "Salaambo, Spirit of Carthage." *The Mentor,* March 22, 1926.

Starr, Kevin. "Prison by the Bay." *Image,* April 2, 1989.

"The Greek World Comes to Life." *The Literary Digest,* July 2, 1927.

NEWSPAPERS

Diario de Yucatán. October 22, 1967.

La Revista de Yucatán. January 1923–January 1924.

New York Times. Alma Reed. March 2, 1923; March 11, 1923; March 18, 1923; March 25, 1923; April 8, 1923; May 20, 1923; August 4, 1923; January 6, 1924; November 9, 1924; November 16, 1924; November 30, 1924; December 7, 1924; May 2, 1926; May 9, 1926; June 4, 1926.

Sacramento Union. January 7, 1919; January–May 1921.

San Francisco Bulletin. 1921–1923.

San Francisco Chronicle. Art Rosenbaum, February 15, 1961; Marian Zailian, April 9, 1961, April 23, 1961; Herbert Carwin, June 5, 1966, November 21, 1966.

San Francisco Examiner. Nadia Lavrova, December 23, 1924; January 4, 1925, June 17, 1928, June 25, 1930, May 6, 1931; May 8, 1931, February 5, 1952, June 11, 1961; Carlos Gutierrez, August 7, 1966; Curley Grieve, December 15, 1972.

San Francisco Morning Call. January 1913–March 1921.

The (Mexico City) News. 1950–November 1966.

INDEX

ABOUT THE AUTHOR

Antoinette May, a former newspaper editor and magazine publisher, is the author of a number of biographies and travel books. A columnist for the *San Francisco Chronicle,* she was the recipient of *La Pluma de Plata,* the highest honor the Mexican government can bestow upon an English-language journalist. May is currently working on a novel placed in first century Rome. She resides in Palo Alto, California.